D0893689

The Art of Willa Cather

The

Art of

Willa Cather

Edited by

Bernice Slote *and* Virginia Faulkner

The Department of English · University of Nebraska–Lincoln
and University of Nebraska Press · Lincoln

Grateful acknowledgment is extended to Alfred A. Knopf, Inc. for permission to quote from the following copyrighted works of Willa Cather: *Willa Cather on Writing*, *Not Under Forty*, and *The Old Beauty and Others*; and to Alfred A. Knopf, Inc. and Hamish Hamilton, London, for permission to quote from the following copyrighted works of Willa Cather: *The Professor's House*, *Shadows on the Rock*, *One of Ours*, *Death Comes for the Archbishop*, *A Lost Lady*, *My Mortal Enemy*, and *Obscure Destinies*. Also to Houghton Mifflin Company and Hamish Hamilton, London, for permission to quote from the following copyrighted works of Willa Cather: *Alexander's Bridge*, *O Pioneers!*, *The Song of the Lark*, and *My Ántonia*.

Library of Congress Cataloging in Publication Data

Willa Cather International Seminar, University of
    Nebraska–Lincoln, 1973.
    The art of Willa Cather.

    Bibliography: p.
    1. Cather, Willa Sibert, 1873–1947—Congresses.
I. Slote, Bernice, ed. II. Faulkner, Virginia,
1913–   ed. III. University of Nebraska–Lincoln.
Dept. of English. IV. Title.
PS3505.A87Z489 1974   813'.5'2   74–78479
ISBN 0–8032–0841–3
ISBN 0–8032–5794–5 (pbk.)

First Bison Book printing: November 1974
Most recent printing shown by first digit below:
1   2   3   4   5   6   7   8   9   10

The publication of this book was assisted by grants from the Nebraska Arts Council, the Willa Cather Centennial Festival Committee, and the Woods Charitable Fund, Inc.

Manufactured in the United States of America

Contents

CONTENTS

A picture section follows page 148.

Introduction

"The Art of Willa Cather: An International Seminar," held in Lincoln, Nebraska, October 25–28, 1973, was a central feature in the year-long series of events sponsored by the College of Arts and Sciences, University of Nebraska–Lincoln, commemorating the hundredth birthday of its most famous alumna. When planning for the Willa Cather Centennial Festival began in January 1972, the idea of a working seminar on the art of Willa Cather was among the first to take concrete shape.

That Willa Cather's art is complex has been acknowledged in a general way. In 1947 Maxwell Geismar said that hers was "one of the most complex, difficult and contradictory minds in our letters." Joseph Wood Krutch in 1951 spoke of her "stylistic subtlety," and W. C. Brownell (as quoted by E. K. Brown in his biography of Willa Cather) said: "I don't know of any art more elusive." Yet the exact nature of this subtlety and complexity still has not been fully explored. Scholars have not given Willa Cather's work the full benefit of their intellectual attention. One critic has suggested that at the turn of the century Willa Cather in her early fiction was using the same technique that Ezra Pound and T. S. Eliot used in poetry a dozen years later; and that although complexities of symbol and allusion were, in her later work, "molded into a style so compact and unobtrusive that on one level, at least, nothing is outside the work," one could only conjecture what would be revealed "if Miss Cather's writing were given the same kind of textual attention that has been given to Eliot, Pound, and Joyce" (*The Kingdom of Art*, pp. 92–93). Furthermore, new biographical findings and new insights into Willa Cather's mind and personality—gained through the reading of many hundreds of letters now available to scholars in special library collections—have only begun to be used in reinterpreting some of her work. Thus, the stated purpose of the seminar was to try in a concentrated period of intellectual and critical cooperation among scholars to clarify meanings and discover directions for study that would yield a more complete understanding of this important American novelist.

Inherent in the planning from the first was the determination that participation in the seminar should not be limited to American scholars. Although the significance of Willa Cather's work as an interpretation of American life, especially in its regional aspects, has long been acknowledged, recently she has emerged as a writer with a predominantly world view who dealt with universal themes and experiences. Even though she grew up and began writing in a period of intense nationalism, Willa Cather had the view of "one world" long before the phrase was widely used. She was concerned with the fusion of cultures as she experienced the process in the immigrant melting pot of pioneer Nebraska; yet her constant emphasis was on the recognition of various ethnic values. As early as 1927, in *Death Comes for the Archbishop*, she wrote of Indians and whites in terms that only now are coming into currency. Her firsthand observation of the acculturation process in Nebraska resulted in the use of materials about European immigrants—"Slavonic, Germanic, Scandinavian, Latin," as she said, "spread across our bronze prairies like the daubs of color on a painter's palette." Also, because of her own unusual intellectual orientation and interests she was able to blend historical and traditional themes with the new American setting and the problems of acculturation. Her ability to transcend national and ethnic boundaries partially explains the respect in which her work is held in other countries. Since she wrote sympathetically of Scandinavians, Czechs, and Frenchmen, for example, one could see why her work would be well received by European peoples; but the reasons for her popularity among the Japanese were not so easy to account for. Clearly, the seminar would be enriched by the participation of scholars from non-English-speaking countries who could tell us why Willa Cather holds such a high place in their lands. Moreover, the scope of the seminar would go beyond the study of one author to the realm of international understanding.

As it was finally constituted, the seminar brought together eighty-five scholars from seven nations, representing forty-four institutions of higher learning. The names of the invited participants and guests appear at the end of this book; there were, in addition, fifty auditors. On Thursday, October 25, 1973, at an afternoon meeting the co-principal investigators, Robert E. Knoll and Bernice Slote, outlined the procedures and the problems to be studied. After the banquet that evening the first of three main speakers, Leon Edel, delivered the opening address in the auditorium of the Sheldon Memorial Art Gallery. (This address, like those of the other main speakers, was open to the public and was televised by KUON-TV, University Television.) Three of the six seminar sections, each directed by an associate investigator who also presented a paper, were held on the morning of Friday, October 26. Section 1, "Willa Cather: American Experience and European Tradition," was attended by all the seminarians. Sections 2 and 3, "Willa Cather and France: Elective Affinities" and "Willa Cather: The Classic Voice," were held simultaneously, with participants attending the section they had previously elected. That afternoon and evening the second and third main speakers, Marcus Cunliffe and Eudora Welty, presented their addresses at, respectively, the Sheldon Memorial Art Gallery and the auditorium of the Nebraska Center for Continuing Education (where all the seminar sections were held and the participants were housed). On Saturday morning, October 27, Sections 4 and 5, "Willa Cather in Japan" and "Italian Perspectives," were held simultaneously; and all participants attended Section 6, "Willa Cather and the Art of Fiction." At the luncheon honoring distinguished guests an unexpected and most welcome bonus was a talk by Alfred A. Knopf. All participants gathered for the concluding discussion by a panel made up of the main speakers, associate investigators, and moderators of the seminar sections, chaired by Bernice Slote. On Sunday, October 28, most of the participants and guests journeyed to Red Cloud to visit Willa Cather's home and other buildings owned and restored by the

Willa Cather Pioneer Memorial, and to tour Webster County
sites associated with her life and work. Although the Festival
Committee can take no credit for it, it was a golden fall day
straight out of the pages of *My Ántonia.*

In editing THE ART OF WILLA CATHER, it has been our intention
to suggest something of the character of the seminar itself—to
show how insights and illuminations are arrived at in the
give-and-take of open scholarly discourse. In September 1973
all discussants were provided with drafts of the papers to be
presented at the seminar sections they would attend, and they
were invited to comment in writing as well as orally during and
after the seminar. Additional material for this book was drawn
from videotaped interviews with the main speakers, the associate investigators, Mr. Knopf, and other participants, and
from transcriptions of the tapes of the seminar sections. Space
restrictions have limited us to only a sampling of the comments
from discussions and interviews, but we are confident that
much of the material we were compelled to omit will be incor-
porated in future articles and books by the seminarians.

Part I, "Reassessments," views Willa Cather's art from a
number of critical perspectives. In "The House of Willa Cather"
Eudora Welty speaks as a writer of fiction on the fiction of
a fellow artist, emphasizing the physical quality and passion of
her work. Marcus Cunliffe, a historian, in "The Two or More
Worlds of Willa Cather," addresses himself to such questions
as why Willa Cather has been relatively neglected by historians
and the extent to which she sheds light on her own age. The
next six papers are those presented at the seminar sections;
each is followed by comments of the discussants. James Woodress advances the thesis that "Willa Cather's importance results
from a successful graft of her native experience on to the roots
and trunk of European culture" and examines the novels in this
light. Michel Gervaud considers Miss Cather's idealization of
French culture—why she came to love France and all things
French, the degree of her familiarity with French literature and
the language, and French influences in her writing. Hiroko Sato
gives us the first account of the reception of Willa Cather's work
in Japan, at the same time affording a glimpse of how American
literature in general is viewed in her country; she then discus-

ses certain facets of Cather's art which have a particular appeal for the Japanese. Aldo Celli also first looks at Willa Cather in a broad context—the image American writers have held of Italy and the Italian image of American literature—before suggesting new modes of interpretation which should contribute to a fuller understanding of Cather's art. James E. Miller, Jr., in his reassessment, has used Henry James's theory of fiction as "a frame to hold the glass" which he focuses on the art of Willa Cather's fiction, scrutinizing her essays relating to fictional theory as well as the novels themselves. Willa Cather is often described as a classical artist, and Donald Sutherland, a classicist, offers some fresh reasons why the adjective is deserved. While he takes account of the many classical allusions to be found in her writings (and the limitations of her knowledge of Latin grammar), his special emphasis is on the classic voice—her extraordinary attention to the expressive qualities of the voice and how it affected her prose.

Part II, "Recollections," opens with Leon Edel's "Homage to Willa Cather," in which he describes some of the unusual problems confronting him when he was asked to complete the biography of Willa Cather begun by the late E. K. Brown, and offers his own assessment of Miss Cather's place in American literature. The delightful reminiscence of Miss Cather by Alfred A. Knopf, her friend and publisher for twenty-seven years, is an expanded version of his informal talk at the luncheon before the seminar's final session. (In Parts I and II, reading notes, signaled by an asterisk or dagger, appear on page; reference notes, indicated by superior numbers, are at the end of the book under the title of the essay to which they pertain, following the Bibliography of Works Cited.)

As the title suggests, Part III, "Afterviews," is a first attempt to review the findings of the seminar. "Definitions and Evaluations" presents a selection of comments and responses to questions from the audience by members of the Seminar Panel, and excerpts from videotaped interviews conducted by Robert E. Knoll and James E. Miller, Jr. Post-seminar papers by John J. Murphy and Warren French comprise the chapter called "Directions: Additional Commentary." In the final chapter, "A Gathering of Nations," Bernice Slote summarizes the international interests of the participants and the variety of cultural views in Willa Cather's own work.

To bring guests from far places and to offer them appropriate hospitality during their stay in Nebraska would have been impossible without generous financial support, not only from the University but from outside agencies and organizations. The Willa Cather International Seminar was made possible primarily by a grant from the National Endowment for the Humanities. Grants from the Nebraska Arts Council and the Woods Charitable Fund, Inc., in addition to supporting other activities of the Willa Cather Centennial Festival, assisted with the publication of this book.

The Willa Cather Centennial Festival was sponsored by the UNL's College of Arts and Sciences, Melvin D. George, Dean, with the support of Chancellor James H. Zumberge and President Durward B. Varner. Committee members from the UNL were Professors Robert E. Knoll, Department of English (Chairman); John W. Robinson, Chairman, Department of English; Bernice Slote, Department of English and Editor, *Prairie Schooner*; John Moran, Director, School of Music; Virginia Faulkner, Editor, University of Nebraska Press; Ron Hull, Assistant General Manager, Programming, University Television; and Norman Geske, Director, University Art Galleries. Other members were: Professor Bruce P. Baker II, Chairman, Department of English, University of Nebraska at Omaha; Mrs. Mildred R. Bennett, President, Willa Cather Pioneer Memorial and Educational Foundation; and Mrs. Maurice Gilmore, President, Nebraska Arts Council.

The scheduled events of the Willa Cather Centennial Festival are concluded with the publication of THE ART OF WILLA CATHER. We hope and believe that it will be a stimulus to scholars to continue developing themes and exploring ideas presented in its pages, and that it will contribute an added measure of enjoyment to Willa Cather's readers around the world.

THE EDITORS

University of Nebraska–Lincoln

Part I

Reassessments

The House of Willa Cather

Eudora Welty

Your invitation to come to the International Seminar of writers, scholars, and critics in commemoration of the centennial of Willa Cather's birth, to speak as a writer of fiction on the fiction of Willa Cather, brings me the very highest honor. I am grateful and filled with humility and pride together in coming before you. The great prize couched in the invitation has come from the incentive it gave me to read all her work again, read it from the beginning. How she refreshes the spirit! The quality that struck me with the strongest force as I read is what I should like to speak about as we meet to celebrate her—the remarkable, and rewarding, physical quality of her work.

"More than anything else I felt motion in the landscape; in the fresh, easy-blowing morning wind, and in the earth itself, as if the shaggy grass were a sort of loose hide, and underneath it herds of wild buffalo were galloping, galloping . . . ." All Willa Cather's prose, like this passage in *My Ántonia*, speaks of the world in a way to show it's alive. There is a quality of animation that seems naturally come by, that seems a born part of every novel. Her own living world is around us as we read, present to us through our eyes and ears and touch.

A cut version of this article appeared by permission of the Willa Cather Centennial Festival Committee in *The New York Times Book Review*, January 27, 1974. © 1974, The New York Times Co. All rights reserved.

Of course it doesn't escape us that this physical landscape is brought home to us in a way that is subjective. "Overhead the stars shone gloriously. It was impossible not to notice them." Thus she rivets our eyes. "The summer moon hung full in the sky. For the time being it was the great fact in the world." Willa Cather would like our minds to receive what she is showing us not as its description—however beautiful—but as the thing described, the living thing itself. To this end she may eliminate its picture, the better to make us see something really there. It was her observation that "whatever is felt upon the page without being specifically named there—that, one might say, is created." "There were none of the signs of spring for which I used to watch in Virginia," says the narrator. "There was only—spring itself; the throb of it . . . . If I had been tossed down blindfold on that red prairie, I should have known that it was spring."

And so the texture, that informs us of so much in her prose, owes more than a little to its function. "It was over flat lands like this . . . that the larks sang." Now we see the land. And hear the lark.

What she has given us is of course not the landscape as you and I would see it, but her vision of it; we are looking at a work of art.

There is something very special, too, about its composition. Look at the Nebraska of her novels as a landscape she might have addressed herself to as an artist with a pencil or a brush. There is the foreground, with the living present, its human figures in action; and there is the horizon of infinite distance, where the departed, now invisible ancients have left only their faint track, cliff dwellings all but disappeared into thin air, pure light. But there is no intervening ground. There is no generation preceding the people now here alive, to fill up the gap between, to populate the stretch of emptiness. Nobody we can see, except the very youngest child, has been born here. Fathers and mothers traveled here, a few hardy grandparents who kept up will survive the life a little while too, and the rest of the antecedents have been left in their graveyards the width of the continent behind.

In this landscape we are made as aware of what isn't as of what is. There is no recent past. There is no middle distance;

the perspectives of time and space run unbroken, unmarked, unmeasured to the vanishing point. With nothing in between, the living foreground and that almost mythological, almost phantasmagorical background are all but made one, as in a Chinese painting—and exactly as in one of the mirages that Willa Cather's people often meet, quite casually, in the desert:

> . . . a shallow silver lake that spread for many miles, a little misty in the sunlight. Here and there one saw reflected the image of a heifer, turned loose to live upon the sparse sand grass. They were magnified to a preposterous height and looked like mammoths, prehistoric beasts standing solitary in the waters that for many thousands of years actually washed over that desert: the mirage itself may be the ghost of that long-vanished sea.

Or that ancient life may be discovered through profound personal experience, through one of her "opening windows." Willa Cather brought past and present into juxtaposition to the most powerful effect. And that landscape itself must have shown her this juxtaposition. It existed in the world where she lived, she had the eyes to see it, and she made it a truth of her art. When the sword of Coronado and the plow against the sun are fused into one in *My Ántonia*, we are seeing another vision of it.

The past can be seen—she lets us see it—in physical form. It can be touched—Thea can flake off with her thumb the carbon from the rock roof that came from the cooking stove of the Ancient People. Thea comes to have intuitions about their lives so close to heart that she could walk the trail like the women whose feet had worn it, "trying to walk as they must have walked, with a feeling in her feet and knees and loins which she had never known before. . . . She could feel the weight of an Indian baby hanging to her back as she climbed." And so Niel, of a later day, in *A Lost Lady*, feels in saying goodbye to it: "He had seen the end of an era, the sunset of the pioneer. He had come upon it when already its glory was nearly spent. So in the buffalo times a traveller used to come upon the embers of a hunter's fire on the prairie, after the hunter was up and gone; the coals would be trampled out, but the ground was warm, and the flattened grass where he had slept and where his pony had grazed, told the story."

5

She saw the landscape had mystery as well as reality. She was undaunted by both. And when she writes of the vast spaces of the world lying out in the extending night, mystery comes to her page, and has a presence; it seems to me a presence not too different from that called up by Turgenev in his magical "Behzin Meadow."

Willa Cather saw her broad land in a sweep, but she saw selectively too—the detail that made all the difference. She never lost sight of the particular in the panorama. Her eye was on the human being. In her continuous, acutely conscious and responsible act of bringing human value into focus, it was her accomplishment to bring her gaze from that wide horizon, across the stretches of both space and time, to the intimacy and immediacy of the lives of a handful of human beings.

People she saw slowly, with care, in their differences: her chosen characters. They stood up out of their soil and against their sky, making, each of them and one by one, a figure to reckon with.

"For the first time, perhaps, since that land emerged from waters of geologic ages," she says of Alexandra in that memorable passage in *O Pioneers!*, "a human face was set toward it with love and yearning. It seemed beautiful to her, rich and strong and glorious. Her eyes drank in the breadth of it, until her tears blinded her. Then the Genius of the Divide, the great, free spirit which breathes across it, must have bent lower than it ever bent to a human will before. The history of every country begins in the heart of a man or a woman."

And the farther and wider she could see when she started out, the closer it brought her, we feel, full circle—to the thing she wanted, the living, uncopyable *identity* of it that all her working life she wrote in order to meet, to face, to give us as well as she knew it in stories and novels.

The lack of middle distance may have something to do with the way the characters in the foreground cast such long, back-reaching shadows. In that lonely stretch of empty and waiting space, they take on heroic stature. And so, Jim Burden tells us—and this has been earned; we have almost reached the end of her novel: "Ántonia had always been one to leave images in the mind that did not fade—that grew stronger with time. . . . She lent herself to immemorial human attitudes which we recognize by instinct as universal and true. She was a battered woman now, not a lovely girl; but she still had that something which fires the imagination, could still stop one's breath for a moment by a look or gesture that somehow revealed the meaning in common things. She had only to stand in the orchard, to put her hand on a little crab tree and look up at the apples, to make you feel the goodness of planting and tending and harvesting at last. All the strong things of her heart came out in her body . . . . She was a rich mine of life, like the founders of early races."

A writer uses what he's been given. The work of William Faulkner—another writer of Southern origin, who was destined himself to live in the thick of his background and who had his own abiding sense of place and time and history—is packed most densely of all at the middle distance. The generations clustered just behind where the present-day characters are in action are in fact the tallest—and the most heavily burdened with that past. Faulkner's ancient peoples, his Indians, whose land was taken away by unjust treaty, who were expelled from their own, their race dispersed and brought to nothing, have made the land inimical to the white man. The slave has cursed him again. History for Faulkner is directly inherited; it has come down to the present with the taint of blood and the shame of wrongdoing a part of it. Along with the qualities of nobility and courage and endurance, there were for him corresponding qualities of guilt; there is torment in history and in Faulkner's wrestling with it, in his interpretation of it. Willa Cather's history was not thus bonded to the present; it did not imprison the present, but instructed it, passed on a meaning. It was pure, remained pure, and in its purity could come and go in crystal air. It had the character and something of the import of a vision. The spirit, and not the blood, received it.

In the world of her novels, history lies in persistence in the memory, in lost hidden places that wait to be found and to be known for what they are. Such history is barely accessible, the shell of it is only fraily held together, it will be loseable again. But the continuity is *there*.

Where does the continuity lie, then? It is made possible, it is carried out, is lived through, by the pioneer. And it is perceived by the artist. And even more profoundly, it exists, for

7

Willa Cather, as a potential in the artist himself; it is his life's best meaning, his own personal, and responsible, connection with the world.

"That stream"—Thea is meditating in Panther Canyon —"was the only living thing left of the drama that had been played out in the cañon centuries ago. In the rapid, restless heart of it, flowing swifter than the rest, there was a continuity of life that reached back into the old time. . . . The stream and the broken pottery: what was any art but an effort to make a sheath, a mould in which to imprison for a moment the shining, elusive element which is life itself—life hurrying past us and running away, too strong to stop, too sweet to lose? The Indian women had held it in their jars. . . . In singing, one made a vessel of one's throat and nostrils and held it on one's breath, caught the stream in a scale of natural intervals."

When Thea holds the ancients' pottery in her hands, her feeling for art is born. When Willa Cather makes her novel one about art, she chooses art not of the word, but of the voice. And not the song, but the voice. She has been able to say everything—it is a dazzling translation—in terms of the human being in a physical world.

The whole work of Willa Cather is an embodiment. The great thing it embodies is, of course passion. That is its vital principle.

She did not come out of Virginia for nothing, any more than she grew up in Nebraska for nothing. History awed and stirred Willa Cather; and the absence of a history as far as she could see around her, in her growing up, only made her look farther, gave her the clues to discover a deeper past. The scarcity of people, a sense of absence and emptiness, set to work in her mind ideas not of despair but of aspiration, the urgency to make out of whatever was there *something*—a thing of her own. She opened her mind to the past as she would to a wise teacher. When she saw the connections, the natural channels opening, she let the past come flooding into the present.

"To people off alone, as we were, there is something stirring about finding evidences of human labour and care in the soil of an empty country. It comes to you as a sort of message, makes you feel differently about the ground you walk over every day," says Tom Outland, in *The Professor's House*.

Eudora Welty

Willa Cather's story conceptions have their physical bases, and their physical counterparts. The shift that took place in her own life when her family moved from its settled home in Virginia to the unbroken prairie of the Divide came about when she was nine years old, so likely to be the most sensitive, most vulnerable year of childhood. Its wrench to the spirit was translated over and over again into the situations in her novels and stories. The shift from one home to another, the shift of feeling, must have become in itself the source of a distinctive fictional pattern which was to fall into place for her; it is the kaleidoscopic wrench to the heart that exposes the deeper feeling there. Not impossibly, the origin of her technique of juxtaposition lay in the Virginia–Nebraska move, too. She worked out some of her most significant effects by bringing widely separated lives, times, experiences together—placing them side by side or one within the other, opening out of it almost like a vision—like Tom Outland's story from *The Professor's House*—or existing along with it, waiting in its path, like the mirage.

Personal history may turn into a fictional pattern without closely reproducing it, without needing to reproduce it at all. Essences are what make patterns. Fictional patterns may well bite deeper than the events of a life will ever of themselves, or by themselves, testify to. The pattern is one of interpretation. There, the connections are as significant as what they join together, or perhaps more so. The meaning comes through the joined and completed structure, out of the worthiness of its accomplishment.

In the novel, relationships, development of acts and their effects, and any number of oblique, *felt* connections, which are as important and as indispensable as the factual ones, in composing the plot, form a structure of revelation. The pattern is the plot opened out, disclosing—this was its purpose—some human truth.

Of course it is a pattern uniquely marked by its author's character; the nature of personal feeling has given it its grain. Willa Cather's revered Flaubert said in a letter, "The secret of masterpieces lies in the concordance between the subject and the temperament of the author." The events of a story may have much or little to do with the writer's own life; but the story *pattern* is the nearest thing to a mirror image of his mind and heart.

The artist needs and seeks distance—his own best distance—in order to learn about his subject. To open up the new, to look back on the old, may bring forth like discoveries in the practice of art. Whether the comprehension keeps to the short perimeter around the present, or runs far back into the past, is secondary to the force, impellment, of human feeling involved: *this* determines its reach.

We need to know only what the work of Willa Cather in its course has to tell us—for it's a great deal—about her independence and courage of mind to guess that Miss Jewett's well-known advice—"You must find a quiet place. . . . You must find your own quiet centre of life and write from that"—would not have been the sign to her it was, unless she had arrived at that fact for herself, deep in her own nature. How could she not have? It was central to her life, basic to her conception of character, of situation, in fiction: the writing of one novel had been able to teach her that. When she read that truth of Miss Jewett's, isn't it likely that she simply *recognized* it? As she recognized, in the Dutch masters when she saw them in Paris, her own intention in a book to come:

"Just before I began the book [*The Professor's House*]," runs a well-known letter she wrote, "I had seen, in Paris, an exhibition of old and modern Dutch paintings. In many of them the scene presented was a living-room warmly furnished, or a kitchen full of food and coppers. But in most of the interiors, whether drawing-room or kitchen, there was a square window, open, through which one saw the masts of ships, or a stretch of grey sea. The feeling of the sea that one got through those square windows was remarkable, and gave me a sense of fleets of Dutch ships that ply quietly on all the waters of the globe."

It is not surprising that the act of recognition is one of the touchstones of her fiction. We see her writing in *The Song of the Lark:* "The faculty of observation was never highly developed in Thea Kronborg. A great deal escaped her eye as she passed through the world. But the things which were for her, she saw; she experienced them physically and remembered them as if they had once been part of herself. The roses she used to see in the florists' shops in Chicago were merely roses. But when she thought of the moonflowers that grew over Mrs. Tellamantez's door, it was as if she had been that vine and had opened up in white flowers every night." And, "Here, in Panther Cañon, there were again things which seemed destined for her." And before that, "When the English horns gave out the theme of the Largo [this is Thea hearing Dvořák's *New World Symphony* for the first time], she knew that what she wanted was exactly that. Here were the sand hills, the grasshoppers and locusts, all the things that wakened and chirped in the early morning; the reaching and reaching of high plains, the immeasurable yearning of all flat lands. There was home in it, too; first memories, first mornings long ago; the amazement of a new soul in a new world; a soul new and yet old, that had dreamed something despairing, something glorious, in the dark before it was born; a soul obsessed by what it did not know, under the cloud of a past it could not recall."

Recognition, we feel, was for Willa Cather a learning process that didn't stop; and Willa Cather was a born learner. The beautiful early story "The Enchanted Bluff" about the boys whose whole wish was to escape from home and who fail in their lives when they never make the break, turned into a chapter of *My Ántonia* that is more beautiful. Here, as in "The Enchanted Bluff," we have children listening and dreaming as a story is being told to them; Jim tells the children about the coming of Coronado and his search for the Seven Golden Cities in the early days, coming right here to Nebraska, where a sword with the name of its Spanish maker was turned up by a farmer breaking sod. And

> Presently we saw a curious thing: There were no clouds, the sun was going down in a limpid, gold-washed sky. Just as the lower edge of the red disk rested on the high fields against the horizon, a great black figure suddenly appeared on the face of the sun. We sprang to our feet, straining our eyes toward it. In a moment we realized what it was. On some upland farm, a plough had been left standing in the field. The sun was sinking just behind it. Magnified across the distance by the horizontal light, it stood out against the sun, was exactly contained within the circle of the disk; the handles, the tongue, the share—black against the molten red. There it was, heroic in size, a picture writing on the sun.
>
> Even while we whispered about it, our vision disappeared; the ball dropped and dropped until the red tip went beneath the earth. The fields below us were dark, the sky was growing pale,

11

and that forgotten plough had sunk back to its own littleness somewhere on the prairie.

The author has come to her quiet center. Nebraska, when she left it, was "Siberia"; now, for her writer's eyes, it is a radiant force of life itself.

The birth of Willa Cather came, as it happens, in the year Mark Twain began writing *Huckleberry Finn*. The authors' worlds were different, their frontiers were different—the events in *Huck* went back, of course, to the 1830s and '40s—but they worked, in a way that came naturally to them both, to something of the same scale. They stand together in *bigness*—their sense of it, their authority over it. The difference I want to mention is not in scale or in authority over it, but in the fictional uses to which the world is put.

Through each of their lands there flows a river. Mark Twain's Mississippi is the wider and muddier. It is the route and channel of adventure to Huck; around every bend as he takes it, the river is both what he's looking for and what he dreads, and it's got for him what he'd not dreamed of till he finds it. It's *experience* he's on raft-level with; it can wash him overboard, he can plunge for it too, and endanger himself and refresh himself and cleanse himself or hide himself, or defy it, or live off it, dream on it, or show off on it. It is his to live through, and he lives through it—comes out at the other end alive, and ready to take off for a new frontier if they try too hard again to civilize him.

Willa Cather's river is filled with grandeur and power too; it too is both danger and rescue, the demander of courage and daring, of sacrifice and reverence and awe; it stirs the heart to a sense of destiny. But the river that waters the plains for Willa Cather is the pure stream of art.

The works of these two are totally unalike except in their very greatest respects, except in being about something big, in the apprehension of the new, and in movement, tireless movement in its direction. And both great writers say: Who can move best but the inspired child of his times? Whose story should better be told than that of the youth who has contrived to cut loose from ties and go flinging himself might and main, in every bit of his daring, in joy of life not to be denied, to vaunt himself in the love of vaunting, in the marvelous curiosity to find out everything, over the preposterous length and breadth of an opening new world, and in so doing to be one with it? The Mississippi River and the unbroken Prairie; comedy and tragedy; and indeed all destinies and destinations, all come subordinate to the charge of life itself. The two novelists remain a world apart, and yet both, at their best, celebrate through the living presence of that world, an undeniable force—the pursuit of truth. They recognize and confront a common evil—the defiling of the proud human spirit.

It is in looking back on Willa Cather's work that we learn how the vast exterior world she shows us novel by novel, a world ever-present and full of weight and substance and stir, visible to us along differing perspectives and in various mutations of time, has been the deliberately fitted form for each novel's own special needs. This world is here to serve her purpose by taking a fictional role, allying itself more or less openly with human destiny. It appears, according to role, a world with the power to crush and suffocate, and the power to give back life; a world to promise everything, and to deny everything; a world to open a way for living, or to close in life's face. It is all her great, ex-panding on-moving world; she has made it hers to take at its own beginnings and follow to its slow eclipse; and, in the full circle of it, to bring home the significance of the solitary human spirit which has elected to bring itself there, in its will and its struggle to survive.

She sought for the wholeness of the form—the roundness of the world, the full circle of life. The vital principle, this passion, has of its own a life—a seed, a birth, a growth, a maturing, a decline and sinking into death, back into the earth; it carries within it the pattern of life on earth, and is a part of the same continuity. It is "the old story writing itself over. . . . It is we who write it, with the best we have," says Alexandra, at the conclusion of *O Pioneers!*.

The emotions of Willa Cather's characters, too, have deep roots in the physical world—in that actual physical land to which they were born. In such a land, how clear it is from the start that identity—self-identity—is hard to seize, hard to claim, and hard to hold onto.

Another of the touchstones of her work, I think, is her feeling for the young. "There is no work of art so big or so beautiful," she writes,"that it was not once all contained in some youthful body, like this one [it is Thea's] which lay on the floor in the moonlight, pulsing with ardour and anticipation." The burning drive of the young, the desire to live, to do, to make, to achieve, no matter what the sacrifice, is the feeling most surpassingly alive to the author, most moving to us. Life has made her terribly certain that being young in the world is not easy."If youth did not matter so much to itself, it would never have the heart to go on," she says, as Thea starts from home. And Doctor Archie, old friend and traveling companion, "knew that the splendid things of life are few, after all, and so very easy to miss." In *O Pioneers!* we read that "there is often a good deal of the child left in people who have had to grow up too soon." Miss Cather has a number of ways to tell us that life is most passionate in the promise, not in the fulfillment.

A strenuous physical life is lived throughout every novel, whether it is the struggle for survival or the keen experience of joy in simple physical well-being; it may reach in some characters the point of total identification with the living world around. It is a form of the passion that is all through Willa Cather's work; her work is written out of it. We see it in many modulations: desire—often exalted as ambition; devotion; loyalty; fidelty; physical nearness and kindness and comfort when it lies at rest. Love? It is affection that warms the life in her stories and hate that chills it. There is reconcilement, and there is pity. There is obsession here too, and so is the hunger for something impossible: all of these are forms of love. And there is marriage, though the marriages that occur along the way of the novels are milestones, hardly destinations; as required in the careful building of her plots, they are inclined to be unavailing. Sexual love is not often present in the here and now; we more often learn of it after it is over, or see it in its results. My own feeling is that along with her other superior gifts Willa Cather had a rare sureness as to *her* subject, the knowledge of just what to touch and what not to touch in the best interests of her story.

What her characters are mostly meant for, it seems to me, is to rebel. For her heroines in particular, rebelling is much easier than not rebelling, and we may include love, too, in not rebelling. It is the strong, clear impulse in Willa Cather's stories. It is the real springwater. It is rebelling, we should always add, not for its own sake as much as for the sake of something a great deal bigger—for the sake of integrity, of truth, of art. It is the other face of aspiration. Willa Cather used her own terms; and she left nothing out. What other honorable way is there for an artist to have her say?

The novels have the qualities and the components of love in proportions all their own, then; and I believe this may point again to the thought that they are concerned not with *two* but with *one*, in the number of human beings—not, finally, with relationships but with the desire in one heart and soul to claim what is its own, to achieve its measure of greatness, to overcome any terrible hardship, any terrible odds; and this desire is served by love, rewarded by love (but its absence or failure never compensated for by love); and most of the time, and at its highest moments, the desire is its own drive, its own gratification. One of its forms is indeed pride; and pride is not punished in Willa Cather's novels, it can be deserved.

"Her voice . . . had to do with that confidence, that sense of wholeness and inner well-being that she had felt at moments ever since she could remember. . . . It was as if she had an appointment to meet the rest of herself sometime, somewhere. It was moving to meet her and she was moving to meet it. That meeting awaited her, just as surely as, for the poor girl in the [train] seat behind her, there awaited a hole in the earth, already dug." And then in the city, at the concert, hearing the music that is to change her life, Thea says, "As long as she lived that ecstasy was going to be hers. She would live for it, work for it, die for it; but she was going to have it, time after time, height after height. . . . She would have it, what the trumpets were singing! She would have it, have it—it!"

How does Willa Cather make this an emotion for which we have such entire sympathy? Its intensity, I think, is the answer—Thea's intensity partaking of Willa Cather's. Thea's music teacher says of her, " 'Her secret? It is every artist's secret—passion. That is all. It is an open secret, and perfectly safe. Like heroism, it is inimitable in cheap materials.' "

This high desire, when merged into other than itself, merges into the whole world. An individuality can be made willing to lose itself only in something as big as the world. It *was* the world, in *O Pioneers!* and *My Ántonia*. It was not the world itself, except in magnitude and undeniability, in *The Song of the Lark* and, consummately, in *The Professor's House*: it was art.

For this novelist, art, as she saw it and perfected it, always kept the proportions of the great world and the undeniability of the world, and it lived for her as certainly as this world lived. And the strongest *felt* relationship, a reader may come to believe, might not be any of those between the characters but the one their creator feels for them, for their developing, passionate lives.

In a landscape this wide and pulsing, it seems not at all out of keeping that the greatest passions made real to us are those *for* greatness, and for something larger than life. Men and women do of course fall in love in Willa Cather's novels and their relationship is brought into clear enough focus for us to put good reliance on; but the desire to make a work of art is a stronger one, and more lasting. In the long run, love of art—which is love accomplished without help or need of help from another —is what is deepest and realest in her work.

There is not a trace of disparagement in her treatment of the least of her characters. The irony of her stories is grave, never belittling; it is a showing of sympathy. She *contended* for the life of the individual. Her attack was positive and vigorous and unflinching and proud of winning. This contending was the essence of her stories, formed her plots, gave her room for action. And she did it without preaching. She lacked self-righteousness, and she just as wholly lacked bitterness; what a lesson *A Lost Lady* gives us in doing without bitterness. It is impossible to think of diminishment in anything she thought or wrote. She conceived of character along heroic lines. For her, the heroic life is the artist's as it is the pioneer's. She equated the two.

Set within the land is the dwelling—made by human hands to hold human life. As we know, the intensity of desire for building the house to live in—or worship in—fills all the Cather novels. It fills the past for her, it gives the present meaning; it provides for a future: the house is the physical form, the *evidence* that we have lived, are alive now; it will be evidence some day that we were alive once, evidence against the arguments of time and the tricks of history.

In her landscape, we learn from both seeing what is there and realizing what is not there; there is always felt the *absence* of habitation. We come to know what degrees there are of the burrow and the roof. "The houses on the Divide were small and were usually tucked away in low places; you did not see them until you came directly upon them," we read of the Scandinavian settlement in *O Pioneers!*. "Most of them were built of the sod itself, and were only the unescapable ground in another form." Mrs. Archie, in *The Song of the Lark*, of whom we are told "such little, mean natures are among the darkest and most baffling of created things," liked to "have her house clean, empty, dark, locked, and to be out of it—anywhere." The Professor's house, shabby and outgrown as it is, is a dated house; but the cliff house, almost older than time, is timeless.

"I wish I could tell you what I saw there, just *as* I saw it, on that first morning, through a veil of lightly falling snow," Tom Outland tells him, in his story within the story. "Far up above me, a thousand feet or so, set in a great cavern in the face of the cliff, I saw a little city of stone, asleep. . . . It all hung together, seemed to have a kind of composition. . . . The tower was the fine thing that held all the jumble of houses together and made them mean something. . . . I felt that only a strong and aspiring people would have built it, and a people with a feeling for design." "The town hung like a bird's nest in the cliff, . . . facing an ocean of clear air. A people who had the hardihood to build there, and who lived day after day looking down upon such grandeur, who came and went by those hazardous trails, must have been . . . a fine people." " 'I see them here, isolated, cut off from other tribes, working out their destiny,' " said Father Duchene, the scholar, " 'making their mesa more and more worthy to be a home for man. . . . Like you,' " he tells Tom Outland, " 'I feel a reverence for this place. Wherever humanity has made that hardest of all starts and lifted itself out of mere brutality, is a sacred spot. . . . They built themselves into this mesa and humanized it.' "

The Professor's House is a novel with a unique form, and to read it is to see it built before our eyes: the making of two unlike parts into a whole under a sheltering third part which

17

defines it and is as final as that verse that comes to recite itself to the Professor's mind. The construction is simple, forthright, and daring. By bringing the Professor's old house and the cliff dwellers' house in combination to the mind, Willa Cather gives them simultaneous existence, and with the measure of time taken away we may see, in the way of a mirage, or a vision, humanity's dwelling places all brought into one. And it was there all the time:

> For thee a house was built
> Ere thou wast born;
> For thee a mould was made
> Ere thou of woman camest.

Tom Outland's story, set into *The Professor's House* like the view from the casement of that Dutch interior, is the objectively told, factual-seeming counterpart of Thea's experience in the Ancient People's cliff houses in *The Song of the Lark*, which was published ten years earlier. Tom Outland's story has a further difference: the tragic view.

It is the objective chronicler for whom the story comes to a tragic end. For Thea, who has seen in her discovery of the Ancient People something totally and exclusively her own, and her own secret, it remained undamaged as a dream. She apprehended it in her own mind, and her own body, as a message for her. Tom Outland's Cliff City was there in the world, and he wanted the world to discover it as he had, to study it, venerate it, share it; and it was taken away from him, broken and desecrated; it brought about not the self-discovery of Thea, but a crisis and a lasting sorrow in human relationship. In the end, it is more of an interior story than Thea's ever was.

"Tom Outland's Story" is written with a compression and strength that the author had already showed us in *A Lost Lady*, and achieves a simplicity that, as it seems to me, nothing else she wrote ever surpassed. Such simplicity is not what a writer starts with; it is what the writer is able to end with, or hopes to be able.

The Professor's House in whole might show us that the novel, in its excellence as a work of art, stands, itself, as a house finished. In so much as it has perfection, perfection has not sealed it, but opened it to us.

A work of art is a *work*: something made, which in the making follows an idea that comes out of human life and leads back into human life. A work of art is the house that is *not* the grave. An achievement of order, passionately conceived and passionately carried out, it is not a thing of darkness. When it is finished, if it is good and sound, somehow all opacity has left it. It stands as clear as candor itself. The fine physical thing has become a transparency through which the idea it was made to embody is thus made totally visible. It could not have been this visible before it was embodied. We see human thought and feeling best and clearest by seeing it through something solid that our hands have made.

"Artistic growth is, more than it is anything else, a refining of the sense of truthfulness." This is said at the end of *The Song of the Lark*. "The stupid believe that to be truthful is easy; only the artist, the great artist, knows how difficult it is." And, Thea's teacher has told her, " 'Every artist makes himself born. It is very much harder than the other time, and longer.' "

In the Cather novels, there is a setting apart of the artist in value, a setting apart of his life from that of other people. Artists, in her considered and lifelong view, are perhaps greater and more deserving to be made way for than other human beings. This could never have been a popular view, but in trying to understand it I think she extolled the artist not for what would seem vanity, or for anything less than a function he could perform—the great thing that only an artist would be able, in her eyes, to do. The artist has a role. Thea, meditating on this role, thought, of the people who cared about her singing, "Perhaps each of them concealed another person in himself, just as she did. . . . What if one's second self could somehow speak to all those second selves?" At base, I think this is an aspect of the Cather sense of obligation to give of oneself. "If he achieves anything noble, anything enduring, it must be by giving himself absolutely to his material. And this gift of sympathy is his great gift," Willa Cather said; "it is the fine thing in him that alone can make his work fine." The artist is set apart the more entirely, all but symbolically, to give himself away, to fulfill the ultimate role of dedication.

Today, neither the artist nor the world holds this idea, and it has faded, along with some of her other strong beliefs (the hero and the heroine, the sanctity of the family), from our own view. Our ideas of history and art are different from hers, as tomorrow's will be different from today's. We have arrived at new places to stand to obtain our own viewpoint of history. Art, since it grows out of its times, is of itself, and by rights, a changing body. But truth?

Truth is the rock. Willa Cather saw it as unassailable. Today the question is asked if this is indeed so. Many of us align ourselves with Willa Cather—I do—in thinking the truth will hold out; but there are many who feel another way, and indeed, I believe, many who would not feel life was over if there were no truth there.

One of the strangest things about art, nevertheless, is that the rock it is built on is not its real test. Our greatest poem made a mistake about the construction of the universe, but this will never bring the poem down.

Yet plain enough is the structure Willa Cather built on these rocks she herself believed were eternal. Her work we, today, see entirely on its own, without need of that support. It holds itself independently, as that future church appears to be doing above the dreaming head of Saint Francis of Assisi in Giotto's fresco. Her work has its own firm reason for existence. And here it stands, a monument more unshakable than she might have dreamed, to the independent human spirit she most adored.

She made this work out of her life, her perishable life, which is so much safer a material to build with than convictions, however immutable they seem to the one who so passionately holds them. It is out of our own lives that we, in turn, reach out to it. Because the house of Willa Cather contained, embodied, a spirit, it will always seem to us inhabited. There is life in that house, the spirit she made it for, made it out of; it is all one substance: it is her might and her heart and soul, all together, and it abides.

[*Sources of quotations from Willa Cather's writings are listed on page 259.*]

The Two or More Worlds
of Willa Cather

Marcus Cunliffe

In 1923 Frederick Jackson Turner, the famous historian of the frontier, remarked that "American history and American literature cannot be understood apart from each other." Most of us would accept Turner's comment as a truism. Yet the problem of the relation between historical and literary approaches is more complicated than that. Thus, so far as I can determine, Willa Cather did not read Turner's enormously influential essays, though they set the pattern for an entire generation of American historians, from about 1900 to 1930; and Turner for his part, though in 1924 he told a correspondent that "a valuable study might be made of the pioneer woman and her place in history,"[1] seems never to have read Willa Cather.

We shall come back later to the parallels and divergences in these two figures. For the moment, my point is that for the purposes of historians, some imaginative writers lend themselves more readily than others to classroom citation. The historian appears to feel most at home with novelists who discuss public issues in their work, or who take stands on issues in their capacity as citizens. In covering the years from 1880 to 1930 or thereabouts, the historian of the United States fastens upon such authors as Edward Bellamy, William Dean Howells, Mark Twain, Frank Norris, Winston Churchill, Sinclair Lewis, and Scott Fitzgerald. He instances Bellamy's *Looking Backward* (1888) as a novel directly concerned with social abuses and social reform. He is fascinated by the development of a social

21

conscience in Howells's novels. He is interested in the more oblique social satire of Twain's *Connecticut Yankee* (1889), in which Twain's illustrator Dan Beard supplied caricatures for a rogues' gallery of contemporary Europeans and Americans. The historian refers students to Norris's *The Octopus* (1901) for a view of the struggle between farmers and capitalists in California, and to *The Pit* (1903) for an account of the frenzied operations of the stock market in Chicago. Churchill's novels supply material for an understanding of political corruption in the so-called Progressive Era. Sinclair Lewis and Scott Fitzgerald are treated as chroniclers of the America of the 1920s. Or the historian brings in those writers who associated themselves with the causes and controversies of their day: Howells for his courageous stand on behalf of Chicago's Haymarket anarchists in 1886, Twain as an anti-imperialist, in the wake of the Spanish-American War, Upton Sinclair and Jack London as socialists, and so on.

Willa Cather, being much less easy to handle, has been comparatively neglected by historians. She is of course less preoccupied with purely local affairs than Sarah Orne Jewett, or with abstractions of behavior than Henry James—two fellow writers whom she much admired, and whose work has likewise not supplied much leverage for historians. Willa Cather is a precise observer. With James we usually have only the vaguest explanation of what his characters do for a living, or how much money they make. In Cather's case the material circumstances are often recorded with some exactness. The dollars and cents are set forth. Financial disasters and successes are fairly prominent in her plots. Some of her characters, we learn, are much affected by the dramas of the time. We are told for example that Rodney Blake in *The Professor's House* (1925) feels strongly about the Chicago anarchists and about the Dreyfus trial in France. But such allusions remain peripheral; they are never at the center of the story.

As for her personal response to public issues, this too seems unemphatic—at least when set beside those of the other contemporary writers I have mentioned. In his lively book *The Landscape and the Looking Glass* (1960), John H. Randall suggests that Willa Cather was considerably influenced by the Populist ferment of Nebraska in the 1890s. This may well be true. But,

Marcus Cunliffe

taking her work as a whole, I do not feel that the Populist outlook was crucial and enduring for her. The esthetic modes of the decade, which Mr. Randall also stresses, strike me as having fixed her attitudes in profounder ways. None of Willa Cather's formidable pioneer women emulates the Populist leader Mary Leese, who urged farmers to "raise less corn and more hell." In the next decade, after 1900, America became highly politicized (to use a jargon word of a later period). Political reform, temperance, women's rights, housing and working conditions, pacifism, conservation: these activities aroused a multitude of energetic and articulate Americans—women as well as men. One thinks for example of Jane Addams, the founder of the Chicago slum settlement known as Hull House, who flung herself into a variety of causes, including that of Theodore Roosevelt's "Bull Moose" Progressivism in 1912. There was abundant opportunity for the writer, through the spread of what Roosevelt called muckraking journalism. Willa Cather, with her editorial job on *McClure's Magazine,* the most lively of all the muckraking periodicals, was set in the midst of Progressivism. Yet for whatever temperamental reasons, she seems to have stood apart from the indignations and aspirations of the Progressive Era. Nor did she seek to attune herself closely to the *Zeitgeist* in later years. Her war novel *One of Ours* (1922) is to my mind a somewhat better book than most critics have been prepared to acknowledge. But it does not reveal a comprehensive grasp of the moods of wartime America or of the immediate postwar atmosphere. Her subsequent treatment of the American scene, for instance in *The Professor's House,* is intelligent but diffuse, as if the author is unsure whether valediction or malediction is the fitter response.

Historians in their classes might have been able to draw upon Cather's writings to illustrate theories of art and literature. Here too she has failed to oblige them. Her ideas on writing are well stated and in my view perfectly sound. But she seems to have declined to jump through the right hoops at the right moment. She did not in the 1890s become identified with the new advocates of naturalism in literature, though self-professedly "Western" writers such as Frank Norris and Hamlin Garland asserted that truth in literature was something that the authors of their region were peculiarly qualified to produce. Willa Cather did

23

not stake out a claim for herself as a woman writer. Though some of her principal characters are women, they display an almost mannish shrewdness and vigor; and in some of her novels the viewpoint is in more ways than one that of a man. Not for Cather, then, the combination of feminine perception and technical experiment evident in the stream-of-consciousness fiction of her English contemporaries Dorothy Richardson and Virginia Woolf. She may in *One of Ours* have expressed an innocent idealism that actually existed. But the historian prefers to conclude that the American experience in World War I was best rendered in the youthful avant-garde prose of John Dos Passos's *Three Soldiers* (1921) and E. E. Cummings's *The Enormous Room* (1922). Her much-quoted observation that the world broke in two in the year 1922 could be taken as her own recognition that she could not imaginatively make the transition from the old universe to the new, in part because she had never sought to keep abreast of literary fashion. So, according to this interpretation, she was able to enjoy talking with D. H. Lawrence when she met him in New York and then through Mabel Dodge Luhan in New Mexico,[2] but would never have been able to stomach most of Lawrence's fiction—any more than she could appreciate James Joyce's *Ulysses* or the plays of Eugene O'Neill. I suppose historians ought not to be blamed too much for their indifference to Willa Cather, seen as spokesman for her time, when some literary critics have also displayed a good deal of uneasiness, and have tended to categorize her as a "traditional" novelist. That may amount to a confession that they are unable to devise any suitable definition or "placing" for Willa Cather.

So much for the superficial problems that have—at least so far as historians are concerned—kept some of us from including her within the familiar range of cultural references. My main argument however is of a different order. It is that each of us is, after all, a prisoner of the *Zeitgeist;* that Willa Cather does, for the historian and possibly for the student of literature, help to shed light on her own age; and that by approaching her from this external position one may gain an additional appreciation of her individual quality. In particular, I wish to examine her as both a product and an exponent of a whole set of tensions between West and East. To some extent these are universal tensions, affecting all "advanced" civilizations at the end of the nineteenth century, and indeed all societies aware of a difference between the provincial life and that of the metropolis.

Within the American framework, it is clear—to begin with —that some Easterners treated the West with a casualness amounting on occasion to contempt. At various times the New Englander Henry Adams observed that the whole country west of the Alleghenies might as well be scrapped. "I do not like the western type of man," was the similar verdict of the New York journalist E. L. Godkin, editor of the *Nation*. The young literary scholar George Edward Woodberry, bemoaning the fate that had exiled him as a teacher at the University of Nebraska, told a Boston friend that the Nebraska faculty was split between Eastern and Western members. Nebraska society was "characterized by blank Philistinism intellectually and barren selfishness morally." The undergraduates were unkempt and wore "shirt fronts of outrageous uncleanness." "This life," he lamented, "requires a hardihood of the senses and susceptibilities of which you have little conception, I fear. . . . I doubt very much whether the hardihood I gain will not be a deterioration into barbarism, not sinew for civilization." In about 1890 the Johns Hopkins historian Herbert Baxter Adams, reared in New England and trained in Germany, was offered a temptingly well-paid professorship at the University of Chicago, which for him was in the West. Pondering the advantages and disadvantages of his present post as against the new future one, Adams drew up a balance sheet. He headed one column "Chicago," the other "Baltimore":

CHICAGO	BALTIMORE
Rush	Quiet
Broken	Continuity
Experiment	Experience
New People	Society
Boom	Conservatism
Advantage	Duty
All new	Assured position
Moving	Settled
Lost	Identification

It is not difficult to guess from this choice of vocabulary that

Adams decided to stay put.[3] For a convinced Easterner, the West was raw, rude, and remote. It was worse than the provinces, in a European scheme, in being not just relatively but almost absolutely uncultivated.

However, as in the case of the European metropolis-provinces polarity, the disdain of the Easterner was often matched by the self-abasement of the sensitive Westerner. A special feature of the American Westerner was that he was often not a native provincial but someone who had come out to the West from the East, and felt he was regressing into barbarism. This was for instance the initial reaction of the young California writer Bret Harte, who had grown up in New York City. In his contributions to San Francisco magazines, during the middle 1860s, Harte sighed at the ugliness of such American place-names as Poker Flat, Red Dog, and One Horse Flat. In another piece he wrote: "The less said about the motives of some of our pioneers the better; very many were more concerned in getting away from where they were, than in going to any particular place." A few years later, as editor of the *Overland Monthly*, Harte poured scorn on the Society of California Pioneers, and claimed that what the West needed instead was a Society for the Suppression of Local Pride.[4]

It was not necessary to be a settler from the East to denigrate the West. Edgar W. Howe, a thirty-year-old newspaper editor in Kansas, poured out his accumulated bitterness in a novel entitled *The Story of a Country Town* (1883). One of the characters in the novel says:

> Haven't you noticed that when a Western man gets a considerable sum of money together, he goes East to live? Well, what does it mean except that the good sense which enabled him to make money teaches him that the society there is preferable to ours? . . . Men who are prosperous . . . do not come West, but it is the unfortunate, the poor, the indigent, the sick . . . who came here to grow up with the country, having failed to grow up with the country where they came from.

Nor was it necessary for a Westerner to apologize for coming East. The classic Dick Whittington-ish story of the ambitious and talented person in all eras and countries is that he demonstrates his ability by leaving the country for the city, the prov-

26

inces for the metropolis. Ambition itself dictates the move; and the consolation for the provinces is that such-and-such a famous individual is "from" their area. They gain or hope to gain a minor glory from what is in fact an abandonment. There is a pathos in this recurrent drama. Sometimes the native sophisticate almost entirely loses his original feeling for the home place, as seems to have happened with William Dean Howells in relation to his Ohio childhood. Sometimes the escaper makes his living out of his store of recollections, as in large part Bret Harte did with California. Sometimes, as with Mark Twain, his best writing deals with the scenes of his early life. Usually, however, he does not go back again except on visits. Missouri-born Twain, comfortably installed in Connecticut, wrote to an old friend in 1876 about Southern politics:

> I think I comprehend their position there—perfect freedom to vote just as you choose, provided you choose to vote as *other people* think, social ostracism otherwise. . . . Fortunately a good deal of experience of men enabled me to choose my residence wisely. I live in the freest part of the country.

But the provinces-metropolis analogy is inexact as applied to the American polarity of West and East, and this not merely because the American "West" was an area whose geographical boundaries and whose other characteristics were continually shifting. There was the further complicating factor that in the American myth, as it has been delineated by Henry Nash Smith and others, the West was never simply the back-of-beyond. It was also, and to a growing degree as the nineteenth century wore on, the land of America's destiny, the locus of the westering impulse evoked in Walt Whitman's poem "Passage to India" (a poem that Bret Harte, incidentally, rejected when it was submitted to his *Overland Monthly*). After his death in 1865 Abraham Lincoln began to be deified as a great Western symbolic hero—the "first American" in the words of J. R. Lowell's Harvard Commemoration Ode. *The American Commonwealth* (1889), a widely read assessment by the Scottish observer James Bryce, insisted that the West was the most American part of the United States. In the traditional legend, the provinces are fatally and irretrievably backward, vis-à-vis the metropolis. In part of

27

the American formulation, the West is not backward but forward: the place of the future.* According to this reversal, in
important respects the "latest" is not to be found in the East but
in the West; and even the "latest" in the limited sense of the
latest fashions in books and clothes was swiftly becoming
available in Western metropolises—including the Chicago that
Herbert Baxter Adams had so summarily dismissed. This other
mood was expressed in Carl Sandburg's *Chicago Poems* (1914):

> I speak of new cities and new people.
> I tell you the past is a bucket of ashes. . . .
> I tell you there is nothing in the world
>   only an ocean of to-morrows,
>   a sky of to-morrows.

As the nineteenth century drew to a close, Westerners were
inclined to argue the strengths of their region as measured by
both kinds of up-to-dateness. The historian Charles A. Beard,
who had grown up in Indiana, later remembered his annoyance
in the 1890s at the prevailing Eastern assumption "that all of us
beyond the Alleghenies, if not the Hudson, were almost, if not
quite, uncouth savages."[5] Frederick Jackson Turner, then a
young teacher at the University of Wisconsin, was exasperated
by an 1891 article in the *Century Magazine* by that proper Bostonian, Henry Cabot Lodge. Lodge analyzed over fourteen
thousand entries in *Appleton's Encyclopedia of American Biography* to prove to his own satisfaction that practically all the
talent in the United States had derived from New England,
New York, and adjacent states. A generation later, in 1926,
Turner offered a rebuttal on behalf of the West in the shape of
an article (*Yale Review*, July 1926) entitled "Children of the
Pioneers." Turner had been working on it for years. His biographer Ray Billington tells us: "It was crammed with the names

---

*Turner too voiced this sentiment. He wrote in 1887: "I am placed in a *new*
society, which is just beginning to realize that it has made a place for itself by
mastering the wilderness and peopling the prairie, and is now ready to take its
great course in universal history. It is something of a compensation to be among
the advance guard of new social ideas and among a people whose destiny is all
unknown. *The west looks to the future, the east toward the past.*" Quoted in
Hofstadter, *The Progressive Historians*, p. 63.

28

of westerners who had succeeded in business, government, and the arts . . . ; his westerners, he believed, gained Lincoln-esque stature by their dedication to the interests of the ordinary people, inventing or writing or worshipping or painting to glorify and instruct the common man.'"*

When therefore Turner delivered his paper "The Significance of the Frontier in American History" at a conference in Chicago in 1893, the moment was exactly right. Instead of bowing to the Lodgeish assurance that the West was, so to speak, on probation and perhaps unlikely to pass the test, Turner declared that everything vitally democratic in American life had developed from the frontier experience. Within a few years every historian of note was beginning to incorporate the Turner frontier thesis in his interpretation of the national past. In Turner's lifetime, to his gratified amusement, references to the frontier spirit even became common in the utterances of politicians. There was the additional gratification that the children of the pioneers were moving into more and more prominence, in their own areas and among the strongholds of the East. He himself exemplified the process by accepting a chair at Harvard with effect from 1910; Harvard had already given him an honorary degree in the previous year.

One reason for the rapid spread of a new congratulatory attitude to the West, already touched upon, was that certain Easterners were not eager to claim kinship with the West out of a troubled sense that the East was no longer the repository of clear-cut, wholesome American values. "Their" America was altering rapidly, and for the worse as they saw it, under the impact of urbanization, industrialization, and immigration. In the West, patrician, Harvard-educated young men like Theo-

*Billington, *Frederick Jackson Turner*, pp. 399–400. The article, "Children of the Pioneers," was reprinted in Turner's *The Significance of Sections in American History* (New York: Henry Holt, 1932), pp. 193–206. In a letter of 23 December 1925 to his friend Mrs. Alice Hooper, Turner says that in the article "I examine whether the prediction of 'barbarism' made for them when their parents were going west—middle nineteenth century—proved true. It's really wonderful what places the children have filled, not only in the world of constructive business where vision was demanded, but also in the realms of art and literature, science, religion etc. etc." Ray Allen Billington, ed., *"Dear Lady:" The Letters of Frederick Jackson Turner and Alice Forbes Perkins Hooper, 1910–1932* (San Marino, Cal.: Huntington Library, 1970), p. 373.

dore Roosevelt and his classmate Owen Wister found adventure, simplicity, manliness—indeed gentlemanliness, for they discerned chivalric qualities in the inhabitants of the great outdoors, especially those of the cattle and mountain territories. Their West, in the words of what is said to have been Roosevelt's favorite song, was the place "Where seldom is heard a discouraging word, / And the skies are not cloudy all day." Their celebration of the natural gentleman, the pioneer, the rugged individualist, is nicely analyzed by G. Edward White in *The Eastern Establishment and the Frontier Experience* (1968). Roosevelt, Wister, and the artist-writer Frederic Remington, extended the romanticizing of the West that was beginning to be essayed in works such as Mark Twain's *Roughing It* (1872) and the stories of Bret Harte. Roosevelt, who had praised the printed version of Turner's 1893 lecture, saw eye to eye with him too as to the future importance of the West. "I think it will be a good thing for this country," he told Turner in an 1896 letter, "when the West, as it used to be called, the Centre, as it really is, grows so big that it can no more be jealous of the East."[6]

Yet we can see that there was much ambiguity in these hymns to the West, whoever sang them. If a Westerner came East, or an Easterner went out West, what did they represent, and to whom? If the West evolved into the Center, in what ways could it remain distinctive? George Santayana, speaking of Whitman, has said that there is a sad contradiction in the very activity of pioneering. Once the pioneer arrives wherever he is going, he begins to "improve"—that is, spoil—the wilderness environment that temporarily ennobled him. The uncertainties are indicated in the device chosen by Bret Harte for the title page of the *Overland Monthly* (which started publication in 1868), as well as in the actual name of the magazine. The founders of the magazine had decided upon a picture of a grizzly bear: an appropriate emblem since California was the Bear Flag state. But the bear on his own did not seem sufficient. Harte's solution was to add a railroad track beneath the bear's paws. Before the change, said Mark Twain, the bear "simply stood there snarling over his shoulder at nothing." With the change, "behold he was a magnificent success!—the ancient symbol of California savagery snarling at the approaching type of high

and progressive Civilization, the first Overland locomotive!"
The transcontinental railroad was then within a year of completion. But what was being symbolized? In a contest with a
locomotive, the bear would clearly lose. The completion of the
railroad would inevitably link California with the East, and
diminish whatever spirit of wilderness the bear typified.[7] In
fact the railroad soon took Harte off to the East, all the way to
Boston and an agreement to produce Western tales and poems
for the *Atlantic Monthly*. And in any case, it had been the Eastern appetite for stories of the Wild West that had made the
dandified Bret Harte realize that he had stumbled upon a literary bonanza. Was the West then truly America's future, in any
but the materialistic sense of a region awaiting exploitation? As
a spiritual heritage, was it not disappearing almost overnight?

This ambiguity is fully apparent in the career of Frederick
Jackson Turner. Did the value of the West for America lie in the
formative, bygone stages of pioneering, as his frontier thesis
appeared to say? He took as starting point in his 1893 paper the
United States census announcement that the frontier as a continuous line of open country had ceased to exist. Yet he was
offended when a critic charged him with having said that the
frontier was ended, and labored to prove that, through the
"children of the pioneers," the West was culturally and materially displaying a favorable balance of trade in relation to the
country as a whole. Having moved to the East from his native
Wisconsin, Turner continued to think of himself as a Westerner. He retained a lifelong affection, indeed a personal need,
for regular re-immersion in wild landscape. But he was never
able to admit to himself imaginatively that his old West might
have had serious shortcomings, in narrowness and crudeness
of spirit, or that the new West might soon become indistinguishable from the East. In *Historians Against History* (1965)
David Noble portrays Turner as one of several American historians who have woven scholarly legends of some splendid
past era but who have been psychologically unable to come to
grips with American evolution up to recent times.

One curious aspect of Turner's view of the frontier West,
which he shared with various Easterners, was that he liked to
think of the pioneers as being pre-eminently of old, that is
"Anglo-Saxon," stock. He knew perfectly well with one part of

his mind that this was historically not so. As a boy in Portage, Wisconsin, he had grown up in a polyglot community.[8] As a scholar he compiled material on immigrant settlement, and recommended graduate students to turn their attention to immigration history. Marcus Hansen, the author of excellent studies on American immigration, was a Turner student. But in some other part of his mind Turner revealed a distaste not only for the city immigrants but also for those on the frontier. This is clearly brought out in the few references to Willa Cather in Turner's printed correspondence. These occur in exchanges with Mrs. Alice Forbes Perkins Hooper, an exuberant and affluent lady who had spent her childhood in Burlington, Iowa, where her father was president of the Burlington railroad. He had extended the Burlington track through Nebraska. Mrs. Hooper had already met Willa Cather by 1913, when she wrote to her friend Turner to say in passing that she had just read *O Pioneers!* and thought it "disappointing." Apparently she expected Willa Cather to "help us sometime"—presumably in lauding the pioneering enterprise of President Perkins. She implied that Willa Cather had failed to capture the atmosphere of Nebraska because she had come to Red Cloud late in the day and really knew little about it. Turner replied facetiously, also picking up a notion of Mrs. Perkins that it would be pleasant to make a return pilgrimage to Nebraska in a private railroad car:

> But is a young thing who doesn't know her own birthplace [?] qualified to write historical fiction anyway? I haven't read *O Pioneers* and I'll *not* until I can make that historical pilgrimage with a real pioneer, possessed of the memory, the maps and the imagination which belong only to oldest inhabitants. . . . As for me, give me Red Cloud *wie es eigentlich gewesen*, or give me nothing![9]

A decade afterward, in *A Lost Lady*, Cather did speak glowingly of the aristocratic boldness and integrity of the railroad builders, as personified by Captain Forrester. But Mrs. Hooper, as she informed Turner, resented the book:

> She drew upon her imagination and our family in Burlington and gave an absolutely false and arrogant impression of my mother and of me tho' she would probably say she had never

heard of us. I didn't care for her a bit when I met her . . . , tho' I must admit some of her stories are excellent.[10]

I leave it to Cather scholars to determine whether there is any foundation for this supposed source of *A Lost Lady*. More relevant to my own account is the agreement of Turner and Mrs. Hooper, as he told her in a letter of March 1925, that Willa Cather and some other novelists had overstressed the non-British side of frontier settlement. He added: "The constructive work of the men of means, bankers, railway builders, etc. will also be recognised again after the present criticism of all things American has died down."[11] Turner's outlook is clarified in a letter he sent in the same year to his fellow historian Arthur M. Schlesinger (another Middle Westerner):

> I imagine that some of the attempts to minimize the frontier theme, in the broad sense in which I used it, are part of the pessimistic reaction against the old America that have followed the World War—the reaction against pioneer ideals, against distinctively American things historically . . . to write in terms of European experience, and of the class struggle incident to industrialism. But we cannot altogether get away from the facts of American history, however far we go in the way of adopting the Old World![12]

It is time to recapitulate the discussion, and to bring it back closer to Willa Cather. In setting her beside Frederick Jackson Turner, the first point to stress is an oddity: the oddity that two writers so distinguished in their respective ways as interpreters of the American Western experience should have had so little to say to one another, directly or indirectly.

The second point is that, in my view, this mutual neglect reveals more of a deficiency in Turner than in Willa Cather. As an imaginative writer she was entitled to be idiosyncratic—to read whatever suited her own needs and to ignore whatever did not speak to her. Turner, as his many admiring colleagues and students have testified, was a compulsively inquisitive and accumulative scholar. He had a feeling for the poetry of his subject. He sought eloquence as well as clarity in his own writing. "I always wanted to be an artist," he told a former student, "tho' a truthful one." He cherished Emerson's phrase "the nervous, rocky West"; and these lines from Tennyson's "Ulysses":

> for my purpose holds
> To sail beyond the sunset, and the baths
> Of all the western stars, until I die.

He was moved by Rudyard Kipling's "Explorer" poem, and also Kipling's "The Foreloper":

> He shall desire loneliness, and his desire shall bring
> Hard on his heels a thousand wheels, a people and a king. . . .
> For he must blaze a nation's way, with hatchet and with brand,
> Till on his last-won wilderness an empire's bulwarks stand.

Turner often, too, recited some lines from Robinson Jeffers's "Californians" in his history lectures. But this appears to me a limited and rather commonplace record.[13] Turner's biographer does not indicate that he ever read Whitman, from whom Willa Cather borrowed her title *O Pioneers!*. He showed some knowledge of Vachel Lindsay's poetry in a letter of 1914, but only a cautious enthusiasm: "I can't say I think he is the authentic voice of the Middle West, as his friends assert." Turner appears to have remained unaware of or unaffected by Lindsay's lovely poem "Bryan, Bryan, Bryan, Bryan" from which Willa Cather took the epigraph—"Bidding the Eagles of the West fly on"—and the title of the final section of *One of Ours*.

A third point is that comparison with Turner strengthens her reputation at the expense of his. In other words, both have been accused of various deficiencies; there is a kind of parallelism in these supposed deficiencies; and Turner's seem to betray a greater deficiency of imaginative scope. Thus, critics have suggested that Willa Cather's mindset was formed quite early, and restricted her. But by this test Turner, too, a dozen years her senior, had a restricted range. After the 1890s he wrote little, and tended to repeat the essential themes he had hit upon by the time he was thirty-five. On the specific matter of immigrant frontier settlement, he appears to have been surprisingly reluctant to admit its significance. The reason, one supposes, is that like Theodore Roosevelt, Woodrow Wilson, and other historical writers of the day, he had formed an emotional image of the frontier West as the embodiment of "pure" Americanism, by which he and they meant old-stock Americanism. Willa Cather, for whatever personal reasons, showed a more original appreciation of the valuable un-Americanness of some aspects of the immigrant contribution, though possibly she may have overemphasized what Turner underemphasized.

This line of inquiry comes dangerously close, one might think, to a negative assertion that if Willa Cather is a defective writer, we will not put her at the bottom of the class because her celebrated historian-contemporary proves to be even worse. That is not my intention. In both cases, something of the quality that made them so excitingly fresh to readers of their day has evaporated, or is now so much part of our imaginative heritage that we take it for granted. Nevertheless, I would like to pursue a fourth point, also expressible negatively—though it leads toward a more positive conclusion. This point, illustrated not only by Turner but by a number of "Western" authors, is that the West in fact offers an extraordinarily elusive and frustrating theme—splendid for manifestoes and brief bursts of oratory but very difficult to handle with subtlety and compassion. The literary shortcomings of, say, Hamlin Garland, Frank Norris, Jack London, and Owen Wister show a tendency to substitute geography for humanity, to be programmatic and declamatory, and to slide into either rancor and self-pity or grandiose sentimentality. Garland shifted in his literary career from bitter little pictures to roseate reminiscence. Norris in his short life could not decide whether the bigness of the West was monstrous or glorious. A comparable stridency and unevenness marred the abundantly gifted Jack London—and can for that matter be detected in the British explorer of other far-off frontiers, Rudyard Kipling. Owen Wister, in company with Roosevelt and Remington, tended to stage heroic but stereotyped melodrama against a spectacular backdrop—making the scenery somehow more interesting than the performers.

The explanation, I believe, lies in the nature of their subject rather than in their own lack of literary ability. No doubt it was a *big* subject, but what precisely *was* it? The West was an embodiment of tender and powerful yearnings in mankind, of the kind hinted at in Wordsworth's phrase "something evermore about to be," or Emerson's haunting juxtaposition of "the grey past, the white future," or Kipling's "Foreloper," or James

Elroy Flecker's *Hassan:* "We are the pilgrims, master, and we shall go / Always a little further." The West was the land of possibility, "a fairer land than prose" as Emily Dickinson put it. Vachel Lindsay caught this quality of make-believe in his evocation of what the Nebraska politician William Jennings Bryan stood for in his campaign of 1896:

> And these children and their sons
> At last rode through the cactus,
> A cliff of mighty cowboys
> On the lope,
> With gun and rope.
> And all the way to frightened Maine the old East
>   heard them call,
> And saw our Bryan by a mile lead the wall
> Of men and whirling flowers and beasts,
> The bard and the prophet of them all.
> Prairie avenger, mountain lion,
> Bryan, Bryan, Bryan, Bryan. . . .[14]

That was the poetic essence of the West, a dream toward which to travel, an area of *becoming* rather than *being*. It has proved an enduring poetic myth, as a host of novels, films, and TV episodes testify. Understandably they concentrate upon the sharpest and most poignant part of the story—the first ranches, the first breaking of the sod, and even more compulsively the journey into the West, the movement of the wagons, the encampments, the Indian raids, and so on. But such sagas are fixated upon a transitory moment, and upon two-dimensional displays of masculinity, of lone-wolf heroism on the part of men who, like Peter Pan in J. M. Barrie's Never-Never Land, resist involvement in the subsequent chapters of the tale.

These subsequent chapters constitute the prose rather than the poetry of the Western story. Historians and novelists have the obligation to put things in sequence, to tell us what happens next. But if what happens next is in some ways a letdown, an anticlimax, as with the later career of William Jennings Bryan, they run into serious difficulties. They can try to confine themselves to chapter one, but that may seem an evasion. They can pretend there was no spiritual deterioration, as I think Turner preferred to do; but that is another evasion, not far removed from the superficialities of mere boosterism. They can turn sour, as Edgar Howe did in his novel of Kansas small-town claustrophobia, or insist that if "Go West, young man" was a stirring injunction, then "Go East, young man (or woman)" was an equally imperative need for talented Westerners. But to portray the West as a psychic wasteland is to miss the poetry, both of exhilaration and of the elegiac, that infuses the prosaic aspects of the theme.

When all these difficulties are considered, it is no wonder that the literature of the West has been so uneven, and so dominated by John-Wayneish, Marlboro-Country clichés of rugged maleness. What is a wonder is that Willa Cather, a woman reared in what might look like the tired fag-end of Late Victorian parlor-culture, was able to turn so much of her situation to advantage. Perhaps she was not able entirely to transcend her difficulties. Now and then I feel she is perilously near to cliché, that she is asserting a truth somewhat editorially, instead of conveying it, and even occasionally against the grain of the narrative; and that she is in such instances rescued in part by the sheer excellence of her prose—a kind of perfection of plainsong.

Nevertheless the achievement is remarkable; and my argument, to reiterate, is not that Willa Cather merely stands out in a field of second-raters, but that she made fine fiction out of alluring yet extremely intransigent material. Thus, to deal for the moment only with her handling of Nebraska, she covers all the basic stages of settlement as enumerated by Frederick Jackson Turner and other historians. There is the unmitigatedly bare landscape as young Jim Burden sees it at the beginning of *My Ántonia:* "I had the feeling that the world was left behind, that we had got over the edge of it, and were outside man's jurisdiction" (p. 7). There are the daunting early struggles of the newly-arrived farmers, recounted for example in *My Ántonia* and in *O Pioneers!*. There is the satisfaction that comes to good farmers from seeing their patch of prairie gradually turn into something fruitful, handsome, and orderly: a prosperity worked for, and fitting. There is the accretion of memories, of vast significance to particular individuals though not related to public events. "Whatever we had missed," as Jim concludes of his lifelong friendship with Ántonia, "we possessed together the precious, the incommunicable past" (p. 372).

Nor does Willa Cather avoid the grubbier sides of Western life. She stresses the drabness and narrowness of the little towns, and the glum resentfulness of some of the farmers. Like William Faulkner, she contrasts the generosity of the older order with the mean rapacity of would-be local tycoons such as Wick Cutter in *My Ántonia* and Ivy Peters in *A Lost Lady*. She reaches up to the present day—her present day—in *The Professor's House*. The gallery of characters is less linked and extensive than with Faulkner's Yoknapatawpha County, but it is surprisingly comprehensive. Moreover, she appreciates the magic of "Eastern" culture, whether represented by college education or by music and the theatre, and freely concedes that those who have the opportunity and wish to take it are likely to head away from the home place, and may become estranged from it. Certain settlers are, so to speak, likely to become unsettled. Kipling says of the pioneer: "He shall desire loneliness, and loneliness shall bring / Hard on his heels a thousand wheels, a people and a king." There is, I think, a tinge of irony but only a tinge, in that précis of the pioneer experience. Willa Cather makes room for it with more honesty than any writer familiar to me.

The reason, I believe, is that with an instinctive wisdom she declined to identify herself as either a professional Westerner, or as one of that band of esthetes in Greenwich Village or the Left Bank who, especially in the 1920s, announced that they were escapees from the prison of the central states of America. With the dispassionate egotism of the genuine artist, Willa Cather abstracted and universalized her own situation. This idea is very well put by Dorothy Van Ghent, who calls Cather's creative spirit "primitive" and "psychologically archaic," and observes that "out of homely American detail"—for instance in *My Ántonia*—"are composed certain friezelike entablatures that have the character of ancient ritual and sculpture."[15] Instead of dwelling upon the uniqueness of the American frontier, as Turner did, she sensed the recurrence of immemorial predicaments and hopes. *Tempora mutantur, nos et mutamur in illis:* both the sadness of frontier failure and the subtler regrets that came from frontier success, had for her a larger dimension, stretching back to the poetry of Virgil and Horace.

It is obvious that she was not a person of a completely equable temperament. In younger life she was a rebel, in middle age increasingly dismayed by what she took to be the progressive vulgarization of the world. Nevertheless there was an assurance in what she wrote. Her likes and dislikes and her convictions were established early. In some respects they appear conventional. But they gave her a frame and a tone, and suggested a literary method. The result is a curiously measured, wise style—that of a tribal elder who can explain the underlying order in even the most disorderly events.

Thus for Willa Cather there simply was no dramatic opposition between West and East, between "frontier" and "civilization." She knew well that there were differences of circumstances, which might be considerable. But she was not committed, as Turner and some of her contemporaries were, to the attractive yet oversimplified East-West polarity. Certainly she knew the strengths and weaknesses of each theoretical mode. Within the sophisticated world, refinement could become preciosity, and art artifice. On the frontier, hardihood could degenerate into callousness, boldness into brutality. She realized that the two extremes existed; she had after all a firsthand acquaintance with both.

Yet to her, frontier and civilization were not so much opposites as coordinates. The true human being in Willa Cather's realm is innately civilized, though books and travel may heighten one's sensibility. The true human being is at home in all environments, and is a respecter both of persons and of places. The false human being, to be found in all environments, is a hater and a spoiler, both of persons and of places. Those are Willa Cather's opposites. They are not complicated. But they work better for literary purposes than the artificial *versuses*, the false male-female, tough-effete antitheses of a good deal of popular frontier fiction—in which for example the reader or viewer is triggered to identify the villain as the man who arrives wearing gloves and a fancy hat, unless this man almost immediately gets into a victorious fight with some local tough and so proves he is not really a corrupt dude, despite appearances. In Cather's fiction, indeed, the pioneer may well be cultivated and—in the best sense of the word—worldly, as with one or two of the priests in *Death Comes for the Archbishop*, or Captain Forrester and some of his visitors in *A Lost Lady*. Nor is

39

he necessarily an innovator, at least not in any reckless fashion. " 'Change is not always progress,' " according to Euclide Auclair in *Shadows on the Rock* (p. 119). As in *Shadows on the Rock*, Willa Cather is fond of comparing good pioneers with bad pioneers. Auclair's patron, Bishop Laval, has respected the needs of the Quebec citizens. His system is overturned by a seemingly more sophisticated cleric in the name of progress. Tom Outland in *The Professor's House* likewise respects the remnants of the Indian mesa culture he has discovered, whereas his companion Blake—though he may believe in justice for the Haymarket anarchists and for Captain Dreyfus—is unable to keep faith with Tom or with the mesa Indians. In other words, Willa Cather refuses to be saddled with the orthodox polarities of supposed East-West behavior. Her proper pioneer is not the spoiler Santayana described, but a conserver and a bringer of beauty. Unlike Theodore Roosevelt, he does not worship the wilderness by killing its animals. In his supreme form, he is as attuned to the ecology as an Indian.

Willa Cather's other main coordinates are time and space. Clearly one of the problems of writing about the West, especially in her time, is that while the space-dimension is extremely large the time-dimension is extremely small. Some writers, as we have seen, shrink the time-dimension to an almost infinitesimally brief period—a sort of imaginary moment suspended between past and future. This could be said, not too unfairly, of the essential idea in Turner's frontier thesis, which is that the initial contact between settler and wilderness brings about a psychic rebirth. In Cather's case, awareness of the time-dimension is among the essential attributes of a true human being. She, and some of her principal characters extend their consciousness of time-past through exposure to the culture of Europe. Her novel *One of Ours* makes an interesting attempt to convey the impact of such an exposure upon an open-minded young man from Nebraska when he goes to France with the American army. In *One of Ours* the theme becomes entangled with other aims. But in her most successful explorations of the time-dimension—Tom Outland's story in *The Professor's House*, *Death Comes for the Archbishop*, and rather less powerfully in *Shadows on the Rock*—she establishes with beautiful economy and authority various previous layers of North American pioneering. If this was her way of reacting against the disagreeable realities of postwar America, she managed to universalize her private concerns, and to transform them into extraordinarily distanced and consoling images. She probably could not have accomplished this had she not been in search of American pasts appropriate to her. Other Americans were involved in similar quests; so for that matter was D. H. Lawrence. Henry Adams, her senior by a generation, had more or less concluded that medieval France was his spiritual home, and that ever since the thirteenth century the world had been going downhill. Van Wyck Brooks, her junior by thirteen years, argued in his first batch of books that while America badly needed a "usable past," it did not truly possess one. The heritage, he thought, was warped and stunted.

It would be too much to claim that Willa Cather singlehandedly supplied the usable past for her country. She did however furnish some authentic and most valuable fragments. They could be no more than fragments or vestiges, like the Coronado sword in *My Ántonia*, because the record itself within the United States was fragmentary and discontinuous. Imaginatively, though, she brought them into a continuum. Figuratively, it could be said that she was the discoverer of the cliff dwellings at Mesa Verde and the pueblo on the plateau at Ácoma. She restored them to the American historical consciousness, and thereby enriched it. I myself, as a wandering student of American history, went to see them a quarter of a century ago, having read about them in Willa Cather, and know that they enlarged the meaning of that history for me.

We come back finally to the question I started with. Why is Willa Cather not given her due in the average history class? In a way the question is misleading. I presume that courses on the history of the frontier do include her. My point was that during her lifetime she did not conspicuously say the right things at the obvious moments. Like all important artists she was essentially a private person, not a platform performer. Yet looking back, we can see that she did after all mirror her own time, in her own ways, and speak for it. She helped her country to understand itself and its momentous, momentary heritage, and she brought dignity instead of rhetoric to such understanding. Perhaps she is too good for the historians, in their everyday teaching. For generally, in spite of what Turner said about the mutuality of history and literature, the historians are ill at ease with first-rate imaginative material. They can get more out of literature that lies nearer the surface, unmistakably signalling its intentions and its provenance.

Her "Americanness" is not in question. But perhaps she is best compared with two other novelist-contemporaries who were not American: Thomas Hardy and Joseph Conrad. None of them lived snugly. All three were deeply aware of the pain, the dislocation, the loss, and the element of heroism, in ordinary lives. All three ranged widely through time and space. They were secret, sympathetic sharers in the hurts and hopes of people who are not full belongers. Hardy, not born into assured status, sensed the anguish of semi-outcasts like Tess and Jude. Conrad, the Polish-born sea-captain, knew that the surfaces of life were merely surfaces. Willa Cather was finely sensitive to the problems of women who refused to accept their conventional sexual-domestic roles, and by extension to the problems of "ethnic" immigrants stranded on the American prairie. Each recognized that, on both a geographical and a psychological plane, the profoundest possibilities of self-knowledge, for people of spirit, are raised not in the well-defined centers of established society but on the equivocal peripheries. What each perceived, we may conclude, was that every worthwhile pioneer is in part an exile—and that such doubleness of insight is both mournful and miraculous.

[*Reference notes appear on pages 259–60.*]

Willa Cather:
American Experience
and European Tradition

James Woodress

Two years ago I decided that it would be good for my character if I taught a section of freshman English. I had been in college and university administration for a good many years and for a long time had not taught any freshman courses. At the first meeting of my class in English 3, which was an introduction to literature, I asked the students to write a theme so that I could get an immediate idea of the state of literacy among them. One of the compositions I received bitterly attacked the freshman English requirement that subjected students to poetry, drama, and fiction for an entire quarter. The author of this theme was an innocuous young man who was only interested, he declared, in becoming an optometrist. He would never, he believed, have to discuss the character of Macbeth or explicate a poem by E. E. Cummings as he fitted his patients with glasses. I did not try to argue with the student. I just made him tighten up his prose and focus his argument more sharply when he rewrote the paper. After he had done that, he sent the theme to the school newspaper as a letter to the editor, and it was promptly printed. So much for part one of this tale.

The next Monday morning the student came in to see me. He had wanted to get his unimportant assignments out of the way so that he could concentrate on the more crucial aspects of preparing himself to become an optometrist, and over the weekend he had read the one novel that was required reading for English 3.

This happened to be *My Ántonia*. After the theme I had received I was certainly not prepared to have the boy say that *My Ántonia* was a marvelous book and that he had hardly been able to put it down until he had finished it. I expressed my pleasure that he had liked the novel, and we discussed it for a quarter of an hour. After the student left my office, I began to ponder this experience.

What was there about Willa Cather, I asked myself, that could evoke such an enthusiastic response from a hostile non-reader, from a student coerced into reading *My Ántonia* in order to pass a course? This boy was about as unsophisticated a reader as I could have found. At the same time what was there about Willa Cather that could evoke just as enthusiastic a response in a sophisticated reader who consumed large quantities of fiction and taught literature for a living? I also had just reread the novel, and my response was equally warm and appreciative. I now have read *My Ántonia* a good many times, and it never fails to move me deeply. What is there about Willa Cather that reaches audiences at opposite ends of the reading spectrum?

My Ántonia now has had a life of fifty-six years. At the start its sales were modest, though Houghton Mifflin's ineptitude seems to have been more than a little responsible; but the book's popularity has grown steadily. It now certainly is a modern American classic, and it is much written about, as the bibliographies of eight or ten persons in this audience will testify. My paper is not primarily about *My Ántonia*, but I begin with it as an example because my pre-optometry student read it and because it is my favorite of Willa Cather's books. *My Ántonia* has not, of course, reached the mass audience of *Ben Hur* or *Gone with the Wind*, but neither do these novels charm the unsophisticated reader and the college professor alike. To explain Willa Cather's genius one needs a theory to account for her appeal to widely disparate readers.

Before I introduce my theory, however, let me review the growth of Willa Cather's reputation, for my theory is the result of a survey of her critical reception over the past sixty years. The early readers of Cather's novels saw different things than we see today. One might say that our present response is like a palimpsest. On the top of the original response we have added another layer of response without obliterating the earlier one.

James Woodress

When I was a graduate student immediately after World War II, the Turner thesis was still a hotly debated historical problem. As you all know, the idea that Turner promulgated in 1893 captured the imagination of an entire generation of American scholars. The notion that American democracy was formed in the crucible of the frontier was beautifully simple. It was a poetic, romantic explanation of why Americans are different from Europeans, and in its beautiful simplicity it was irresistibly attractive. By 1947, however, the Turner thesis had been under attack for a decade, and although Turner as bard of his time and place won a niche in history, he has not been the dominant conceptualist for a long time. The debate over the truth or falsity of the Turner thesis belongs among the controversies of another era, and his work now is only a chapter in American historiography.

Willa Cather's rise to critical importance in American literature occurred during the years of Turner's greatest acceptance. As the first writer to make fictional use of Nebraska, she published *O Pioneers!* in 1913 at a time when Americans were ready to have their past interpreted romantically. By 1913 the closing of the frontier was nearly a generation in the past. *O Pioneers!* was followed by *The Song of the Lark*, *My Ántonia*, *One of Ours*, and *A Lost Lady*, all of which had to do with the settling and growth of the West. These novels were to non-historians and novel-readers the fictional counterparts of the Turner thesis. By this time the Turner thesis already was passing into mythology, and any American who thought at all about his country's past believed in its uniqueness and cherished the myth of the frontier. He held firmly in his mind the image of pioneers clearing the forests, tilling the virgin prairie, and settling and populating the brave new world. Whitman, of course, in the poem that Willa Cather used for the title of her first Nebraska novel, had anticipated Turner, just as Crèvecoeur had done earlier in the eighteenth century in his essay, "What Is an American?"

With *Death Comes for the Archbishop* in 1927 Willa Cather reached the peak of her lifetime reputation. In it she achieved a great critical success, and because the novel also was a great commercial success she extended significantly her already large audience. In the following decade, however, during the 1930s when proletarian literature and Marxist criticism were in vogue, when the public was reading James T. Farrell's *Studs Lonigan* and Dos Passos's *U.S.A.* trilogies, Willa Cather's reputation declined. The problems of the Great Depression forced Americans to examine their assumptions closely and to grapple with social and economic issues. The problems of the 1930s seemed unprecedented, and the poetic version of American experience offered by the Turner thesis turned somewhat sour after the 1929 stock market crash. In this decade the Turner thesis began to be attacked, and Willa Cather's reputation underwent a partial eclipse. Cather was not quite in the predicament of William Dean Howells in 1915 when he wrote to Henry James: "I am comparatively a dead cult with my statues cut down and the grass growing over them in the pale moonlight."[1] Yet when she died in 1947 she probably would not have been put into a volume such as Jackson Bryer edited in 1969 called *Fifteen Modern American Authors*. In this volume, which perhaps establishes the canon of our major twentieth-century writers, Cather is in the company of Anderson, Dreiser, Faulkner, Fitzgerald, Hemingway, Steinbeck, and Wolfe, to list only the writers of fiction. If this work had been published in 1940, I think that John Dos Passos or Sinclair Lewis would have taken precedence over Willa Cather.

Since Cather's death her reputation has grown steadily. E. K. Brown's splendid biography, which Leon Edel completed in 1953, was a milestone, and both of her publishers, Houghton Mifflin and Alfred Knopf, kept her books in print. The insistence of the New Critics on close reading also was influential, for they stimulated an entire new generation of American scholars to reread their texts. Willa Cather, it turned out, was an author who could stand rereading, and her novels, which earlier had been classed as regional literature, written more or less in the realistic tradition and celebrating the taming of the wild land, were discovered to be full of myth and symbol. Critics of the 1950s and 1960s found her novels romantic rather than realistic, rich in texture and design, and constructed with consummate artistry. So unobtrusive was the art that earlier readers often had missed the virtuosity of the performance.

What makes Willa Cather's work significant *and* attractive is the fact that her novels actually do contain what the original readers thought they saw, as well as the depth, richness, and complexity that the postwar critics have seen. Thus I come to my thesis: Willa Cather's importance results from a successful graft of her native experience on to the roots and trunk of European culture. Or to change the metaphor, her appeal rests on the happy marriage of the Old World and the New. The New World experience in her novels gives them character and drama, color and romance—the emotional content. The Old World experience provides the texture, the ancient myth and symbol, the profundity—the intellectual content. The reader who plunges into Sinclair Lewis, for example, is likely to hit his head on the bottom, but with Cather there is no danger. The reader can dive as deep as he wishes and stay down until he has to come up for air. The reader who enters the world of Thomas Wolfe, to cite another example, is overwhelmed by the astonishing vitality of his work, but, as Lionel Trilling notes, he is dismayed by "the disproportion between the energy of his utterance and his power of mind."[2] It is the intellection coming from the European tradition that gives the reader room to swim in Willa Cather's fiction. One would not accuse Cather of writing intellectual novels, but the intellectual content is there, well assimilated and carried along lightly by the emotional content. The emotional content, I think, owes its vigor to Cather's Nebraska experience and to the commitment she was fond of calling "the gift of sympathy."

My assignment for this conference is to consider Cather's life in relation to her art. The thesis I have just stated follows from such an examination. The relationship between Willa Cather's experience and her fiction is close and important, but the experience is of two kinds. There is the experience of the body, the contacts with people like Ántonia, the adventure of living in Nebraska, the tales of immigrant farm women heard first hand. Also there is the experience of the mind, the vicarious travel through books, the contacts with France, Rome, and the world through poetry, fiction, and drama. Cather's fiction is a subtle blend of the two kinds of experience. Her roots in the soil of Webster County are deep and well nourished, but at the same time her knowledge and use of Old World culture is substantial and pervading. The warp and woof of her fabric is native American, but threads of European culture are woven into the texture. *My Ántonia* is an instructive novel to examine from the standpoint of the author's life and reading.

Character and drama, romance and color—in short, emotion—are present in this novel in large quantities, and they derive chiefly from the author's nostalgic memories of her own experiences. Ántonia was a real person whose father did commit suicide and who did end up as the richly fulfilled wife of a Bohemian farmer. She lived to reap the bounty of the virgin prairie she had helped subdue, and she raised a large and attractive family. Jim Burden, the narrator, is a fictional persona for Willa Cather, whose experiences growing up in Nebraska closely parallel his. She may not have met Ántonia when she lived on her grandfather's farm, but she knew her well when she worked as a hired girl for the Miners across the street, and the friendship continued as long as Willa Cather lived. The title-character of "Neighbour Rosicky" in *Obscure Destinies*, moreover, is Ántonia's husband. Thus the story of the immigrant family transplanted from the Old World to the New is authentic. It encapsulates the whole story of the settlement of America. It is a romantic tale as it filters through the golden haze of Jim Burden's middle-aged memories. It has the same simple, clean lines of Turner's poetic explanation of American experience and the frontier. Willa Cather fixes memorably the image of the pioneer farmer on the western plains in that famous passage that occurs during the picnic with the hired girls. It comes just before Jim leaves Black Hawk for college, and it punctuates the end of his childhood and the end of the pioneer era. As the sun sets over the prairie Jim and the girls look across the high fields toward the horizon. There silhouetted against the setting sun is a great black object. Startled, they spring to their feet and strain their eyes toward it:

> In a moment we realized what it was. On some upland farm, a plough had been left standing in the field. The sun was sinking just behind it. Magnified across the distance by the horizontal light, it stood out against the sun, was exactly contained within the circle of the disk; the handles, the tongue, the share—black against the molten red. There it was, heroic in size, a picture writing on the sun. [P. 245]

As a metaphor for the Westward Movement, what could be more appropriate than this plow against the sun? Turner's poetic view of the frontier and Willa Cather's remarkable image are of a piece in their romanticizing and mythologizing of the American West.

Two of the girls in this passage, as you will recall, are Lena Lingard and Tiny Soderball, Scandinavian friends of the Bohemian Ántonia. Although the novel is mostly about Ántonia, it deals also with the lives of the other two immigrant girls, who also pursue the American dream in their own way. Tiny, who makes a fortune in mining, ends up living in San Francisco and looking after her investments, while Lena, who learns to be a dressmaker, succeeds as a businesswoman. Willa Cather has taken pains here to round out the American success story. Tiny is a female Horatio Alger who strikes it rich, and Lena—among other things—is a Benjamin Franklin type who works hard, builds a business, prospers, and remains devoutly attached to the work ethic. All three of the girls are representative of the new American, and they are part of the romance as well as the reality of the frontier.

There are plenty of other immigrants in the novel as well, all in the process of being Americanized. Jim's grandparents have German neighbors, as did Willa Cather's grandparents, and there are the Danish laundry girls, the Bohemian Marys, Anna Hansen, Ole Benson, the rascally Krajiek, who cheats the Shimerdas, Anton Jelinek, the saloonkeeper whose cousin Cuzak turns up at the right moment to marry Ántonia, Selma Kronn, the first Scandinavian girl to get a job in the Black Hawk high school, and so on.

The frontier experience also supplies ample drama and melodrama in the novel. One of the early episodes describes Jim's heroic killing of the rattlesnake when Jim and Ántonia as children visit the prairie-dog village. This melodramatic scene, which only could have taken place on the frontier, makes authentic use of native American materials and provides a somber contrast to the lyrical descriptions of the western landscape. Later the suicide of Ántonia's father dramatizes the blasted hopes of immigrants who could not cope with the challenge of the New World. While many immigrants pursued and realized the dream of success, the streets of America were not paved with gold for everyone. Mr. Shimerda was one of the failures. The two Russians, Pavel and Peter, also were victims of the harshness of life in the new country. They had escaped the horrors of Russia only to succumb to the rigors of Nebraska. Throughout the novel the incidents that give life and color and emotion to the narrative are fashioned from Willa Cather's

memory of actual experiences or memories of stories she heard
from the immigrant farm women she visited or from members
of her family, particularly her father.

Now let us consider *My Ántonia* from the standpoint of texture, complexity, allusion, that is, in terms of Old World experience. These are the elements that I think derive chiefly from
Willa Cather's intense interest in classical and modern language
and literature, the reading experiences she absorbed like a
sponge during her adolescent and college years. The texture
and complexity come from the use of detail, from myth and
symbol, from quotation and allusion. The detail is spare and
never obtrusive, for Willa Cather's theory of writing involved
paring away detail, as she explained in "The Novel Démeublé."
She stripped away all unnecessary elements so that only the
essence of a scene or character was left. She approved of Dumas
père, who had said that all one needed to make a drama was one
passion and four walls.

Here are some of the essential details she chose to use. When
Jim Burden goes to college he hangs a map of ancient Rome and
a photograph of the theatre at Pompeii on his walls. Then he
studies the classics under Gaston Cleric, who exerts a profound
influence on him. He develops a passion for Virgil and in a
moving chapter Willa Cather's persona Jim prepares his lesson
from the *Georgics*. The book is open to the passage, "*Optima dies
. . . prima fugit*" (p. 264). Jim sits in his room reflecting on the
dying Virgil at Brindisi, who must have remembered his youth
in his native *patria* on the Mincio near Mantua where he had
been born. Jim himself has left his village of Black Hawk, the
Nebraska prairie, Ántonia, and his family. He is beyond childhood now and on the threshold of adulthood. His destiny will
take him to the eastern cities and make a corporation lawyer out
of him. As Jim sits reflecting on this passage, there is a knock
on the door, and in comes Lena Lingard, who now is a dressmaker in the state capital. Thus Jim's musing over the passage
from Virgil, "*Optima dies . . . prima fugit*," is interrupted by a
part of his past walking in on him. This scene is marvelously
suggestive, and the theme from Virgil weaves into the fabric of
the novel a subtle unifying thread. The theme is so appropriate
for Jim's musings and inserted so unobtrusively, however, that
the effect on the average reader is probably subliminal. This is

what I mean by rich texture and complexity resulting from Willa Cather's immersion in Old World culture. There is intellectual excitement here when one realizes how well Cather has juxtaposed the pull of the past and the charm of the present by linking across the millennia Brindisi and Lincoln, Mantua and Black Hawk (that is, Red Cloud).

Another scene late in the novel, also rich in myth and symbol, illustrates intellectual content perfectly assimilated in evocative prose. This is the chapter that in real life actually inspired the entire story. During Willa Cather's return to Red Cloud in 1914 she went to see Annie Pavelka, who then was surrounded by her large brood of children and after the vicissitudes of her early life, the death of her father, her years of work in town, and her desertion by a faithless lover, she had reached a happy middle age. Something clicked in Willa Cather's brain when she visited this friend of her childhood, and there the idea for the novel was born. The scene is adroitly managed as the middle-aged Jim Burden goes to see Ántonia. The children and Ántonia show him the farm, which after the years of struggle is a cornucopia of the earth's bounty. They go down into the cave, where Jim sees shelf upon shelf of preserved fruit and barrels of pickles. After inspecting the fruit cellar, Willa Cather writes:

> We turned to leave the cave; Ántonia and I went up the stairs first, and the children waited. We were standing outside talking, when they all came running up the steps together, big and little, tow heads and gold heads and brown, and flashing little naked legs; a veritable explosion of life out of the dark cave into the sunlight. It made me dizzy for a moment. [Pp. 338–39]

I think it has the same effect on the reader. The scene is rich in allusion and metaphor, the explosion of life out of the dark womb: Ántonia the earth goddess, mother earth, the madonna of the cornfields. "She was a rich mine of life, like the founder of early races," sums up Jim at the end of the chapter. With its suggestion of ancient fertility rites and myth and its setting on the Nebraska prairie Willa Cather here has linked her Bohemian immigrant woman to the old story of man and the earth. Yet it is done very simply and quietly and the unsophisticated

51

reader hardly notices the richness of the texture and the art of its creator. The passage reverberates in the mind, however.

There also are other skilful uses of Cather's "book-learning" in the novel. The earliest is the rattlesnake episode, which I have cited already as an effective bit of indigenous material. Jim Burden's summary reference to dragon-slaying is a subtle link between the American frontier experience and its cultural antecedents—all the literary examples as well as a myriad of visual representations of dragon-slayers. All the elements of myth are here: the adoring maiden who says in her broken English to the young dragon-slayer: " 'You is just like big mans' " (p. 46); the hero's reflection after the killing that the snake seemed "like the ancient, eldest Evil"; and then the hero's triumphant return to his admiring people. It is all there nicely naturalized in the Nebraska setting. Cather also gives the scene a neat touch of twentieth-century irony at the end, as she has Jim reflect on the basis of later experience that his exploit actually was pretty lucky: his dragon was well-fed and lazy and an easy mark for a ten-year-old St. George.

Later in the novel, in the same scene that contains the famous plow against the sun, Cather makes good use of history and legend. The story that Jim tells the hired girls about Coronado's wanderings through the Southwest and perhaps as far as Nebraska effectively connects the Nebraska landscape, which apparently had nothing but geologic history, with all the ancient legendary quests as well as the history of the Spanish penetration of North America. The metal stirrup and sword that give rise to this account were found by a farmer turning the sod of the virgin prairie, and Coronado, recalls Jim, supposedly died of a broken heart in his futile quest for gold. This bit of history not only embellishes the narrative, but it also allows Willa Cather to remind the reader that the death of Ántonia's father, which is a recurring theme in the novel, also took place in the same wilderness that for him too had refused to yield up its treasure.

The final example of literary material I want to cite is the theatre scene in Lincoln (pp. 272–78) in which Lena and Jim attend a performance of *Camille*. It is a second-rate production by a mediocre road company, but Jim and Lena are enormously moved by the pathetic drama as it unfolds to the accompani-

ment of Verdi's music from *La Traviata*. In this episode the
literary material reenforces the events that are taking place in
the novel. The renunciation of love for duty to family is about to
be enacted as Jim and Lena part. Gaston Cleric in the novel
plays the role of the elder Duval in the play as he calls Jim to
follow his destiny to Boston and to stop " 'playing about with
this handsome Norwegian' " (p. 289). This time instead of
myth to enrich the texture of the fiction Cather has gone to
nineteenth-century French literature and Italian opera. It is a
very effective and romantic scene, and I suspect that many of
the readers of the novel in the past half century have remembered the great Greta Garbo movie of *Camille*, or they have
grown up loving Verdi's musical version of the sad romance of
Violetta and Alfredo.

How Willa Cather acquired the experience of the body and
the mind that went into her fiction is a familiar story to this
audience. Without going into great detail, I should like to
summarize a few facts before proceeding to further speculation.

The experience of growing up first on the farm and then in
Red Cloud between her ninth and sixteenth years left indelible
pictures on her brain. Although the Cathers moved west fourteen years after the transcontinental railroad had been built in
1869, and Red Cloud had been founded the following year, the
town in 1884, the year the Cathers settled there, still was full of
people who remembered the pioneering days when the buffalo
roamed the prairies. The Cathers arrived at a historical moment: the frontier of the hunter had vanished farther west, but
the frontier of the farmer still existed a few miles out of town.
Had the Cathers moved to Nebraska a decade later, Willa would
have been too late for first-hand contact with the new Americans while their experience still was fresh.

Willa Cather's account of her childhood experiences in talking to immigrant farm women in Webster County is well
known, but I want to remind you of a comment she once made
to an interviewer: she said that after a morning of visiting these
women she went home in a state of excitement: "I always felt,"
she recalled, "as if they told me so much more than they said
—as if I had actually got inside another person's skin."[3] This
was the way her mind worked, and when she created a character like Ántonia she literally felt as if she were in the skin of her

character while writing the novel. A friend once told her that great minds like Shakespeare or Balzac got thousands and thousands more distinct mental impressions every day of their lives than most men in a lifetime.[4] So did Willa Cather, and this kind of grasping imagination produced the vivid reality of her Nebraska characters and background. She was in Henry James's phrase "one of the people on whom nothing is lost."[5]

After she left Red Cloud in 1890 to go to Lincoln and later after she left Lincoln to work in Pittsburgh, she never cut her ties to Red Cloud. The distance merely gave her perspective, and even during the years after 1906 when she settled permanently in New York, in a real sense she never had left Nebraska. I think this is an important point to make because eventually she did leave Nebraska, both figuratively and literally, following her mother's death and her final trip to Red Cloud in 1931. Thereafter she never returned to Nebraska, and after publishing *Obscure Destinies*, which had its inspiration in that last visit to Red Cloud, I think her work declines. I would include in the novels of her decline *Shadows on the Rock*, which owes nothing to Nebraska, along with the last two, *Lucy Gayheart*, which *is* about Nebraska, and *Sapphira and the Slave Girl*, which is a good but not great novel. But down to 1931 she returned again and again to Nebraska and the Southwest from which she drew her fictional strength. The indelible childhood and adolescent experiences of the body ripened in her maturity and were strengthened and reenforced as she revisited the West of her youth. Even when she first left Lincoln to work in Pittsburgh, the pull of Nebraska was strong, and in an early story, "Tommy, the Unsentimental," published just two months after she went to Pennsylvania, she has her heroine say: " 'It's all very fine down East there, and the hills are great, but one gets mighty homesick for this sky . . . . Down there the skies are all pale and smoky. And this wind, this hateful, dear, old everlasting wind . . . . I used to get hungry for this wind! I couldn't sleep down there.' "[6] Tommy had just returned from a year in an Eastern school and was overjoyed to be back on the prairie. This was Willa Cather's feeling, too, as long as her brothers and sisters and parents were still in Nebraska.

There was plenty to nourish the mind in Red Cloud even though it was a young prairie village. You all will recall Mr. and

Mrs. Wiener, who lived just around the corner. They both spoke French and German and had a well-stocked library, which Willa Cather had the use of. Their fictional portraits in "Old Mrs. Harris" are memorable, and the picture drawn there of Vickie Templeton lost in the world of books as she reads in the Rosen library is highly evocative. Willa Cather's life of the mind began there. Of course, the Cathers also had a good many books, and if you want a detailed accounting of this topic, Bernice Slote treats it fully in her introduction to *The Kingdom of Art*. Among other writers the Cathers had Dickens, Thackeray, Scott, Ruskin, Carlyle, Shakespeare, Ben Jonson, some translations of the classics, and the inevitable *Pilgrim's Progress*.

The Wieners were not the only cultivated people in Red Cloud to leave their mark on Willa Cather. There also was Will Ducker, the Englishman who clerked in a store and loved the classics. Willa Cather had learned Latin in high school, Ducker gave her lessons in Greek, and together they read both Latin and Greek authors. This interest in the classics looms large in Cather's literary career, and she continued her interest in Latin and Greek after she went to the University. Another neighbor who introduced Willa Cather to Old World culture was Julia Miner, the immigrant daughter of the first oboist in Ole Bull's Royal Norwegian Orchestra. When the vicissitudes of life made her the wife of a Nebraska merchant, she installed a new Chickering piano in her Red Cloud parlor and played, as Mrs. Harling does in *My Ántonia*. Willa Cather never learned to play the piano, to be sure, but she developed a passion for listening to music, and the influence of Mrs. Miner on Willa Cather certainly was important. There also was the derelict and alcoholic music master named Schindelmeisser, who wandered into Red Cloud from God knows where and gave piano lessons. When he could not teach Willa Cather to play, her mother kept him coming so that her daughter could listen to him play and talk about the life of a professional musician in Europe. He turns up very significantly, you will recall, as Professor Wunsch in *The Song of the Lark*. The extent to which music influenced Willa Cather's fiction in theme and form is a large subject, about which Richard Giannone already has written a very good book.[7] I can only mention the subject here, but the point I want to make is that in the raw, prairie town of Red Cloud a decade after the buffalo trails had become streets there were ample springs of Old World culture from which to drink.

Later Willa Cather's college courses were devoted mostly to English literature, French, Greek, Latin, and German. She was good enough in Latin to teach it in a Pittsburgh high school later when she got tired of being a journalist, and there are many evidences of her interest in Greek throughout her works and particularly in her poetry. Her command of German was never more than adequate, though during her Pittsburgh years she was exposed to things German through her friend George Seibel, even while she and Seibel read French classics together. She already had begun reading German literature back in the Wieners' Red Cloud library as a child, and in addition she developed a lifelong enthusiasm for German opera. French was her best language, but her perpetual love affair with France and French civilization is too well known to need elaboration here. I think her account of meeting Flaubert's niece in Aix-les-Bains in 1930, as told in "A Chance Meeting" in *Not Under Forty*, epitomizes her Francophilia. Her knowledge of Flaubert's works and her indebtedness to him are very important. But Flaubert was only one of the many French writers she knew well. If one thumbs through the index to *The Kingdom of Art* and *The World and the Parish*, he will find many French writers listed: Hugo, Valéry, Balzac, Daudet, Maupassant, Gautier, Loti, Mérimée, and others. She was fluent in written French and very well read.

It seems to me that there are no other writers of Willa Cather's generation who were as well educated as she and who also drew their literary material, so to speak, from their grass roots. Certainly the erudition of Pound and Eliot, for example, are not to be questioned, but Pound's lifetime pilgrimage took him from his birthplace in Idaho to his final resting place in Venice, and Eliot, who was born in Mark Twain's Missouri, ended up in England. E. A. Robinson is a better example, for he was a poet-scholar whose best work is rooted in his native Tilbury Town. But among prose writers one would have to look perhaps to Thornton Wilder, Vardis Fisher, or Robert Herrick to find novelists who are also rather formidably erudite. But Wilder is only a second-rank writer, and Fisher and Herrick are at least third magnitude.

Among major novelists of the first half of this century Willa

Cather seems unique in this respect. Run down the list of fiction writers included in Bryer's *Fifteen Modern American Authors*: Anderson, Dreiser, Faulkner, Fitzgerald, Hemingway, Steinbeck, and Wolfe. The only college degrees in the group are Wolfe's A.B. and M.A. from North Carolina and Harvard. Fitzgerald was not a very serious student at Princeton, and Steinbeck's time at Stanford did not lead to a degree. Dreiser had one year at Indiana University, and Faulkner only took courses at the University of Mississippi. Anderson had little formal schooling, and Hemingway went directly from Oak Park High School to the Kansas City *Star*. What experience of books there is in the works of these writers comes from self-education.

Faulkner certainly was well read and put his reading to good use in his fiction (though he would not admit it), and he stuck to his native Mississippi for most of his literary material. His importance, it seems to me, derives, as Willa Cather's does, from the literary use of what he knew best, from which comes the emotional impact, as well as in the exercise of a cultivated mind, which is the source of the intellectual content in his work. Hemingway also wrote intensely out of his own experience, and there is more intellectual substance and cultural tradition in his writing than he would have admitted. As with all good writers, he grapples well with the intractable materials of life; but his education was spotty and his reading highly eclectic.

The other writers in this group all have produced major fiction, but their importance does not, as Willa Cather's does, rest on such a balanced mixture of the author's life of the body and life of the mind. Wolfe's education was comparable to Cather's, though quite different, and his use of native materials is an eloquent aspect of his writing. But his fatal flaw, his inability to control the form, diminishes the total impact of his work, and the lack of intellection in his writing I have already commented upon. Steinbeck was a thoughtful, conscientious craftsman whose novels of the thirties dealing with his native California are significant works. But when he left California for the East his work fell off, and *The Winter of Our Discontent* is a pale work beside *The Grapes of Wrath* or *In Dubious Battle*. Here the parallel with Willa Cather is interesting and instructive. I think that a writer uproots himself from his native soil at his peril. Would Faulkner's later work have been worth bothering about if he had settled down permanently in Hollywood when he went there in the mid-thirties to doctor scenarios?

Willa Cather's novels from her first use of Nebraska in *O Pioneers!* through *Death Comes for the Archbishop* generally have this double strength of experience from life and experience from books. *O Pioneers!* creates in its heroine Alexandra Bergson a Swedish pioneer who tames the wild land and grows up with the country. The novel is planted deep in the life of the Swedish immigrant in Nebraska, as Cather realized when she wrote on the flyleaf of her presentation copy to Carrie Miner Sherwood: "This was the first time I walked off on my own feet. . . . In this one I hit the home pasture and found that I was Yance Sorgeson and not Henry James."[8] *O Pioneers!* anticipates *My Ántonia* in being the romantic tale of the molding of new Americans in the crucible of the frontier, and has the universality of all peoples settling new lands anywhere. At the beginning when Alexandra takes over the farm following her father's death and faces the future with confidence, Willa Cather writes: "For the first time, perhaps, since that land emerged from the waters of geologic ages, a human face was set toward it with love and yearning. . . . The history of every country begins in the heart of a man or woman" (p. 65). Meanwhile, the tragic subplot of this novel seems less derived from the author's Nebraska experience than from literary analogues. Alexandra's beloved younger brother Emil falls in love with Marie Shabata, the wife of a Bohemian farmer. This love leads to a star-crossed doom that ends with the brutal slaying of Marie and Emil by the enraged husband, as the lovers meet under a white mulberry tree. One is reminded of the legendary death of Pyramus and Thisbe under a white mulberry tree or perhaps a medieval story with which the murder has some closer parallels: the death of Paolo and Francesca at the hands of the enraged Gianciotto Malatesta, as told in Canto V of the *Inferno*. Or one might cite *Romeo and Juliet* and *Tristan and Isolde*.

Cather's next novel, *The Song of the Lark* (1915), has its basis in her experience growing up in Red Cloud, her aspirations to dedicate herself to art, and her interest in music and musicians. The novel was suggested by the life of Olive Fremstad, the Wagnerian soprano, whom Willa Cather met during her work on *McClure's Magazine.* The Swedish singer had grown up in Minnesota while that state was still in its pioneering era and had worked her way to stardom. Willa Cather's own childhood and Fremstad's struggles to become a singer furnish the emotional material of plot and character. Again the work is rooted in the Western actuality—authentic memories and experiences. Again there is intellectual content blended into the novel through Cather's nurture in cultural tradition. This time it is the world of Wagnerian opera, the myth of Orpheus and Eurydice, and Thea Kronborg's speculations on the nature of art and the artist's role in creative endeavor.

Willa Cather's novel after *My Ántonia* was *One of Ours* (1922), inspired by the death of her cousin in France during World War I. It is the poorest of her works because the intractable materials of her cousin's life did not yield themselves wholly to her control. Yet this novel once again fuses Western experience with European tradition. The hero's early life on the farm is as well portrayed here as comparable material in any of Cather's best work. Only after Claude Wheeler goes to war does the novel slip out of the author's grasp. Even then, however, the author's love affair with France and French civilization saves part of the story, as she creates effective scenes that take place far behind the front lines. There is allusion and quotation here too in Cather's use of Shakespeare and other literary material, and the last section which deals with the hero's death was written with *Parsifal* in mind.[9]

Her next novel was *A Lost Lady* (1923), another work laid in Red Cloud, and again the new and the old, the actuality and the cultural roots exist together. The lost lady is a kind of Emma Bovary of the prairie, and her husband, Captain Forrester, is one of the pioneers of the state. These characterizations were based on real people, Silas Garber, one of the founders of Red Cloud, and his younger wife. The Garbers were the lord and lady of the manor in Red Cloud when Willa Cather was growing up, and their memory is evoked admirably. At the same time the parallels between Flaubert's novel and *A Lost Lady* echo in the reader's mind and place Cather's work in a literary tradition.

The Professor's House, which followed *A Lost Lady* in 1925, does not take place in Red Cloud but in a college town beside Lake Michigan. The Professor, however, is a self-portrait of Willa Cather, and the book is written out of the deepest kind of experience, as Leon Edel's well-known essay on this novel makes very clear.[10] The Professor had grown up on the prairie, and his cultural ties to Europe are numerous and strong. He is the historian of the Spanish colonialization of North America and has often been in Spain in pursuit of his research. He also is a tremendous Francophile who studied in France as a young man and who now cultivates a French garden behind his modest, middle-class house. The narrative structure of the novel owes a debt to three sources, as Willa Cather explained: to early French and Spanish novelists who inserted novellas into their novels; to a vague effort to imitate in literature the sonata form in music; and to the Dutch genre painters in whose pictures there often is an open window looking beyond the interior of the foreground.[11] These artistic models from literature, music, and art justified the insertion of "Tom Outland's Story" as a story within a story, but the tale itself owes its inspiration to the solid impact of the Southwestern experience on Willa Cather.

Death Comes for the Archbishop (1927) only could have been written by an author familiar with the Old World and the New. This was the novel Willa Cather was most proud of, and it culminated fifteen years of interest in the American Southwest. In 1912 when she first visited Arizona and New Mexico, she fell in love with that area and in subsequent years went back again and again. The ancient and contemporary life of the Pueblo Indians and the history of the Spanish penetration of that area captivated her. Already she had used this material in *The Song of the Lark*, and again in "Tom Outland's Story." When she finally came to write her novel of the Southwest, the background material was as much a part of her as her Nebraska material had been earlier. Her grasping imagination rendered the actuality of mesa and desert with a highly satisfactory verisimilitude.

The sources of this novel in the European cultural tradition, however, are equally strong. It is, of course, a historical novel, and the quality of the performance is directly proportionate to the author's grasp of the historic materials. Cather's long romance with France and French civilization enabled her to create a believable French priest and his vicar as her leading characters. Her deep interest in the history of the Catholic Church in the Southwest gives the tale authenticity, and it is perhaps a tribute to this sense of actuality that the notion was widespread at the time the novel appeared that Willa Cather had been coverted to Catholicism. Throughout the novel there is skilful mixing of the culture and traditions of the Catholic Church and its priests with the culture of the Indians and the descendants of the Spanish *conquistadores*.

The literary and pictorial sources of this novel are just as interesting as the historical materials. The frescoes of the life of Saint Geneviève in the Pantheon in Paris by Puvis de Chavannes provided one inspiration; the Holbein woodcuts entitled *Dance of Death* provided another. She had seen the frescoes during her first trip to Europe in 1902, and one of the Holbein woodcuts, one recalls, depicts death coming for an archbishop. Both of these sources from the visual arts suggested the possibility of doing a book in which the materials were organized in a series of tableaux-like legends rather than dramatically. She also had in mind *The Golden Legend*, as she once explained.[12] In that work of medieval ecclesiastical lore the saints' lives and martyrdoms are no more emphasized than the trivial events related in the collection. An undramatic effect from casual ordering was what she was striving for. This is a somewhat disingenuous explanation, however, for the novel certainly has unity and structure, but what interests me particularly is the very considerable leaning on cultural traditions in the writing of this most artful of novels. *Death Comes for the Archbishop* is a masterpiece of cultural assimilation and first-hand observation written at the peak of Willa Cather's career when she was fifty-four years old. In it she blends the reality of the Southwest and the artistic traditions of Europe.

I come now to the end of this essay with a restatement of my thesis: Willa Cather's importance lies in her ability to fuse the experience of America with the tradition of Europe in a series of superbly conceived and skilfully executed novels. She is no more a regionalist than Faulkner or Shakespeare but a novelist with international appeal. As Sarah Orne Jewett once wrote her: "One must know the world *so well* before one can know the parish."[13] Willa Cather knew both the parish and the world, and while her best novels are planted firmly in her native earth, their appeal and influence are universal. It is her ability to get into the skin of Ántonia and to breathe life into the inert facts of Nebraska in the 1880s that enchanted my pre-optometry freshman. It is this same talent plus the disciplined technique, the myth, the symbol, the allusion—all the products of a thorough

REASSESSMENTS

assimilation of cultural tradition—that kindle and keep burning
my own enthusiasm.

[Reference notes appear on page 260.]

COMMENT

*Discussion concerned Willa Cather's use of Old World and New World
material, her appeal to both sophisticated and unsophisticated readers, and
her handling of persons, places, and incidents taken from life.*

ELLEN MOERS: . . . I think we have moved on again in relationship to
the Turner thesis to yet another tradition, where there's much more
interest today in the heterogeneity of the American historical experience. . . . Here in Nebraska the pioneers were not people with names
like Smith, Brown, and Jones, but they have names like Shimerda and
Shabata and Pavelka. This is a complexity, it seems to me, to be added
to the idea of Cather's dealing with the old and the new. As she was
very well aware, she herself came from "old" people, that is, good,
solid, Eastern-seaboard Virginia stock. And the "new" people she en-
countered were crude, poor, not well spoken, servant people who had
illegitimate children, and were dirty people—and I want to put it as
she must have heard it in her own day. I think this is very much in the
books as much as her sense that the old world, the rich world, the
cultivated world is the European world. . . . But it's complicated in
Willa Cather; that is, the old is also the new in Willa Cather, and she is
very aware of it. She was doing something very bold in using immigrants, using what today we call ethnic people to stand for old and
deep and superior kinds of civilization.

JOHN H. RANDALL III: I was impressed when rereading *My Ántonia*
recently in how often Ántonia was angry at Jim Burden, and was
wrong—especially in the middle section of the book when she's working for her brother Ambrosch. I think it is evident that Willa Cather
did see the crude side as well as the cultured side. . . .

BRUCE BAKER: I feel that the new generation of student readers, unsophisticated though they may be, may well bring to Cather this sense
of the European tradition. At least my students in Omaha whose
names are Pokorny, Sturek, Motek, are reading with a sophistication
that I think we were not capable of before recent critical work suggesting the many levels of classical and European tradition lying beneath
the surface, sometimes out on the surface, of Cather's work. The unsophisticated reader may well bring to Cather a knowledge of the
European tradition, not merely the intellectual tradition, but the folklore, the customs, the habits of mind, the kind of things that made the

James Woodress

American experience and which Cather so beautifully assimilated. They have assimilated it, too, because they are the generation that followed. I therefore look forward to the ethnic revival as being a very important part of the scholarship concerning Cather.

MARGARET O'CONNOR: One of the most important concepts brought out in this paper is the idea of the underlying complexity that exists in a work, with the sense that it can be read on so many levels. The achievement is very similar to what William Butler Yeats was trying so much to say in his own work about the role of the artist, and about nonchalance as an achievement. . . .

VICTOR HASS: I am not a scholar, and I am impressed by the atmosphere. I'm just a working newspaper man, but I do believe that people like me who just read get more out of the books than you. I'm not bothered by all this. I just read Cather and I glow. And I think maybe that's what she meant us to do—just glow. All these complexities —you're over my head. Nevertheless Cather was writing for me. . . .

GEORGE GREENE: She was writing for people, perhaps, with a kind of temperamental affinity, as Conrad was. This is not an academic posture so much as the human stance. It's more inherent than it is acquired, and I think, in that sense, what Mr. Hass is saying is a useful counsel so long as we don't make it into a doctrine. . . .

SISTER ISABEL CHARLES: I think there's a genuineness. Ellen Moers was talking about the kind of people that were the characters in Willa Cather's books. But there was for those people a genuine respect, a diving into what they really are, which I think people react to right away. Whether it is the freshman in college, or the senior in high school, or the newspaperman, whoever reads it gets that genuine response to human value. I think that's the thing, with all the complexity, that makes something worthwhile.

ELLEN MOERS: May I add a small parenthesis? I am thinking of someone who may never have read *My Ántonia*, perhaps a European, who might pick it up one day and find with absolute astonishment that this marvelous, golden, hazy figure of Ántonia is a girl who, as we say, is "knocked up" and has an illegitimate baby. This is not a matter of accident. Cather chose to celebrate a figure who is sexually not respectable, and she is very much aware of what she is about. This is a complexity we haven't even opened up—the whole feminine side of this book and all the books, because Ántonia is, after all, like Marian Forrester in *A Lost Lady*, someone who preferred life on any terms. . . .

BLANCHE GELFANT: I think that Ántonia gets her credentials by the end of the novel very, very strongly. She's obviously not a wayward girl, but she's somebody who in every way exemplifies an ideal of femininity and motherhood so that whatever has happened with

Donovan is taken care of by the end of her life in the book. . . . There is nothing very extraordinary about Ántonia's illegitimacy insofar as she vindicates herself by becoming a true mother, breeder of men, and so forth. And her marriage, as I read it, is conceived of in completely asexual terms. When Jim comes back and looks at her husband, he's very pleased to find that they are like friends, and being like friends this is a safe kind of marriage. But the other girls who have a life of the body . . . they end up somehow being taken care of, taken out of the scene, out of their femininity. They end up being business people. So I think that we have a rather deceptive image of how sex is treated, and how women are treated, in the book. . . . .

VICTOR HASS: I always felt the Pavelka-Shimerda existence was the tag end of an earlier frontier concept where it wasn't easy to get married, and people often set up house and prayed that the circuit preacher would get there before the baby arrived, and that some of this mentality certainly must have flowed over into the Pavelka frontier, this casualness, this acceptance of it.

BLANCHE GELFANT: Antonia, it seems to me, is very severely punished after she has the baby. . . . She's brutalized, and masculinized, so that I don't think it's a casual incident in her life. . . .

MARGARET O'CONNOR: The acceptance of the illegitimacy . . . suggests a view of the culture of the people, not just of the town but of the farm outside. It is against the picture of the revolt of the village, against the small-mindedness of the town, that Ántonia grows in stature with the way she accepts the birth of her child. . . . It's become part of life, and it becomes part of the life that is affirmed in the novel.

An important consideration not brought out in the discussion pertains to the time in which Cather wrote. In 1918 Cather evinced a great amount of temerity in writing so openly. The reactions shown by Ántonia, by Ántonia's older brother and mother, and by the Widow Steavens seem to cover the gamut of possible reaction by those of Catholics and Protestants in a provincial community. And speaking of Cather's temerity to write openly of illegitimacy, the book includes a total of five such cases, beginning with the marriage of Ántonia's parents and including the foibles of the three Marys. As Randall points out in *The Landscape and the Looking Glass*, through her writing technique Cather lets us see the Ántonia illegitimacy from five persons away, her way of downplaying the whole incident.

MILDRED R. BENNETT

Willa Cather and France:
Elective Affinities

Michel Gervaud

In many respects Willa Cather's works reflect her deep admiration and love for France. For some mysterious reason France
and the French seem to have never disappointed her or hurt her
feelings, whereas she was prompt to pass harsh judgments on
her own country and fellow citizens. Even when in *Shadows on
the Rock* she alludes to the horrors of the Ancien Régime in
seventeenth-century France through the unfortunate Jules, alias
Blinker, a former torturer in the king's prison at Rouen, her
veneration for our country, its values and past, remains undi-
minished. Tyranny did not preclude good manners, though she
preferred to see them preserved and allied to the spirit of freedom in the young and daring French-Canadian Pierre Charron.
I believe the only objectionable thing she ever found in our
country were the "hungry French fleas" that in September 1902
nearly spoiled her first trip to Avignon. But the splendors of the
City of the Popes, among them ten-course meals in a dining
room with a Gothic ceiling, were soon to soothe her ill-humor
and to convince her forever that "people know how to live in
this country," even if they take baths in washbasins and go to
bed by candlelight.

When confronted with the picture of France she draws in her
novels, a French reader cannot help feeling moved, flattered,
but also ill at ease, for unless he is particularly chauvinistic, he
is aware that he is presented with an idealized vision of his

country. Reality in France has always had its negative aspects, and some of its most glaring weaknesses might have rightly inclined Willa Cather to praise it more moderately had she been less partial to it.

But whether or not she overidealized France is, after all, of little moment. The France she loved may represent just a myth. Yet, apart from the fact that myths refer to some fundamental truth, however elusive and fragmentary, external to man or within him, they stimulate his imagination and heart and, as such, are essential to religion, art, literature. Such was the appeal of France to Willa Cather: it fecundated and nourished her creativeness, in combination with other sources of her inspiration like the Nebraska of her youth, the Southwest, or artistic values. So one may consider that the shortcomings which have marred French civilization are negligible when opposed to the part which Miss Cather's vision of France played in the shaping of her genius and the orientation of her inventive powers.

Out of the articles collected by William M. Curtin in *The World and the Parish*, which, together with *The Kingdom of Art* edited by Bernice Slote, offer the Cather student a very valuable source of information regarding Willa Cather's early writings and, consequently, the genesis of her interests and art, I have taken this enthusiastic statement about France. After praising Dumas *fils* (she was a fervent admirer of Dumas *père* as well) she declares:

> Stopping to think of it, most things come from France, chefs and salads, gowns and bonnets, dolls and music boxes, plays and players, scientists and inventors, sculptors and painters, novelists and poets. It is a very little country, this France, and yet if it were to take a landslide in the channel some day there would not be much creative power of any sort left in the world. Some psychologist said that all Frenchmen are more or less insane, but fortunately it is an insanity that so often takes the form of genius. [*The World and the Parish*, p. 223]

I doubt whether the readers of the *Nebraska State Journal* were ready to fully agree with the twenty-two-year-old critic as to France's outstanding merits. At any rate, it would be hard to find more lavish praise bestowed on a nation. Later, Willa Cather was to learn how to express her admiration in a more

Michel Gervaud

sedate manner, but my impression is that she never really substantially revised that early judgment. Once she had acquired a conviction she clung to it whether or not it met with the prevailing views of her contemporaries. It is a well-established fact that she could only like or dislike intensely. Admiration was the food of her inspiration. In 1939, discussing a chapter about her art in Margaret Lawrence's book *The School of Femininity*, she wrote to Mrs. Carrie Miner Sherwood that Miss Lawrence seemed to have understood she could write successfully only about places or people for whom she had great admiration, which for her was really love.[1] The subjects of her novels are a perfect illustration of this remark.

As to the origins of her Francophilia, Miss Cather's biographers have pointed out the influences she received during her childhood in Red Cloud. In her famous interview with Latrobe Carroll in 1921 she said: "I think that most of the material a writer works with, is acquired before the age of fifteen."[2] Without doubt those formative years in Red Cloud were to be of paramount importance in the shaping of her personality and tastes. If, as she was prone to deplore, Nebraska had no past of its own, the immigrants brought to it a rich one, and she made the most of the wealth of traditions and cultures at her disposal in this patchwork of nationalities. However raw life was there in those days, there were enough interesting people in and around Red Cloud to stimulate the mind of a gifted and curious child such as the young Willa. Her biographers have in particular stressed the role played by the Wieners, the talented Jewish couple who spoke German and French, in the intellectual growth of the young girl. It was through Mrs. Wiener, who was of French origin, that Willa got acquainted with French literature. Other factors encouraged that interest: the French-Canadian settlements to which, for instance, she could go "to hear a sermon in French" as she recalled in "Nebraska: The End of the First Cycle." She liked their songs, dances, cheerful mood, and liveliness, which she was later to evoke in a little-known short story, "The Dance at Chevalier's" (1900), and especially in *O Pioneers!*.

The aura with which she was to surround almost everything that was French owes some of its brilliance to the plays and operas she saw at the Red Cloud Opera House. *The Count of*

67

Monte Cristo, particularly, was to enchant her imagination. When in 1902 she visited Marseilles and the Chateau d'If, probably remembering the thrill with which she had once watched the play, she wrote: "This prison and its island . . . were quite as important to me, quite as hallowed by tradition, quite as moving to contemplate, as Westminster or Notre Dame."[3] Thus the often modest actors who played in a remote little prairie town were contributing, unsuspectingly, to the awakening of a literary talent which, one day, would with sovereign ease embrace the cornfields of Nebraska and the most dazzling aspects of the Old World. But even before Red Cloud, during her early Virginia years, Willa Cather may have become acquainted with France through the wife of Dr. Love, the doctor who delivered Willa Cather into the world. Mrs. Love was the daughter of the United States minister to France during the reign of Napoleon III. So, as a young girl, she had grown up in the glittering world of the French Imperial Court, and in her house she had beautiful objects brought from France. Willa Cather may have seen them; she may have heard fascinating stories relating to the Third Empire or other periods of French history. All her life she remained a friend of the Love family and corresponded with Mrs. Love's oldest daughter, although unfortunately the correspondence has been lost.[4]

Willa Cather's sensitivity to French culture was to become more and more refined during her student years in Lincoln and later when she went to Pittsburgh. It is difficult to evaluate how much French she learned in her classes at the University. She probably improved her reading ability but got little training in the practice of the language. That certainly was not her instructor's fault: just as, when she was younger, she was keen about musicians but showed no zest for practicing the piano with her German music teacher, in the same way she took little interest in French grammar and was bored by exercises. How typical of Willa Cather! Her enthusiasm suffered no restraint. She wanted to enjoy French literature, not a set of dry rules.

The amount of French she picked up in the course of numerous stays in France is not easy to assess either. It may be supposed that eventually she learned a good many everyday idioms in the company of her faithful French cook, Josephine, who spoke no English and who "translated into French cuisine

Michel Gervaud

the materials she could find in the New York market."[5] On the whole, it may be safely assumed that her understanding of written French was very good, that she was able at least to carry on a simple conversation in that language, and that she had little trouble in understanding it when spoken by educated people. The French phrases which her characters use quite frequently in several of her novels are correct most of the time though they occasionally contain a few mistakes (or misprints?) and even may look clumsy. In *Death Comes for the Archbishop*, for example, when she makes Doña Isabella exclaim: *"Ah, mon père, je voudrais mieux être jeune et mendiante, que n'être que vieille et riche, certes, oui!"* the structure of the sentence is influenced by English and is hardly grammatical in French.* At times one is led to suspect that she preferred to thumb through her dictionary rather than look for qualified advice. Of course that is but a minor fault of hers and does not make her books less valuable. Such slips simply tend to prove that she was far more versed in French literature than in the language proper. In "A Chance Meeting" she frankly acknowledged her limitations in that field; she would have liked to speak to the old lady who turned out to be Flaubert's niece, but at first she dared not: "I am a poor linguist, and there would be no point in uttering commonplaces to this old lady; one knew that much about her at a glance. If one spoke to her at all, one must be at ease."[6] Fortunately, much to the American novelist's relief "Caro" happened to speak English.

Yet, whether she was a poor linguist or not, Willa Cather had at any rate a keen perception of the cadence and musicality of French. In the same essay she points out the beauty of the final sentence of *Herodias*, "where," she writes, "the fall of the syllables is so suggestive of the hurrying footsteps of John's disciples, carrying away with them their prophet's severed head . . . : *'Comme elle était très lourde, ils la portaient al-ter-na-tiv-e-ment'."* † In *One of Ours* Claude, reading the in-

Death Comes for the Archbishop, p. 191. See also p. 176: Doña Isabella, a Kentucky girl brought up in Louisiana and educated in a French convent, "had done much to Europeanize her husband. . . . She spoke French well, Spanish lamely."

†*Not Under Forty*, p. 22. It should be noted that *v* forms one syllable with *e–ve*. One should read *"al-ter-na-ti-ve-ment."*

69

scription "*Mort pour La France,*" thinks that the word France is "a pleasant name to say over in one's mind," whereas another American soldier remarks that " *'mort'* seems deader than dead.' It has a coffinish sound" (pp. 335–36). In 1902, landing in Dieppe she noticed that "the very porters spoke in smooth, clear voices that phrased the beautiful tongue they spoke almost as music is phrased."[7]

Willa Cather was so inclined to use French in her books that sometimes she seems to have taken for granted that all her readers were conversant with the language. "A Chance Meeting" contains extracts from Flaubert's correspondence with his niece, and the last page, relating the death of Madame Franklin Grout, is a clipping from the *Journal des Débats*, entirely in French, naturally. *Shadows on the Rock* requires now and then the help of a dictionary and even a translator! Yet in the case of *One of Ours*, as she wrote once to Dorothy Canfield Fisher, she tried to use easy-to-recognize French words so that people in Red Cloud who did not have a French dictionary would know what she meant.[8] Indeed, using French freely in a few of her novels—far more than any other language, including German—was not prompted by any desire to impress her readers or write for American Francophiles (though there must have been many among her audience). In her eyes French when she resorted to it was indispensable to the meaning and tone of the novel. A normal device when she dealt with French characters, it was also a way of indicating cosmopolitan sophistication in her American heroes and above all a certain turn of mind, an attitude to people and things, as in the case of Professor Godfrey St. Peter (who, not surprisingly, is very much like Willa Cather at one particular stage of her life). French also served to broaden perspective, to relate the Old World to the New. It helped the writer to anchor (one of her favorite words) her novels on a solid layer of culture. However, among the various motivations that prompted her to use that tongue there must have been the sheer delight she found in handling an idiom she loved. In *One of Ours* she communicated this admiration to Claude, the Frankfort boy whose reactions she describes as he listens to Madame Joubert:

> He admired the way she roused herself and tried to interest them, speaking her difficult language with such spirit and preci-

sion. It was a language that couldn't be mumbled; that had to be spoken with energy and fire, or not spoken at all. Merely speaking that exacting language would help to rally a broken spirit, he thought. [P. 303]

As we can see, Claude may be an unsophisticated lad, but he is receptive to the rhythm of this foreign language and obscurely perceives that it reflects the mind and ways of a people. In fact, Claude's sympathetic attitude toward French is his passport to the appreciation of a civilization for which he will eventually die. Listening to French enlightens Claude's soul. It is an invitation to discover a purpose in his life.

Through Claude we can see how seriously Miss Cather considered French. She did not regard it as a mere drawing-room language, as Anglo-Saxon people sometimes do. To her it referred to a living culture, popular and aristocratic, and to its highest expression, literature. Her biographers have indicated the part which, at Lincoln, the Westermanns and the Canfields played in further acquainting the young Willa with European traditions. As stressed by Brown, "Mrs. Canfield's cult of art, nourished by her association with French artists and her broad reading of French literature, was important to Willa Cather—it strengthened her in the aesthetic attitude she was forming in her years at Lincoln."[9] She always admired Dorothy Canfield for her knowledge of French and the way she felt at ease in France.

During her Lincoln years she must have begun to relish a style of life—manners, conversation, good food—which to her became inseparable from her understanding of Europe and France particularly. At the Westermanns or the Canfields culture was not cut off from everyday life as at the University; it suffused in the most natural way the activities of the family. That is what Claude Wheeler, whose youth had been spent in a cultural desert, notices immediately and enjoys at the Erlichs, missing it cruelly when he is forced to return to his father's farm. He will find it again in France at the Fleurys. It is something in the house, in the atmosphere, a way of life maintained in spite of the war, which he admires but at the same time envies bitterly, as he feels out of it. He is like "a wooden thing amongst living people . . . . tongue-tied, foot-tied, hand-tied" on account of the barren dullness of his native environment

71

(pp. 355–56). That "feeling about life"—an expression found in *Shadows on the Rock* which to Willa Cather, just as to the dying Madame Auclair, distinguished the French people from the others—that feeling she perceived distinctly in our writers.

Willa Cather's imbibing of French literature was to be intense and prolonged until her last years. At Lincoln she began exploring it on her own and not "under the chilling guidance of an instructor," as she says a little unkindly in "A Chance Meeting."[10] The selection of her articles in *The Kingdom of Art* and *The World and the Parish* from 1893 through 1902 constitutes an impressive list of French authors, books, and plays discussed at length and most of the time in warm laudatory terms. Introducing Miss Cather's review of Pierre Loti's *The Romance of a Spahi*, Miss Slote estimates that by the spring of 1896 the young woman was familiar with most of the important French writers—at least those of her time, I would like to add, as one does not find many allusions to French authors anterior to the nineteenth century in her works, criticism or fiction.* Written in her mature years, "A Chance Meeting"—to mention once more this remarkable essay which reads like a captivating short story, a true one—shows how deeply involved she was with the finest literature produced in our country. Moved by her conversation with Flaubert's niece, Willa Cather wrote these revealing lines about the effect which this extraordinary encounter produced on her: "The old lady had brought that great period of French letters very near; a period which has meant so much in the personal life of everyone to whom French literature has meant anything at all."[11]

As we can see, the phrase "personal life" suggests much more than the mere enjoyment derived from the company of Flaubert, Balzac, Mérimée, or Maupassant. To her those writers had brought "a refining of the sense of truthfulness" which is the essence of artistic growth, as she says in *The Song of the Lark*, an integrity of language and vision, as in the case of Flaubert, which certainly to her went beyond purely esthetic matters.[12]

*The Kingdom of Art, p. 365. One of Cather's rare references to seventeenth-century authors occurs in a 1902 *Journal* article sent from Paris: "When you hear a play of Molière's given at the Français . . . you begin to realize what respect for tradition means" (*The World and the Parish*, p. 919). Another is the allusion to Pascal, mentioned in the text below, in *Death Comes for the Archbishop*, p. 267.

Michel Gervaud

The French authors she revered helped her to achieve a conception of France which had begun to form in her mind before her visit to that country at the turn of the century. If she respected Zola as a powerful craftsman dedicated to his art, he nevertheless repelled her because he hurt her own sense of beauty and clashed with her vision of French culture and perhaps society, too. Of him she said: "Artistically, he is an anomaly; a Frenchman, of the land of light phrases and elegant expression, his heavy, labored style smacks almost of the Teuton."[13] Willa Cather had no appreciation for books "full of repulsive odors," as she called Zola's *Le Ventre de Paris.* The ugly, the sordid did not attract her. The suggestion that Zola might be at least partly right in his description of French realities does not seem to have crossed her mind. Zola contradicted her sense of French history and traditions: "To him the faith that builded Notre Dame, the treasures of art in the Louvre mean nothing. He sees Paris and all the world saturated and steeped in sin, ready to fulfil its doom."[14] Indeed, for Willa Cather this slimy "Caliban" had no place in the fair garden of France!

The French spirit as she had come to apprehend it through her favorite novelists and also through famous artists— Mounet-Sully, Emma Calvé, and particularly the great Sarah Bernhardt ("typically and entirely French," combining "coquetry and Parisian capriciousness" with a savage force)* —represented in her eyes a mixture of rationality and passion, strength and versatility. When so many puritan-minded people clung to the idea of French frivolity, when even the subtle Henry James found our values exquisite but corrupt, Willa Cather on the contrary was always aware of the innate gravity of a civilization which plunged its roots into a remote Latin past. She scolded Mark Twain for having declared "that all French literature was indecent because he had read Zola's *La Terre* and had found it so." Not that she disagreed with Twain about that particular book, but she had chosen the case as "a

---

*The Kingdom of Art, p. 118. In 1892 Willa Cather had admired Sarah Bernhardt's *La Tosca.* The play was performed entirely in French—"a lesson in pioneer sophistication," observes Miss Slote (p. 116). In October 1900 when Bernhardt came to Washington, D.C., with five plays in French, Cather went to see her four nights in succession (*The World and the Parish*, p. 813).

good example of the unfairness of our usual estimate of French literature."[15]

Willa Cather was never prudish. Even after she had taken refuge in the orderly world of the past and traditions—as is often said with some oversimplification—her morality as reflected in her novels cannot be described as conventional. In *One of Ours*, Claude does not find much wrong about the excursions for mushrooms in the forest around Beaufort, which are so popular among his men and the village girls. In her college years, she had enjoyed reading Daudet's *Sapho*, then considered daring. When she was in Pittsburgh and went to the Seibels once or twice a week to read French she did not hesitate to indulge, as Mr. Seibel said, in devil's food cake like Anatole France's *Le Lys Rouge*.[16] When Paul Verlaine died in 1896, she defended him against the attacks of Max Nordau who had called the French poet "a repulsive degenerate." Praising his poetic genius she denied the Philistines the right to judge Paul Verlaine: "You cannot judge an artist by ordinary standards because his duty is to do extraordinary things."[17] That unpuritanical attitude so often to be observed in her writings facilitated without doubt her understanding of French patterns of conduct and her exploration of French literature, and she never let her esthetic judgment be biased by a genteel sense of propriety.

When in the summer of 1902 Willa Cather and her friend Isabelle McClung visited Europe (more exactly, England and France) for the first time, it was for the Nebraska girl a confirmation of what she already knew and felt about France as much as a discovery of it. She liked England, but except when she came across the vestiges of Latin or Norman civilization, she was rarely thrilled by it. By contrast, even before her landing in Dieppe she was sharing the excitement of her French and Italian fellow passengers. As James Woodress writes, "In a sense she too had come home."[18] One cannot deny that at that time she must already have been highly prejudiced in favor of France. Though she had admired the London monuments, she had loathed the bleak aspects of its slums and populace. In France, where she could have noticed as much griminess, she was disposed to pay attention to its attractive aspects only. She must have nurtured in her mind a pre-established vision of our

Michel Gervaud

country that acted as a selective filter: such is the power of love to blind one to the faults of the beloved object and sharpen the perception of its finer qualities! From her delightful account of her experiences in France it is easy to see how much the "Daughter of the Frontier" felt at home in that country. Almost everything she saw could be related to a past, a culture she was familiar with. Of course, as reported by E. K. Brown, she was to say later that "it takes the right kind of American to go to France—one with character and depth and a passion for the things that lie deep behind French history and French art."[19] No one could have been more qualified than she to represent that sort of American. Claude Wheeler, despite Brown's opinion, fits that description only in part. True, he has a desire to understand a country and a people but his previous knowledge of French culture is rather limited, and however sensitive he is, it is difficult to fully credit him with the character and passion alluded to by Willa Cather. He evidently lacks the long years of preparation which made her stay in France such a "great imaginative experience." This happy, passionate encounter with a culture "on its own soil, in its age-old stronghold," to quote Edith Lewis again, left a deep imprint on the young woman.[20] The emotional and intellectual impact of that discovery of France in the flesh can be traced in her novels again and again. The references she henceforth made—places, monuments, people, customs—were not bookish but directly borrowed from her observations of French reality. However, unlike Balzac whom she had accused of cataloguing material objects, she did not strive for literalness in her evocation of the concrete aspects of France. Like Mérimée she believed in the necessity to select significant details. Thus, with a few deft strokes she suggested the greenness of a Normandy landscape, a sunny morning in a garden carefully taken care of by an elderly French couple, the warmth of the Auclairs' living room in Quebec, "the girls of a charity school . . . in hideous dark uniforms and round felt hats without ribbon or bow, marshalled by four black-bonneted nuns" on a Paris street.[21] In her evocation of French places and scenes she succeeded in creating this "emotional aura" which, as she states in "The Novel Démeublé," gives high quality to a novel.

Of her first visit to Paris we have—curiously enough—mostly

75

an account of her pilgrimage to the graves of the writers she admired, at Père Lachaise Cemetery. One could be disappointed with such a choice if one did not know the outstanding role artists and creators occupied in her mind. Significantly, her vision of Paris is more historical than esthetic, in her 1902 letters at any rate. She sees Paris "dominated by Notre Dame and the Invalides and the columns of victory," notices the way the French commemorate their great men by naming their streets after them: "Nearly every street in Paris bears the name of a victory—either of arms or intellect."[22] Paris, by the way, did not inspire her as the subject of a novel; nevertheless, it was never absent from her life and works. She was very fond of Victor Hugo's *Les Misérables* and especially *Notre Dame de Paris*. From those novels she had derived a romantic vision of the city: "Do you want to know what it was like to live in the Paris of the fifteenth century? . . . Then read *Notre Dame*. It is a perfect representation of Gothic art and of the life which fed the roots of that art."[23] After her first visit in 1902, Willa Cather was to make repeated and prolonged stays in the capital of France. In June 1920, for instance, she settled in Paris for almost two months. She had still to write the last part of *One of Ours*, which is about Claude's French experience. As Brown writes, "From her absorption in the past of the city she drew what she felt she had needed: a feeling of the meaning of French civilization and culture as a whole."[24]

In *The Professor's House* Paris provides the melancholy St. Peter (of mixed stock, French-Canadian and American, incidentally) with nostalgic remembrances of his happy student years in France, when he was living with the Thieraults in Versailles. Evocations like "the sky was of such an intense silvery grey that all the grey stone buildings along the Rue St. Jacques and the Rue Sufflot [sic] came out in that silver shine stronger than in sunlight" (p. 102) capture the atmosphere of Paris in late fall, the quality of the Ile-de-France light which brings out the brightness of the pink dahlias bought by young St. Peter in the street. In the same novel, Willa Cather enjoys mentioning the names of monuments, buildings, streets, restaurants—Foyot, Lapérouse—names of celebrities: Emile Faguet, Anatole France, Paul Bourget. The Professor would have liked to spend a summer in Paris with Tom Outland: "He had wanted to revisit

Michel Gervaud

certain spots with him: to go with him some autumn morning
to the Luxembourg Gardens, when the yellow horse-chestnuts
were bright and bitter after rain; to stand with him before the
monument to Delacroix'' (p. 260). In short, the Parisian
memories of St. Peter furnish a counterpoint to the disen-
chanted bitter mood which characterizes the novel.

The history professor is haunted, just as Willa Cather was, by
the memory of the Paris cathedral "standing there like the Rock
of Ages, with the frail generations breaking about its base" (p.
270), a recurrent symbol in Catherian fiction of permanence and
strength endowed with profound spiritual significance.
Medieval religious architecture as a key to the understanding of
French civilization which Willa Cather found, as we have seen,
in Hugo and later in the French historian Michelet is nowhere
more essential than in the last part of *One of Ours*. Claude, on
the day after his landing in France, visits the Church of St.
Ouen in Rouen. Despite his lack of sophistication, the young
man is not totally unprepared for this first encounter with
Gothic art; "he had read more or less" about Gothic architecture. At Lincoln he had written a thesis on Joan of Arc. As a
child, he had often imagined her in "a luminous cloud, like
dust, with soldiers in it . . . the banner with lilies . . . a great
church . . . cities with walls" (p. 56). However, Claude admits
that "it had nothing to do with these slim white columns that
rose so straight and far,—or with the window, burning up there
in its vault of gloom." In the twilight of the ancient church, the
soft glow of the rose window "with its purple heart" surrounded with deep silence and stillness, the revelation of the
beauty of the past comes to Claude together with the awareness
of the slow passing of centuries during which that civilization
had been shining, undisturbed like "the purple and crimson
and peacock-green of this window" (p. 292). George N. Kates
remarked that the 1902 account of her visit to the cathedral of
Rouen offered many similarities to the passage in *One of Ours*
describing Claude's impressions in the Church of St. Ouen.[25] It
is indeed more than plausible that the emotions she herself
experienced were so intense that twenty years later she could
convincingly communicate them to an inarticulate but sensitive
farm lad from Nebraska.

After Paris and Rouen, Avignon was to synthesize for Willa

77

Cather the ultimate meaning of French medieval architecture. In Avignon more than anywhere else she found "a life rooted in the centuries." Edith Lewis wrote that "on her many journeys to the south of France, it was Avignon that left the deepest impression with her. The Papal Palace at Avignon . . . stirred her as no building in the world had ever done."[26] In 1898 she had written of "the great cathedrals [which] reared their towers of impregnable stone, like the very fortresses of God."[27] The fortified Papal Palace, discovered four years later, admirably fitted that description; dominating the town and the region around from the top of Rocher des Doms, it stood once at the center of Christendom. Willa Cather certainly had in mind that vision of austere beauty allied to abiding order and faith when in *Death Comes for the Archbishop* she made Father Latour decide to build a Midi Romanesque cathedral in Sante Fé, which would rise above a vast, primitive, and still half pagan land. As a matter of fact, when he discovered the hill "gleaming gold" from which the stone for the chapel would be quarried, he and Father Vaillant were reminded of Avignon:

> "When I look up at this rock I can almost feel the Rhone behind me."
> "Ah, you mean the old Palace of the Popes, at Avignon! Yes, you are right. . . . At this hour, it is like this." [P. 242]

Thus Avignon at the very beginning of her literary career became for Willa Cather the perfect symbol of the church and the rock fused together, from which, a quarter of a century later, she derived her conception of the Sanctuary, materialized by Ácoma and the Rock of Quebec, where men, whether heathen or Christian had been "yearning for something permanent, enduring, without shadow of change" (p. 98). The Rocher des Doms may also have had another meaning more worldly but nevertheless important in the opinion of a woman who, though less "gourmande" than Colette, the French novelist, was fond of the good things of life—such as *petits fours*, vintage wines, salad dressing, and a ripe Camembert cheese. As Kates very aptly suggested: "The idea of cultivation achieved upon barrenness, of art and labor conquering nature . . . appealed strongly [to her]."[28] Indeed, materially as well as spiritually what was originally barren had become fruitful: the popes in

Michel Gervaud

exile had succeeded in planting a beautiful Italian garden on the
Avignon "bald rock." In the same way, the French missionaries
wherever they went in America set out gardens and orchards,
as Father Latour did near the Tesuque Pueblo, north of Santa
Fé, growing "cherries and apricots, apples and quinces, and the
peerless pears of France." For Willa Cather, gardens were part
of an "art de vivre" beneficial to man: thus by having fruit trees
planted, the Archbishop wanted to encourage the Mexicans "to
add fruit to their starchy diet." On the other hand, she invested
gardens with a biblical, almost sacred character: Latour was
fond of quoting his "fellow Auvergnat," the seventeenth-
century scientist and philosopher Pascal who once said that
"Man was lost and saved in a garden" (p. 267). From what
precedes, it is quite clear that to Willa Cather the French eminently knew how to spiritualize earthly matters, with their
" 'sense of proportion and rational adjustment,' " their ap-
titude for conciliating zeal and order, faith and reason, their
capacity to organize (p. 9). Those traits explain why Latour's
spiritual venture in New Mexico always retained the character
of a civilizing process, and it is no heresy to suggest that Willa
Cather was more interested in the cultural developments of his
enterprise than in the intrinsic value of the religious cause he
championed.

Thus Willa Cather's whole life, interests, work, strikingly
show how deep her affinities with France were. All that we
know about her ratifies Edward Wagenknecht's opinion that
she had "an essentially French appreciation of civilization, of
the amenities of life."[29] Elizabeth Sergeant wrote that Willa
Cather once told her that the French "have values, aims, a point
of view, and have acquired wisdom from the enduring verities.
One did not find anything of the sort in the Middle West."[30]
The latter remark is highly revealing: even as a child, hungering
for beauty, rich cultural traditions, impatient with her environment, she turned to the Old World and particularly France,
discovered through its literature. Later, at every stage of her
life, she always found in French civilization what she was looking for: when she was craving independence, when she was
rejecting harsh provincial molds, France offered her noncon-
formity. In her mature years, when she had reached respectability (but never complacency!) and needed stability in a fast-

79

changing world, she found in French life a reassuring sense of
the past, a devotion to lasting values, a leisurely pace of life
which the brutal growth of commercialism and machine-made
materialism in America had destroyed in her lifetime, much to
her distress. As modern life, in her view, was becoming more
and more shallow, she, on the contrary, was looking for deeper
and deeper certainties and she found some of them, at any rate,
in our culture. Naturally it would be only too easy to show how
much her vision of French civilization was subjective. She saw
only what was best or thought best in our country, its highest
achievements in the fields of thought, art, society. Yet manifes-
tations of pettiness, stupidity, arrogance, intolerance, Parisian
superficiality or provincial suffocation, blindness to artistic
values (as evidenced notably by the bourgeois of Aix en Provence, including its academics as well, who in his lifetime ignored the genius of the native-born painter Cézanne) were not
rare in the France of her time, just as nowadays. Because she
was not interested in these facts she was hardly aware that the
same economic laws that ruled the United States were at work
in the Old World, and that in the field of machine-made
materialism the French lagged only a little behind America. She
never anticipated, I hope, that one day Paris's noble perspectives would be destroyed by ghastly office buildings erected by
the frantic speculators of today, or that the lovely fishing har-
bors on the Mediterranean shore would be turned into gaudy,
sprawling holiday resorts. On the other hand, one would be
very naive indeed to think that she was actually blind to all of
France's blemishes. As Brown wrote, "Willa Cather had an extraordinary power of obliterating from a historic scene its modern encrustations."[31] One could aptly apply his remark to her
general vision of France. That she was not deluded about a
country dear to her heart is furthermore shown in Mrs.
Wheeler's reflections on the meaning of Claude's death on the
battlefront in France: "He died believing his own country better
than it is, and France better than any country can ever be. . . .
She would have dreaded the awakening."[32]

One may wonder then why, if Willa Cather could indulge in a
kind of selective blindness toward the French, she could not do
the same toward her own country. It was perhaps because the
mistakes of a pioneering technological civilization were too

blatant to be forgiven, because she loved the United States too much to remain serene in front of changes which affected the quality of American life for the worse, according to her.

However, to the last she remained faithful to her country. Contrary to what may have been said, I do not think that in everyday life she ever felt alienated in her own land. She never was an exile like Henry James or Edith Wharton. She many times declared that she could only write in America. Even when she was enjoying her stays in France she might suddenly be overcome with nostalgia. She did not let the Frenchness of her culture kill her native roots. America and France, in her life as in her fiction, were always related. Actually certain French landscapes reminded her of her homeland. The wheatfields beyond Barbizon made her think of those of the Divide, with their Lombard poplars. Claude going "deeper and deeper into flowery France" was thrilled at the sight of the "familiar" cottonwoods growing along the green valleys. "He felt they were a real bond between him and this people" (pp. 288–89). "The brown merry old women" she had observed in 1902 gleaning in the fields, were the sisters of Ántonia and the cheerful grandmothers described in "The Bohemian Girl."

In *The Professor's House*, she wrote how St. Peter "had succeeded in making a French garden in Hamilton" (p. 14) in which he grew beautiful flowers. In the same way Willa Cather's French garden was adorned with the finest blossoms of an ancient culture, but, like the French marigolds and dahlias of the Professor, they drew their brightness and vigor from the rich soil of the New World.

[Reference notes appear on pages 260–61.]

COMMENT

There were comments pro and con on whether or not Willa Cather idealized French civilization. Also discussed were Flaubert's influence and a possible emphasis on France as linked with the Catholic Church or religious matters in the fiction.

ELLEN MOERS: I thought it was a marvelous paper because you left things very complex. I particularly liked the term "selective blindness." One aspect of Cather's writing about France gives us a kind of laboratory experience in which to examine that always puzzling question: how much did she know? How much did she see? How much did she refuse to see? And if she consciously eliminated the sordid, the cruel, the rough, what does it do to the work? I for one think that she eliminated it only to lower it to a very deep level and that she is not so much a celebrant of the ideal, she is not so sentimental, she is not so purely nostalgic, whether writing about Nebraska or France. The case I'm referring to is to me one of the great puzzles in Willa Cather . . . and that is that piece "A Chance Meeting," which is fascinating because it is not fiction, it purports to be a journalistic, an autobiographical account of a meeting with a woman. And my question is, how much did Willa Cather know about Madame Grout? I have not seen anywhere, either in writers about Flaubert, who don't seem to know the Cather piece, or in writers about Cather, who don't seem to know, or who perhaps have forgotten, this lady, who was, if I can briefly summarize—and I refer you to the Enid Starkie biography of Flaubert—perhaps the worst bitch in nineteenth-century French literature. She was indeed Flaubert's niece. She also perhaps killed Flaubert. She sucked him dry, little Caroline; she took his money, she refused to give him affection, she went off to Germany during the Franco-Prussian war and bet that the Germans would win, to the horror of her uncle; she stood at his funeral haggling with the publishers over the rights to Flaubert's books. She indeed was the apple of his eye, the daughter of his sister who died in childbirth, but the story of Flaubert's relationship with his darling niece Caro is one of the most hair-raising episodes in the history of French literature. And for anyone who loved Flaubert as much as Cather did, and characteristically her favorite book was that very cruel work, *Salammbô*—I wonder whether—how much she knew. She had read the letters to Caroline. I wonder whether she could have remained completely ignorant of the role of this woman, who was a very tough cookie, and who is interestingly like, though in a nonfiction form, so many of the puzzling heroines of Cather's last work. She's a Myra Henshawe, in a way, where one is always wondering, is this a celebration, is this an inversion of the ideal, what are these elements of cruelty, nastiness, where are they buried in the work? I think they're very effectively buried, and I'm just curious about this. Have you any ideas about her own knowledge or of how much she decided not to tell, or was she just ignorant?

DALMA BRUNAUER: I wonder whether Cather could not have seen her as, let's say, Père Goriot looks at his daughters. They sucked him dry and hated him and abandoned him in the hour of his death and yet they're the apple of his eye. It is possible to have ambivalent feelings like that and love and despise the person at the same time.

ELLEN MOERS: But look at the way Cather handles that material . . . .

Michel Gervaud

It is not simply a representation of beautiful old French culture where everybody lives the literature (which, as we know, is not true), and where the past is always important, and isn't it wonderful, I just met someone who is related to the great Flaubert and in America we don't have this sort of deep civilization. I think that little sketch is much more than that. There is a woman who is frightening, who has a rather fearsome relationship to the younger Willa Cather, who insists, in that very hot weather, on going to the concerts, and so on. There are tensions I think even in a chance meeting that are somewhat like the tensions in her portraits of all mature women in the fiction.

BRUCE BAKER: The affinities you point out, Professor Gervaud, find their way often into various symbolic motifs of the novels, a direction we might well want to pursue after we leave here today. For instance, in *Death Comes for the Archbishop*, there is a kind of union of cultures, the bringing together of these affinities, in such things as the planting of the garden where you get not only the French culture but the native culture as well, brought together in a very beautiful way—the seeds and bulbs from France, remember, and the fruit trees from St. Louis, and, planted nearby, the native trees. It seems to me that the subtle kind of art beneath art we've been talking about in this conference is very much evident in that kind of quiet passage that suggests so much more than it says by bringing these affinities into a kind of symbolic mold.

Professor Gervaud observes that Willa Cather's French is occasionally clumsy and cites Doña Isabella's use of the language in *Death Comes for the Archbishop:* " 'Ah, mon père, je voudrais mieux être jeune et mendiante que, n' être que vieille et riche, certes, oui!' " Doña Isabella's speech is indeed clumsy and hardly grammatical in French, but perhaps this was intended by the author. The portrait of Doña Isabella owes something to Chaucer's characterization of the Prioress in the *Canterbury Tales* (See M. A. Stouck, "Chaucer's Pilgrims and Cather's Priests," *Colby Library Quarterly 9* [June 1972]: 531–37), and it may be that Miss Cather wanted to suggest Doña Isabella's affectations in this subtly ironic fashion. Professor Gervaud says that the structure of the sentence is influenced by English; Chaucer says of his affected Prioress, "And Frenssh she spak ful faire and fetisly, / After the scole of Stratford atte Bowe, / For Frenssh of Parys was to hire unknowe."

DAVID STOUCK

Willa Cather in Japan

Hiroko Sato

In her famous essay "Escapism," Willa Cather says that "the themes of true poetry, of great poetry, will be the same until all the values of human life have changed and all the strongest emotional responses have become different—which can hardly occur until the physical body itself has fundamentally changed."[1] If you believe these words, as I do, it would not seem to be necessary to explain to you why Willa Cather has been popular in Japan. However, it is generally believed that between our two cultures lies a difference as vast as the Pacific, a difference which makes it difficult for us to understand each other; it is, then, quite natural for many to be puzzled about Japanese enthusiasm for Willa Cather and her works. Therefore, I will try my best to satisfy you, and in the process to illuminate a side of Willa Cather that might have passed unnoticed by American readers.

Before discussing the Japanese appreciation of Willa Cather's works, perhaps it will be helpful to say a few words about how American literature in general has been regarded in Japan and about the images of America we have formed through our encounters with American literary works. Our contact with Western culture began only a hundred years ago, except for very limited contacts with Spanish and Dutch people; and the foreign literary works that Japanese people came to know were those by French, Russian, German, and English authors. It was from their reading of these authors that Japanese people began to shape their ideas about Western literature. As the tendency

Hiroko Sato

of the time was to regard anything European as superior, European literature served as a guide and a standard to Japanese readers in their appreciation of literary works.

With a few exceptions, American literary works came into Japan comparatively late, primarily after World War I. First the writings by the nineteenth-century Romantics were introduced, and then came the works of Floyd Dell, Upton Sinclair, and Theodore Dreiser, whom we called proletarian writers. Their books struck many Japanese people as rather crude and irregular, and they decided that American literature was inferior to European literature. As a consequence, until the mid-1930s books by American writers were not treated as literary works, but generally were read in order to learn about social conditions in America, or, as in the case of the works of the New England Renaissance, as philosophical tracts. Japanese people failed to understand the almost limitless range of the American imagination which had created so much variety in its literature. After the introduction of proletarian literature, the images we had about Americans can be summarized thus: Americans were concerned only with the pursuit of material success; they didn't try to understand human nature; they were ignorant and ill-educated people—look at the language the characters use!

It was in this atmosphere that Willa Cather was introduced. Her work first became known to Japanese scholars and students of English literature when some of her novels—*A Lost Lady*, *The Professor's House*, *My Mortal Enemy*, and *Lucy Gayheart*—were made available in inexpensive Tauchnitz editions in the late 1920s and early 1930s. A few people came to love her work in these years, but it is incorrect to say that her novels immediately aroused great interest and enthusiasm among the Japanese people. Miss Cather was regarded merely as one of the many new writers who had emerged after World War I. In *Contemporary American Literature*, published in 1935, Matsuo Takagaki, who was perhaps the first reliable scholar in the field of American literature in Japan, mentions Willa Cather's name three times, referring to her as a writer of the Midwest, together with Sinclair Lewis and Edgar Lee Masters, but saying nothing further. Apparently he came to know about her through such books as Carl Van Doren's *Contemporary American Novelists:*

85

1900–1920 (1922) and Stuart Sherman's *Critical Woodcuts* (1926), and his treatment of Willa Cather in his own book indicates that no real interest in her works had yet arisen. In fact, Willa Cather's novels were not actually introduced to the Japanese reading public until just before World War II. First came *Lucy Gayheart*, which was translated into Japanese in 1939 as part of a series called "The Great Novels of the World"; next, a translation of *Shadows on the Rock*, which was brought out the following year. It seems to me significant that two of Miss Cather's novels were translated at a time when the relationship between our two countries was at its worst and when anything American was suppressed in Japan. There must indeed be something in her novels that is attractive and appealing to the Japanese mind.

The quiet, yet long-lasting enthusiasm for Willa Cather began soon after World War II; though it has died down a bit, it has continued and will continue. Three books of biographical criticism have been published, and innumerable articles have been written on her and her works. Almost all of her novels, some essays (such as "The Novel Démeublé"), and short stories like "The Sculptor's Funeral," "Paul's Case," "The Enchanted Bluff," and "Neighbour Rosicky" have been translated. "Paul's Case," and "Neighbour Rosicky" are among the most popular English textbooks in Japan, and Willa Cather is one of the most popular writers among women English majors in Japanese colleges and universities, as the number of graduation theses on her attests.

Now let us probe into this Cather enthusiasm and find reasons for it. Admittedly, it is a difficult task, for no Japanese writer has ever clearly stated what aspect of Willa Cather's novels charmed and attracted him. Japanese critical writing is of little help on this point, as the writers usually only interpret what has been said about her and her works by American scholars; they rarely offer their personal appreciation. Therefore, my discussion will present conjectures, based in part on my own experiences with her novels. But to show you that my speculations are not wholly unfounded, let me quote the comments made by four well-known Cather lovers, in which they try to convey the "incommunicable" something that attracts them to Willa Cather's novels.

The first comment comes from Momoko Ishii, a noted writer of children's books as well as a Cather scholar. She was among those who first became acquainted with Willa Cather's novels through the Tauchnitz editions in the late 1920s. In a brief article titled "Willa Cather and I," she writes: "Since my childhood I hadn't had a book which could be called 'my own.' But after I read Willa Cather's *A Lost Lady* when I was a college junior, I felt that I had found a 'book of my own.' " When I asked Miss Ishii in a recent interview why she felt like that, she told me that she had found Willa Cather a person who had the same sense of values and the same yearning for things of beauty as her own. Another woman writer, Tsuneko Nakazato, writes in her introduction to a translation of *Lucy Gayheart* that she was struck by the French flavor of that novel and was amazed by Miss Cather's skill in handling the cruelty of human destiny in such a restrained and subdued way. In 1940, only a few months before the beginning of the war between the United States and Japan, Saburo Yamaya, a famous scholar in the field of American literature, said that very few American writers had as noble and pure a mind as Willa Cather, and he praised her artistic intensity and her perpetual endeavor to make her novels perfect. The last and perhaps the most revealing comment on Willa Cather was made by Koji Nishimura, a professor of English literature, a few years after the war. "Among contemporary American writers," he said, "I love Willa Cather best. I am fascinated by Thomas Wolfe, challenged by Faulkner and Hemingway, and stimulated by Dos Passos. I respect these writers, but at the same time I feel repelled by them because their imagination and the worlds they create are so completely different from ours. With Willa Cather, it is quite different. What I feel toward her is a deep and quiet love. The first Cather novel I read was *My Ántonia*. What peace and comfort that novel gave me in the desolate and hopeless period soon after the war!"

We Japanese are usually charmed with a foreign literary work when we find something familiar in it, along with a definite identification with its native place. I think that this principle can be applied to Willa Cather's novels. The most obvious though not the most important reason for her popularity in Japan is that, compared to other major American writers, Miss

Cather's novels are closer in plot, structure, characters, and theme to the European novels which we Japanese have been accustomed to reading. There are, however, more important reasons why her novels seem more familiar and easier to understand than the works by her compatriots. One of them, I think, is her attitude toward nature. To discuss this point, I will begin with a comparison between her attitude and that of other American writers.

As seen by Japanese eyes, the most striking thing about American literature in general is the overwhelming sense of space caused by the very vastness of American nature. Such a vastness is alien to the Japanese experience. Charles Olson begins his book on Herman Melville, *Call Me Ishmael* (1947), with the following statement: "I take SPACE to be the central fact to men born in America, from Folsom cave to now. I spell it large because it comes large here. Large and without mercy." To many American writers, nature, which in America is equated with wilderness, is something mysterious, unknowable, and powerful. It often rejects all human approaches; it is something that is opposed to civilization. Man struggles tragically against a powerful and merciless nature, trying to see what lies behind it, as in Melville's *Moby Dick*. Sometimes man escapes into it from "the sound of the hatchet," as do Cooper's Natty Bumpo and Mark Twain's Huckleberry Finn. In this case nature is regarded as something that will be destroyed by the advance of civilization. Often it is thought of as a source of vitality, as when Thoreau says that "we need the tonic of wilderness"; but even then nature is something which is separated from civilization and man stands separate from nature. When American literature, especially the literature of Romanticism, was introduced into Japan, we could not understand it because of the difference between the American concept of nature and our own. Since the beginning of our history, we have coexisted harmoniously with nature, and that relationship is one of the bases of our culture. If you look at a Japanese traditional painting titled "A Snowstorm in the Deep Forest," for example, you will indeed see a forest in a snowstorm but you will also see a small, inconspicuously-drawn farmhouse or two at the edge of the picture.

Another point of difference is that in Japan when we refer to

nature we are usually speaking of a definite locality. Even the
moon is often described in connection with a place-name, as
"the moon seen from such-and-such hill." On the other hand,
nature as it is referred to by American writers rarely has a local
identity. It is a mental fabrication.² In Willa Cather we find a
quite different approach. The nature in her novels is clearly that
of Nebraska, New Mexico, Arizona, or Quebec; it always has a
definite local flavor. To her, nature is revealed in specific details. However, to a certain extent she does hold the usual
American concept of nature. At the beginning of *O Pioneers!*,
the small town of Hanover is described as "trying not to be
blown away" (p. 3). John Bergson in the same novel "had the
Old-World belief that land, in itself, is desirable" but he has
found the wild land of the Divide "an enigma" (pp. 21–22).
Now after his eleven-year struggle with the land he is so exhausted that he is "quite willing to go deep under his fields and
rest" (p. 25). To men like him and Mr. Shimerda in *My Ántonia*
the land seems merciless, unknowable, and full of violence as
well as immense. The narrator of *My Ántonia*, Jim Burden, says:
"Between that earth and sky I felt erased, blotted out" (p. 8).
Essentially, though, Willa Cather differs from other American
writers, for Jim has said earlier that this immense land is "the
material out of which countries are made" (p. 7).

Willa Cather thinks of nature as an object of "love and yearning" and as something that will respond to these emotions.
Also, nature has law and order and to exist harmoniously with
it man must obey and reaffirm nature's law in his everyday life.
Alexandra Bergson, the heroine of *O Pioneers!*, becomes a successful pioneer farmer, and "it is in the soil that she expresses
herself best" (p. 70). So it has become clear to us Japanese that
Willa Cather never thinks of nature as something opposed to
civilization, but rather that without the harmonious coexistence
of nature and man no civilization can be founded and developed. Therefore she fiercely resents such exploiters of nature
as Bayliss Wheeler in *One of Ours* and Ivy Peters in *A Lost Lady*.

In *My Ántonia* there is one scene which Willa Cather's
Japanese admirers invariably point out as the most impressive.
It is the scene in which Jim Burden, on a picnic with Ántonia
and several other hired girls, sees a plow left standing in a field
magnified by the horizontal light of the setting sun: The plow

"was exactly contained within the circle of the disk; the handles, the tongue, the share—black against the molten red" (p. 245). This well typifies Willa Cather's idea of the relationship between man and nature. Nature, represented by the sun, and the plow, a human tool for cultivation, harmonize beautifully and create the magnificent scene. (Though a plow sometimes symbolizes human will to conquer nature, Willa Cather clearly differentiates tools used by hand like a plow and labor-saving machinery like a tractor. Her dislike for the latter is most evident in *One of Ours*.)

The harmonious coexistence of nature and man also becomes one of the main themes of *Death Comes for the Archbishop*. Father Latour plans for the cathedral in Santa Fé to be in "the right style for this country" (p. 243), not like those "horrible structures" American builders have put up without regard to local characteristics. Willa Cather develops this idea somewhat more deeply when she writes about the Indians' relationship with nature. On his visits to various small Indian villages in his diocese, Father Latour notices and comes to admire the Indian way of passing through a country without disturbing anything; he thinks that "it [is] the Indian manner to vanish into the landscape" (p. 233). This is similar to the Japanese or Oriental attitude toward nature and brings Willa Cather's world nearer to us, in spite of the immensity and power of the nature she described.

In discussing my second point, which concerns her attitude toward the family, I will again begin with a comparison between Willa Cather and other American writers. I think one of the characteristics of typical American heroes is their peculiar state in society; they are alone, almost without any family relationships. Ishmael in *Moby Dick* was brought up by a stepmother; at the end of the book he is floating alone on the sea, and is saved by the *Rachel*, whose captain is looking for his own lost son. Thus the book ends without any change in Ishmael's state; he remains a "stepson." Huckleberry Finn, whose father is a drunkard, is no better than an orphan, and the book ends with Huck planning to run away to the territories when he hears that the Widow Douglass is going to adopt and "civilize" him. Jay Gatsby in *The Great Gatsby* was born of "his platonic conception of himself"; he denies his actual parentage in order

90

to be faithful to his dream and dies alone, without being understood by anybody. In *A Farewell to Arms*, Frederick Henry, who has found his only certainty in Catherine's embrace, at the end of the novel bids farewell to her dead, statue-like body and leaves the hospital alone. I have named only a few representative heroes of American fiction, but they all share the quality of being outsiders in a society where the family is the basic unit; they are all travelers in life, forever seeking two contradictory things—freedom and a framework that will restrict that freedom.

Like other typical American heroes, the protagonists of Willa Cather's novels are almost always children of broken families. Jim Burden and Tom Outland are orphans; Alexandra Bergson and Ántonia Shimerda lose their fathers early in the novels in which they figure; Niel Herbert and Cécile Auclair are motherless. Even those protagonists who have both parents, like Thea Kronborg and Claude Wheeler, are outsiders because of their great abilities or unusual yearnings. At the end of each book, however, the protagonist appears firmly rooted in life after having found the object of his or her search. Alexandra not only becomes the most successful farmer on the Divide, but also marries Carl Linstrum in her real life while in her dream life she is united with "the mightiest of all lovers," a being whose "shoulders seemed as strong as the foundations of the world" (pp. 282–83). At the novel's end she is depicted as a goddess of fertility. Ántonia, who feels that "the ground is friendly" on the prairie, finally marries Anton Cuzak and raises a large family. Having seen her in her orchard surrounded by some of her ten children, Jim Burden thinks that "she lent herself to immemorial human attitudes which we recognize by instinct as universal and true" (p. 353). She is "a rich mine of life, like the founders of early races," and Jim himself feels satisfied as he shares "precious, incommunicable" memories with her.

Niel Herbert in *A Lost Lady* and Tom Outland in *The Professor's House* find what they have been looking for, at least partially. As a young man Niel witnesses the decline and fall of Mrs. Forrester, the beautiful wife of a true pioneer, but in his middle age he comes to be glad that he has known her, for "she had always the power of suggesting things much lovelier than herself" (p. 172); she has given him an assurance of beauty in this world. The orphan Tom Outland finds his mental parentage among the ruins of the cliff dwellers on the mesa, a place for which he feels "filial piety" (p. 251). Moreover, a mummy found among the the ruins, named "Mother Eve" by his companion, stays in the canyon even after all the other artifacts have been removed. The most ideal picture is found in *Shadows on the Rock*. The motherless Cécile Auclair refuses to leave Quebec, then a small and precarious frontier settlement, because of her love for the rocky place. Later she marries Pierre Charron, a friend of the Indians and a fur trader, and bears four sons who are described by Bishop Saint-Vallier as "true Canadians" (p. 278). Here the image of the founder of an early race is realized. We Japanese are especially charmed by Willa Cather's recurrent presentation of the mother-figure as the symbol of beauty and the foundation of human society.* The question of the mother-figure is particularly interesting to us, because since the beginning of our Westernization about a hundred years ago, the family system in Japan has been disintegrating; hence, we have largely lost the mother-figure. With this loss has come a sense of rootlessness, and now the search for the mother-figure is one of the major themes of contemporary Japanese literature.

Various interpretations and explanations have been given of this conception of the family. Some say that Willa Cather could not accept the fluidity of American society, and as an alternative tried to create something stable and definite in her novels. In his discussion of *The Professor's House*, Leon Edel points out that the sense of displacement she experienced in her own life aroused in her the desire for permanence.[3] Perhaps her admiration for European civilization had something to do with this feeling. Whatever the reason, her attitude toward nature and her yearning for stability through the establishment of a family indicate her larger desire to create something permanent and beautiful in America.

I now come to the third point of my discussion, Willa Cather's concept of art and civilization. These words from a

---

* A very sophisticated and interesting discussion of Willa Cather's idea of the family appears in John H. Randall III, *The Landscape and the Looking Glass: Willa Cather's Search for Value* (Boston: Houghton Mifflin, 1960), pp. 108–14, but I think my approach to the question is more basic.

published letter she wrote about *Shadows on the Rock* serve as a good illustration: "A new society begins with the salad dressing more than with the destruction of Indian villages."[4] Willa Cather seems to be saying not only that a new society begins at home, but also that creating and refining even an insignificant thing like salad dressing can be an art if it is done with devotion and imagination. It can be a foundation of civilization. In this sense, all her protagonists can be called artists, regardless of their actual vocation.

Here again Willa Cather seems unique among American writers. Certainly her artists share to a certain extent a general characteristic of American artists which an English critic summarizes as follows: "The American artist has ever felt more at home in unsocialized space than within any social order."[5] If we modify the words "any social order" to "the present American social order," this statement expresses the situation of Willa Cather's artists at the beginning of her novels. They all suffer from the limitations and circumscriptions of the society in which they live. Midwestern small towns like Hanover, Moonstone, Black Hawk, and Sweet Water are full of ugliness. Such eastern industrial cities as Pittsburgh are "grimy" with human desires for material success swirling on their streets. Jealousy and vulgar, raw passions fill the minds of the people in such societies. In that Willa Cather's artists are living in an uncongenial society, they are quite similar to such other artists in American fiction as Melville's Pierre Glendinning, James's Roderick Hudson, London's Martin Eden, and Dreiser's Eugene Witla. However, the destiny that awaits these other artists is quite different. Their art is an affirmation and assertion of their individuality and strong vitality; the only place provided for their self-expression is the society in which they live, and they find it unacceptable. Sometimes their strength brings them material success, but what they face at the end is total isolation and alienation. Therefore, they either commit suicide or, as in the case of Eugene Witla, remain outsiders. At the end of *The Genius* Eugene stands alone, gazing up into "sparkling deeps of space."

Willa Cather's artists, in contrast, feel quite at home in unsocialized space, but instead of standing alone and gazing up into "sparkling deeps" they begin to work at building a new and better society to colonize that unsocialized space. Some people might criticize this attitude by saying that it shows Willa Cather is too weak to face the immensity of the universe, or even that her artists' desire to build a new and better society is contradictory, for they turn their backs on one society to create yet another restrictive structure. But I think her notion is an inevitable outcome of her view of human beings; she believes that man is, like the cliff dwellers in *The Professor's House*, endowed with "some natural yearning for order and security" (p. 221). Alexandra Bergson, for example, creates a beautifully ordered, fertile farm by accepting the laws of nature through her communion with the Genius of the Divide. Similarly, Thea Kronborg in *The Song of the Lark* recovers from the distractions of her life in Chicago among the Indian ruins in the Southwest. Thea learns of the "glorious striving of human art" which had already existed in the human heart "when men lived in caves" (p. 399), and combines it with her love for the sand hills of Colorado, which stretch out to "drink the sun" (p. 276); then her singing becomes full of noble power.

Art is certainly an expression of human individuality, which Willa Cather defines as the human desire for order, beauty, and security. But she seems to believe that art, hence civilization, is made up of a "long chain of human endeavour."[6] This is perhaps what James Woodress calls "perpetuation of tradition."[7] Individuals "for a little time cast a shadow in the sun,"[8] as the French colonists did on the rock of Quebec, as the Indians did on the rock of Ácoma, and as the European immigrants did on the prairies in Nebraska. After they are gone, the next generation will come along and carry on their spiritual yearning for things of beauty. Speaking of the onion soup Father Vaillant is making, Father Latour says: "'I am not deprecating your individual talent, Joseph, but, when one thinks of it, a soup like this is not the work of one man. It is the result of a constantly refined tradition.'"[9]

Willa Cather also insists on the importance of the locality, as I mentioned earlier in discussing her attitude toward nature. Her idea is best symbolized by the cathedral in Santa Fe, which Father Latour planned to have "the right style for this country." Although it is designed by a French architect in Midi Romanesque style, it is built of the golden-red rocks of the Southwest.

Also, the location is ideal: "the Cathedral lay against the pine-splashed slopes as against a curtain. . . . the towers rose clear into the blue air, while the body of the church still lay against the mountain."[10]

But Willa Cather is not an ordinary traditionalist, and here we come to her most attractive quality. Surely she is sympathetic with people like Mr. Shimerda and Euclide Auclair who cling tenaciously to the Old World culture, but who are presented as defeated. She does not insist on a blind imitation of European culture in America. The closing lines of *O Pioneers!* are: "Fortunate country, that is one day to receive hearts like Alexandra's into its bosom, to give them out again in the yellow wheat, in the rustling corn, in the shining eyes of youth!" (p. 309). It is not the continuity of the outward forms, but that of hearts, that Willa Cather praises. This continuity comes in the forms of growing vegetation and hopeful youth—truly American images. People with souls "new and yet old"[11] are those who add one link of refinement to a culture and who carry it on to the future.

Here we may wonder how it is possible to realize a spiritual heritage in a new world. In *Death Comes for the Archbishop* we find the following passage:

> There is always something charming in the idea of greatness returning to simplicity—the queen making hay among the country girls—but how much more endearing was the belief that They [the Holy Family], after so many centuries of history and glory, should return to play Their first parts, in the persons of a humble Mexican family, . . . in a wilderness at the end of the world. [Pp. 282–83]

The idea expressed here corresponds to the famous passage in *My Ántonia* in which Jim Burden reflects on Gaston Cleric's interpretation of Virgil's *Georgics*. Cleric has explained to his students that when Virgil said "I shall be the first, if I live, to bring the Muse into my country," he meant that he hoped to bring the Muse to "the little rural neighbourhood on the Mincio where the poet was born" (p. 264). This is perhaps one of the most significant things said by Willa Cather. The Muse symbolizes the spirit that lies at the base of a civilization. Man facing nature with love and yearning will learn what the most fundamental thing for human society is and subsequently will know how to express it. Thus Ántonia and Cécile begin by founding families, the simplest form of society.

It is quite true, as David Daiches has written, that Ántonia's "rooting of herself in the American soil . . . is not achieved at the expense of repudiating her European past."[12] In speaking to Jim Burden of her father, a symbol of the sophistication and refinement of European culture, Ántonia says that " 'he's been dead all these years, and yet he is more real to me than anybody else. He never goes out of my life' " (p. 320). She inherits from him the spirit that lies behind the old European culture, but her eyes are turned toward the future while his were always turned back to the past; and the place to which she brings this spirit is not peaceful Bohemia, where the social structure has been established for centuries, but the Nebraska wilderness. And from her communion with nature she comes to learn the best way to express the spirit she has inherited. Nature in America has a power to simplify the human mind until it becomes clear to a man which are the most vital and fundamental of human desires. Thea Kronborg in Walnut Canyon finds that "her ideas [are] simplified, [become] sharper and clearer. She [feels] united and strong."[13] Father Latour refuses to go back to France in his old age, because nothing in European culture could "make up to him for the loss of those light-hearted mornings of the desert, for that wind that made one a boy again."[14]

Because Willa Cather's beliefs that anything that is made with imagination and a desire for beauty is a work of art, that civilization is a linking of individual efforts, and that "some natural yearning for order and security" is innate in man are quite similar to what we Japanese have always believed, we can easily sympathize with her. However, when it comes to the idea of a "return to simplicity" and the idea (in T. S. Eliot's words) that "the culture will have to grow again from the soil," the situation is different. We are almost as surprised and struck as by Jay Gatsby's famous words: " 'Can't repeat the past? Why, of course you can.' " Willa Cather even applies her idea of simplifying to her method of writing, as exemplified in her essay "The Novel Démeublé." Though she firmly believes in the continuity of spiritual heritage, she denies the continuation of outward forms if it occurs without reference to locality. This idea, together with those of simplicity and renewal, indicates to us that Willa Cather attempts to deny the passage of physical time, which in turn is a denial of history. We Japanese feel history too keenly to be able to deny it. We feel, nonetheless, that despite her differences from other American writers Willa Cather is a true American writer, for her innocence and naiveté are possible only in America, where the immensity of space is the most important fact to man. There is a certain validity in Lionel Trilling's criticism that "her own work is a march back toward the spiritual East—toward all that is the antithesis of the pioneer's individualism and innovation,"[15] but I cannot wholly accept it.

Through comparing Willa Cather with other American writers and with us Japanese, I have tried to suggest which of her ideas are interesting to us and why. Because of the limited time and for the sake of a unified theme, I have had to omit certain points of interest to us Japanese, such as her subtle treatment of sexual matters.

In conclusion, I would like to add a few words about why Willa Cather is especially interesting to the people of the younger generation in Japan. Recently, the idea of anti-progress has been seriously discussed among us, because when we reflect on our time we realize how difficult it is to know what is the most important and fundamental thing in life. Our lives seem burdened and complicated by all kinds of distractions and unnecessary trivialities. We come to notice that Willa Cather's idea of a "return to simplicity" and renewal is quite similar to the idea that lies behind the search we are engaged in for the primal root of human existence, though her approach is fundamentally esthetic while ours is sociological. Amazed by the irony of time that makes the most conservative the most radical, we feel deep admiration for her keen insight in foreseeing the destiny of this materialistic civilization some fifty years ago, when most people still believed in the possibility of scientific and material progress.

[*Reference notes appear on pages 261–62.*]

COMMENT

The discussion dealt with bibliographical information, especially regarding Willa Cather's popularity in Japan, and with varying concepts of her treatment of man and nature and of her attitude toward the family.

I like Professor Sato's discussion of landscape and ideas of art and civilization in Willa Cather's fiction, but I find her discussion of Cather's attitude to family a little confusing. Willa Cather's protagonists frequently come from broken families and to her list of Cather orphans Professor Sato might add Myra Henshawe, who was raised by her uncle, and Lucy Gayheart whose mother is dead. There is also Bartley Alexander in Cather's first novel whose origins, like those of Jay Gatsby, are obscure and who might be similarly described as self-engendered. I am not sure, however, that Cather's protagonists, as Professor Sato suggests, always wind up "firmly rooted in life" or that they find the object of their life's search. One has to distinguish between an ideal presented in the book and the protagonist's realization of that ideal in his life. Ántonia serves at the end of that novel as an ideal mother-image for the central protagonist, Jim Burden—her farm in the West is an innocent refuge that he emotionally craves for—but she does not resolve the tension in Jim's life between his mature desire for a sophisticated life and career in the East and his instinctive yearning for a "home" in the country of his childhood. Her life can never be a complete way of life for Jim. Claude Wheeler is a notorious example of a man who finds an ideal (the idea of French civilization) but who is far from realizing it or being "firmly rooted in life." The great disillusionment in store for him if he had survived the war is made explicit at the end when the author says: "He died believing his own country better than it is, and France better than any country can ever be." As with the other American heroes that Professor Sato mentions (Ishmael, Huck Finn, Gatsby) the dream for Claude is preferable to the reality. Niel Herbert and Tom Outland never become fathers or husbands and we do not see Cécile Auclair, the only one of Cather's protagonists to raise a family, after she has grown up and married. Professor Sato's argument that Cather places high value on the family is irrefutable, but I don't think Cather protagonists are any more successful than their American fictional contemporaries in realizing this ideal in their lives.

DAVID STOUCK

What Willa Cather hated most about a modern world was its fluidity; the things of today would in all likelihood be gone by tomorrow. Indeed, "things"—as pejorative a word as "they"—were not meant to last much longer than a figurative twenty-four hours in the world of now. The momentum of constant change—the new replacing the old and the newer overtaking the new—sometimes frightened her or made her querulous, even petulant.

Her only protection from an ever-widening circle of alteration was to find sources of stability for herself and the characters she created. Surely for many of her people the family could serve as a fixed center; it could provide the order and discipline, the intelligence and love that one found in nature before it was abused by human greed and exploitation.

Her attitude toward the family, however, is ambivalent. "The Best Years" and *Shadows on the Rock* are, we suppose, Miss Cather at her most nostalgic about her own family life. Whatever personal needs nostalgia satisfies, it nevertheless roseates truth. We can, for example, appreciate the cleverly wrought experimental structure of *Shadows on the Rock*, but cannot take seriously the Auclair family as a realistic portrait. Think of Cécile with a head cold, Cécile who "was kept in bed for three days—in her father's big bed, with the curtains drawn back, while her father himself attended to all the household duties." Considering whether to bring anyone in to help him, he rejects the notion: "'Mais, non, nous sommes plus tranquilles comme ça. . . .' That was the important thing—tranquillity," as he and Cécile drew together in perfect harmony. The Auclair family is sentimentalized beyond belief so that Cécile is very much like Esther Summerson, the one character in Dickens who brings us to the brink of esthetic despair. M. Auclair is so reasonable and yet so much a man of untarnished conviction that he is less credible than Mr. Quilp, who eats hard-boiled eggs with their shells on.

On the other hand, Willa Cather can create realistic family situations—strong portraits of immigrant family life where the only stability comes from an unquenchable desire to survive and in truth not all do survive. The Shimerdas represent a magnificent family grouping —the grasping mother whose greed is motivated by a need to keep her family alive; a father so sensitive that he would rather die than witness the dehumanizing of his children; the surly Ambrosch who sends Ántonia to work "in the fields from sunup until sundown." But Ántonia's ardor can never be significantly diminished, whether she worked like an animal in the fields goaded by her family, or whether she worked in kitchens for other families like the Burdens or the Harlings. Whatever the abrasions she suffered from her own kin or the less visible scars she allowed to form during her days with the Harlings, she saw the family as equatable with permanence and ordered stability. It is no wonder that at the end of the novel she emerges as the earth mother whose own fertility is inseparable from that of the earth. The realistic Ántonia, who was often bullied by her own family and yet who believed in any family as the core of human continuity, is transformed into an allegorical figure. What is magnificent about the portrait of Ántonia, surrounded almost always by some family or other, is that the transformation is literarily valid.

Except in those few instances when Willa Cather romanticized family life beyond the willing suspension of disbelief, she was all too aware of the tensions and blind selfishness that could erode family feeling. From *O Pioneers!* and *The Song of the Lark* to *Lucy Gayheart* and *Sapphira and the Slave Girl* Miss Cather's judgment of the family was often strengthened by bitterness. And bitterness can be an esthetic tool for one who believed in "creative hate." What rapport can there be between the mythic Alexandra, whose "eyes drank in the breadth of [the Divide]," and her brothers Oscar and Lou, the embodiment of those superficially real Nebraskans "scudding past those acres where the old men used to follow the long corn rows up and down?" It is only Alexandra's visionary power, a power paradoxically rooted in the soil, that allows her to triumph over Oscar and Lou, who stupefy themselves with the immediate reality of drudging habit and erratic fussiness.

There is no rapport either between Thea and her sister Anna, so incapable of thought that "her opinions about the smallest and most commonplace things were gleaned from the Denver papers, the church weeklies, from sermons and Sunday-School addresses." It is only Thea's talent that allows her to triumph over Anna's triviality. Because Thea acknowledges her own desire, she also takes in stride the truth that "the world is little, people are little, human life is little." Obviously a similar tension exists between Pauline and Lucy Gayheart, but Lucy has permitted herself to be crushed. For her—if we can alter Thea's dictum—"everything is far and nothing is near." The struggle Lucy makes to stay alive when she knows she is about to die is futile only because she has died a long time before.

In short, the family can be a center of trial; and a person's power to survive, even to triumph—and death can occasionally be a form of triumph—stems from his inner resources and sense of values. The family is a world in miniature. Those who plod along or feel no rough edges comply with a pattern of conformity that may be indigenous to the family or the society of which it is a part. But within many families, no matter how prosaic their occupation or activity, there is a dynamic creative impulse. Sometimes this impulse suffuses a whole family. When this happens, as it does to Rosicky's family, his own life—even in death—was "complete and beautiful." Old Mrs. Harris, abused by the indifference of her family, chooses to die alone but her desire for giving and doing passes on to Victoria and Vickie; they "had still to go on, to follow the long road through things unguessed at and unforeseeable." Sapphira too had this creative impulse, evident in the way, as a young woman, she helped manage the farm at Back Creek and evident in the way she never capitulated to death. But she could not share her desire; it was too selfish, too rigid for that. Still its essence permeated her household. It gave courage to Rachel, making her "rebellious toward the fixed ways which satisfied other folk." And it animated the runaway slave Nancy, branded by her mother as one who fought against her "natural place in the world."

Willa Cather's image of the family was never one but many and hence unpredictable. Certainly she hoped it might be a place of refuge where one garnered the strength to "follow the long road." Sometimes it was that but then it was a rarity or simply a sentimentalized portrait. The family was too much like the flawed world. But there were many ways to encounter this world and so too there were many ways to face one's family.

EDWARD A. BLOOM and LILLIAN D. BLOOM

Hiroko Sato's experience in Japan reminded me of my experience in writing about Willa Cather in Hungary. When I was a freshman at the University of Budapest in 1943, I was one of only five English majors; when I submitted my doctoral dissertation on Willa Cather in 1948, I was told by my adviser that I was the first person to have written a doctoral dissertation on an American author at a Hungarian university.

The first work of Willa Cather to be published in Hungarian translation was "Paul's Case." The translator was the excellent László Cs. Szabó; the editor of the anthology was Professor Joseph Remenyi. This was in 1935. Later the same year a translation of *Death Comes for the Archbishop* came out, the work of Kázmér Pogány, published by Szent István Társulat, Budapest. *Shadows on the Rock*, in a translation by Iván Boldizsár and with an introduction by Mária Blaskó, was published in 1937 by Franklin Társulat, Budapest. Then, strangely enough, at the peak of the last year of World War II, *Sapphira and the Slave Girl*, originally published in English in 1940, came out in Hungarian translation in 1944. The translator was László Kéry, the publisher Szöllösy könyvkiadó, Budapest. How they got hold of a book so recent and what prompted them to publish an American book during that unpromising year is a mystery.

In 1963, Gábor Thurzó wrote an essay on Willa Cather for a volume, in Hungarian, *American Literature in the Twentieth Century* (Amerikai irodalom a huszadik században). No new translations of Willa Cather are mentioned in the bibliography. I am convinced, however, that if Hungary had a free publishing market, the works of Willa Cather would by just as popular in Hungary as they are in Japan.

As for the works by Willa Cather in English, the situation in Hungary again resembled that in Japan. The inexpensive Tauchnitz editions could be found, by diligent search, in either the library of the English Institute at the University, the central University Library, or the American Library. At the time of my dissertation, only one full-length book on Cather had appeared, René Rapin's. I knew of its existence but was unable to obtain it. Several essays were available, however, both by and about Willa Cather. My introduction to her, however, came through none of these but through a chance meeting of an Armed Services Overseas Edition of *O Pioneers!*.

The same values which Miss Sato found appealing for Japanese readers would also appeal to Hungarian readers. In many respects, they resemble the traits which distinguish another woman who was a pioneer of mind and spirit, Murasaki, writing in eleventh-century Japan. Among Hungarian writers, the closest analogue would be Willa Cather's close contemporary, the novelist Margit Kaffka.

DALMA H. BRUNAUER

Italian Perspectives

Aldo Celli

On considering the general plan of the seminar it seemed to me more appropriate to limit myself to identifying certain problems and concerns as points of departure for clarification and discussion. Thus, I thought, first, to elaborate on the interplay between Willa Cather and Italy and Italian readers; second, to approach some of the dimensions of Willa Cather's art on the basis of critical assumptions and arguments that have spread throughout Italy and may directly influence the appreciation of her books there as well as in other parts of Europe. Willa Cather's writings allow different modes of interpretation, and it would seem of interest to consider their contribution to the understanding of her art on a practical rather than a mere theoretical level.

To begin, I would like to glance at those few instances in which Italy and Italians are in some way present in Willa Cather's writings. There is no doubt that she refers to Italy much oftener and more meaningfully as the seat of the classical world of ancient Rome and Greece and of their mythology than to contemporary Italy. Quotations of the former kind may be easily found. I recollect a case which, by the way, seems to me indicative of Willa Cather's world view and metaphorically significant for the understanding of her as a writer and as an artist. It is a memory referred to by Elizabeth Sergeant in *Willa Cather:*

A Memoir, telling of a meeting with the novelist while she was writing *My Ántonia*:

> She then suddenly leaned over . . . and set an old Sicilian apothecary jar of mine [elsewhere referred to as a "Taormina jar"] . . . in the middle of a bare, round, antique table.
>
> "I want my new heroine to be like this—like a rare object in the middle of a table, which one may examine from all sides." [P. 139]

The geographical location is in Italy, but it is not the Italy of her own day. It is an idea: the idea of a harmonic fusion which Greek civilization acquired on Italian soil. In other words, it is a symbol of the greatest moment of classical art and at the same time of the plural signification of the object of art and the artistic sign.

As in the case of many American writers, it was the great classical tradition that first stirred Willa Cather's interest—a vision of Italy that was also the result of an atmosphere which had permeated the American literary and artistic worlds. For a long time there persisted an interpretive dichotomy: on the one hand, Italy was a happy dreamland, blessed by God, a source of light, joy, and liberating energy, home of the glories, pleasures, and forces of nature; on the other hand, it was a land of magic, of mysteries, of sin, of intrigues, of evil. To these was added the myth of Catholicism, the fascination of the most spectacular and arcane aspects of the life of the Catholic Church. It is an Arcadian, medievalist kind of myth with flashes of Carnival. Let me remind you how Thomas Jefferson described his visit to Italy—"a peep into Elysium"—and of the words of Henry Adams: "[In Rome] the lights and shadows were still medieval, the shadows breathed and glowed full of soft forms felt by lost senses. No sand-blast of science had yet skimmed off the epidermis of history, thought, and feeling. . . . Medieval Rome was Sorcery." Henry James had exclaimed on entering Italy, "At last—for the first time—I live! For the first time I know what the picturesque is." And what had Hawthorne to write in his diary? "More and more, in Rome, the visionary splendour of St. Peter's took possession of my imagination—it was the world's cathedral. The more I observe the Catholic Church the more I realize the perfection with which it answers the exigency of human frailty." And, writing of Florence, "I walk on the smooth flags of Florence for the mere pleasure of walking and live in its atmosphere for the mere pleasure of living. I hardly think there can be a place in the world where life is more delicious for its own simple sake." And finally a view of Venice by James Fenimore Cooper: "Venice held its vicious sway, corrupting alike the ruler and ruled, by its mockery of those sacred principles which are alone found in truth and natural justice." Thus the myth was built up, fascinating, irresistible, contradictory.

Whatever is said about Italy in Willa Cather's writing is framed in this myth. The Rome visited by Albert in "Double Birthday" is Italy conceived as the land of Arcady, of Elysium, and in " 'A Death in the Desert' " the dream is also localized, this time in Florence: "[Katharine] dreamed of youth and art and days in a certain old Florentine garden."[1] We may consider in this connection the epic-Arcadian paganism of the Italian boy Caesaro in "Behind the Singer Tower."[2] Italy may become a memory and serve as a background, an emblem, a fixed allegory. Consider, for example, the emblematic use of Venice at the end of *The Song of the Lark*:

> The many naked little sandbars which lie between Venice and the mainland, in the seemingly stagnant water of the lagoons, are made habitable and wholesome only because, every night, a foot and a half of tide creeps in from the sea and winds its fresh brine up through all that network of shining waterways. So, into all the little settlements of quiet people, tidings of what their boys and girls are doing in the world bring refreshment; bring to the old, memories, and to the young, dreams. [P. 581]

Italy is also the land of the beautiful, and of evil, of glory and decadence, in the middle of unhealthy localities. In *My Ántonia*, Gaston Cleric's health is "enfeebled by a long illness in Italy" (p. 257), contracted as a result of contemplating the glories of its ancient past. "He had wilfully stayed the short summer night [at Paestum], wrapped in his coat and rug, watching the constellations. . . . It was there he caught the fever . . . of which he lay ill so long in Naples." Willa Cather's comment follows immediately: "He was still indeed doing penance for it" (p. 261).

It is difficult to deduce her attitude toward the contemporary

Italian because of the scarcity of references, but she does refer sometimes to Italians who have emigrated to the United States. In such cases she seems to tend to present them as the fruit of the negative aspect of that myth of Italy I have talked about —the fruit of the "fall" and the "decadence." Compared with the other immigrants, the Italians are weak, unsuited to the great adventure of the West. In *My Ántonia*, for example, Otto Fuchs, recalling his mining days, tells of the bucket that traveled across a three-hundred-foot-deep canyon, about a third full of water, carrying the workmen to the mine.

> "Two Swedes had fell out of that bucket once, and hit the water, feet down. If you'll believe it, they went to work the next day. You can't kill a Swede. But in my time a little Eyetalian tried the high dive, and it turned out different with him. . . . I happened to be the only man in camp that could make a coffin for him." [P. 109]

Or Italians carry out activities that are rather unrespectable, unimportant, like the Vannis and their dancing pavilion in Black Hawk. The allusions to contemporary Italian life may be reduced to anecdotes which seem out of context and are without a pertinent reference, as when, in "Double Birthday," Elsa gives a bunch of violets to Dr. Engelhardt: " 'Hey, you take me for a Bonapartist? What is Mussolini's flower, Albert? Advise your friends in Rome that a Supreme Dictator should always have a flower.' "[3] Another example is the reference to Queen Margherita in *My Ántonia*:

> "Ever since I've had children, I don't like to kill anything. It makes me kind of faint to wring an old goose's neck. Ain't that strange, Jim?"
> "I don't know. The young Queen of Italy said the same thing once, to a friend of mine. . . ."
> "Then I'm sure she's a good mother." [P. 342]

On Italian culture Willa Cather quotes Dante, the obvious and certainly the greatest author, he too having entered the myth that nineteenth-century American culture had built around Italy. In one case, however, the reference historically concerns Rome; it occurs in *My Ántonia*, and it is made to the lines in

106

which Statius talked about the *Aeneid*.* In another case, in " 'A Death in the Desert,' " the recollection is emotional, the quotation obvious: "And in the book we read no more that night."[4]

From the foregoing it is apparent that the Italian reader would not have been moved to read Willa Cather's books for reasons that involve any direct relationship between the writer and his country. However, there is a parallel to be drawn: just as Willa Cather has included that fraction of Italy that she mentions in a myth manufactured by the culture of her country, so the Italian readers have, to some degree, enveloped her writings in another myth created in Italian culture about America.

It was to a large extent the Fascist dictatorship with its censorship and its distortion of the real conditions of the democratic world that brought the Italians to the discovery and framing of an American myth. Many Italian readers of the 1930s, stimulated also by D. H. Lawrence's *Studies in Classic American Literature*, tended to see the whole of American literature, for better or for worse, under the sign of primitivism, however inspired. The Italian writers in this period who were most strongly engaged socially and politically looked to American literature, in truth to America itself, as a means of reacting against the state of Italian culture. They saw American literature as a positive factor, as new blood to be transfused into the (for them) sick and bloodless body of Italian literature, the more so that in this land of "nature" they also saw the land of liberty, of the democracy scorned by Fascism. The terse factuality of American style was felt as a relief from the the turgid bombast of propaganda. To readers suffocated by conformism the Americans brought a breath of liberty. The work of the Americans was felt to be a synthesis of "all that Fascism pretended to deny and exclude," and sowed "the first doubt that not every-

*The quotation, apparently from memory, is from Canto XXI of the *Purgatorio*: "Nel tempo che 'l buon Tito, con l'aiuto/ del sommo rege, vendicò le fóra/ ond' uscì 'l sangue per Giuda venduto,/ col nome che più dura e più onora/ era io di là," rispuose quello spirto/ "famoso assai, ma non con fede ancora./ . . . Al mio ardor fuor seme le faville,/ Che mi scaldar, de la divina fiamma/ onde sono allumati più di mille;/ de l'Eneïda dico, la qual mamma/ fummi, e fummi nutrice, poetando" (82–87; 94–98). As Gaston Cleric translates it to Jim: "I was famous on earth with the name which endures longest and honours most. The seeds of my ardour were the sparks from that divine flame whereby more than a thousand have kindled; I speak of the 'Aeneid,' mother to me and nurse to me in poetry" (pp. 261–62).

thing in the world civilization had ended with Fascism." In its own way American literature thus "helped not a little to perpetuate and to nourish the political opposition among 'reading Italians'."[5]

Thus Willa Cather was welcomed as an element in the myth; she was, in fact, represented with "The Sculptor's Funeral" in *Americana*, a sort of "manifesto" of the myth, with an introduction by Elio Vittorini which was forbidden by Fascist censorship.[6] Translations from Willa Cather had been made even earlier, but it was during this vivid revival that we had the largest number of them. Her novels, however, were fascinating above all because of the story of the immigrants, in which the human and religious values that founded the great American nation could be recognized, and which showed the notion of a heroic and moral way of life: an ideal admired not so much for its institutions as for its human qualities. As Vittorini pointed out:

> Willa Cather had drawn attention to the legend of the pioneers and the realistic note which went with it, with the same need to reach metaphysical satisfaction; and she reached it in the rhapsodical, enchanted landscapes . . . in the psychological escapes and their evocative concentration. . . . What did Willa Cather do? What did Gertrude Stein do? What did Sherwood Anderson and Eugene O'Neill do later on, and the poets, their equals? Still impressed by the realist legend, they set themselves to intensify what they believed they could get out of it forever, the psychological processes, and to translate it, along lines that would remain psychological, into a superior legend, into metaphysics. But they didn't succeed in shaping a real legend, something ordinary, outside the ordinary course of events. Everyone attained his own type of metaphysics in its own form.[7]

And Vittorini's are some of the soundest comments written in Italy about Cather.

But not many years later America lost its mythological and mythical fascination. Such a change can be exemplified by the very same critics previously cited, Vittorini and Pavese. In 1946 Pavese wrote:

> We were accustomed to considering the United States as a country which entered world culture with a warm, persuasive, and

unmistakable voice only in the decade which followed the great war. . . . We shared the sensations of those "young Americans" of being new Adams, alone and resolute, who had come out, not from Eden but from a jungle, freed of all burdens of the past, fresh and ready to walk on the free earth. . . . But now it turns out that those young Americans were wrong. . . . In reality it was not American culture which was renewed from its foundation in those years; it was we who came in serious contact with it for the first time.[8]

America and its literature were no more a myth: Italians had found in American literature realism and naturalism, sincerity and spontaneity—an image of a new culture, a new civilization, a new aspect of humanity, a wide, almost limitless sense of nature. They had found in it a spirit of freedom, of liberty, of full expression of the individual, a full democratic spirit. All these aspects of American literature are true and do exist; but American literature is much more complex and various, richer and more profound than they would indicate. With the loss of their enthusiasm for those particular aspects, Italian readers and critics discovered other elements essential to the understanding of that literature. Obviously, the list of American writers read and studied grew larger, but many names almost disappeared as new names were added.

As for Willa Cather, her writings received other interpretations. She was felt closer to a certain European characteristic, rich in "a sensitivity, a restless, a vague intellectualism,"[9] defined as more European than American. She was also perceived as a writer endowed with a certain "Latin spirituality"; and such a spirituality was opposed to American "realism." In her works Italian readers have felt vibrating a profound interest in life, but above all in the mystery of life; and therefore a profound interest in death. These interests explained to some Italian readers why Willa Cather has given such importance to ancient traditions, to the heroic and mysterious past. Other readers have noticed that her work is distinguished by its timbre, comparable to the airy freshness of Katherine Mansfield and the sophisticated awareness of Virginia Woolf. Her characters have been seen as portraits, as physiognomies of the soul, rather than as embodiments of conflicts. It has been noticed that because her novels depend more on character than on plot and concentrate everything on the soul, she succeeds in communicating the spiritual essence but makes her characters static, similar to the figures in a conversation piece. It is apparent that the judgments of American criticism have often been repeated. However, the Italian reader has also discovered that Willa Cather revealed a tendency toward intimism, a way of romantic evasion, "a need coming from the heart."[10] I may even point out a resemblance, a similarity in style, with certain Italian novels and short stories of the period immediately after World War I—a leaning toward autobiography, lyricism, depth, a search for emotions, and a rummaging among inner recollections.

By 1960, however, hardly any writing about Willa Cather is to be found, except of course in histories of American literature. The general trend has moved toward what is thought of as complex, ambiguous, "profound" writing, and many critics do not consider Willa Cather's work as such. It is my own conviction that her writings could be scrutinized very profitably in the light of new modes of interpretation. The brilliant work done by American scholars entitles us, for a practical purpose, to avoid analyzing her novels according to certain patterns which, more or less disguised, are gained from a type of critical reading that began with and was appropriate to a narrative tradition typical of the nineteenth century. This could also lead to the conclusion that her books are not novels in that tradition. We feel that we need not limit ourselves to defining her novels according to their themes, and also we may avoid hunting for symbols, a task that can take in even more territory and lead us farther astray. There are many possible symbols, and they can branch out into an infinity of pathways that may cause us to lose our way.

One might begin with carefully checking her modes of narration, her devices of style and organization; and by investigating the movement of her narrative along the syntagmatic and paradigmatic axes. Willa Cather's method of composition turns out to be a complex narrative network, fascinating many readers and irritating others. In her books the paradigmatic, or vertical, axis, with clues, information, description, small tales on the side, etc., is very dense, variegated, and with all kinds of rhythms and tonalities—from the brief, sudden, interpolated

110

allusion, to the long description, to the story within the story.
Everyone has noted how Willa Cather makes abundant use of
descriptions (her sweeping brushstrokes on the landscape);
how she introduces psychological backgrounds, and, not infre-
quently, real moral judgments directly expressed. Her fiction
abounds in little domestic episodes, little adventures in the
fields, observations on the state of the harvest, of the livestock,
on the weather; a correlation between daily life, ordinary activities, atmospheric mildness and severity. Right on the
paradigmatic axis one meets many of the writer's most widely
known passages.

Contrary to the expansion of the "informative" elements, one
notices the dryness, the essentiality, and the concise nature of
the elements that fill up the nodal centers of the actions. The
most important episodes, the fundamental happenings—the
acts of love, the announcements of death and of marriage, the
abandonments, the reconciliations—happen along short or very
short tracts. The nodal elements of the story are revealed sometimes only through the sudden, unforeseen, and isolated use of
a central word. That variegated and very dense web of clues
may meet up with the story at any moment.

It is by watching how and when these elements meet that one
of the secrets of Willa Cather's art can be discovered. In fact, the
clue-giving, informative, descriptive, and even observational
passages very frequently assume new meanings when they are
read in contrast with the story. The story is in its turn enriched
and amplified, and it even justifies itself in the light of these
other elements. It is significant, for example, that Willa Cather
uses the time element especially at the crossroads of the two
axes of her modes of narration. Characteristic of her narrative
technique is also the pause in time and space around the central
elements of the story. She creates a temporal separation, a suspension that serves, in a certain sense, to distill everything that
has been narrated previously. The endings of her novels and
tales are displaced in time; they assume a retrospective function. There is a constant care in dating what she narrates, and
she tends to fix everything in time; almost every chapter in her
novels and almost every paragraph in her short stories begins
by identifying a specific time and then elaborating on it. This
often leads her to establish a time, after which she locates a

space within which an event will take place. Take these two examples from *A Lost Lady*:

> Thirty or forty years ago, in one of those grey towns along the Burlington railroad . . . . [P. 9]
> One winter afternoon, only a few days before Christmas, Niel sat writing in the back office . . . . [P. 34]

And these from *O Pioneers!* and *My Ántonia*, respectively:

> One January day, thirty years ago, the little town of Hanover, anchored on a windy Nebraska tableland . . . . [P. 3]
> I had been living with my grandfather for nearly three years when he decided to move to Black Hawk. [P. 143]

Her narrative is characterized by the presence of constants, systematic recurrences. Such constants help to establish the characteristic rhythmical movement of her prose.

There is a corresponding parallel in the repetition of highly privileged words that form real lexical constants. This does not come about only at the level of the single word, the "key words," but includes the grammatical and syntactic levels as well. To all this we may add the frequent use of the codified patrimony of stereotypes, proverbs, popular sayings, the uncertain phrasing of the foreigner, the commonplace often disguised behind a quotation in another language.

In every case her language appears significant. No matter what approach is used to the art of Willa Cather, one feels the need of a careful consideration of her linguistic devices. Her prose tends to assume a rhythmical register that varies according to the psychological situation of each event narrated. A fast rhythm, for instance, is produced on several levels, whether it is phonic, or lexical, or syntactic. Take this example from *A Lost Lady*:

> Quick as a flash, as if it were a practised trick, with one of those tiny blades he slit both the eyes that glared in the bird's stupid little head, and instantly released it. [P. 24]

At the lexical level we find a prevalently monosyllabic structure; at the syntactic level we find short sentences simply and coherently linked to one another, but supported by devices of rupture or transposition—such as the attributive "quick as a flash" placed in the first position and remote from the subject, in such a way as to give pre-eminence to the action itself in contrast with the person acting. At the phonic level, in the line of the suggestive presence of the liquid sound in "flash" one has a reverberation of the iterated *l* (seven times). The rapid flow of the *l* is accompanied by the regular repetition of the *s*'s, two present in each phrase (as many as eleven times), that unites sinister connotations to the sense of suddenness of the action. A fast rhythm is frequently produced by a syntactic transposition of the verb which is placed at the end of the sentence. Such a syntactic device comes together with related lexical choices: "Up and down, backward and forward among the tangle of branches it flew" (*A Lost Lady*, p. 24).

On the other hand, a slow rhythm is built up on an ampler, more easy flowing style, with a more relaxed and calm syntax, and with a predominance of multisyllabic words, as in this passage from *A Lost Lady*:

> When the blue shadows of approaching dusk were beginning to fall over the snow, one of the Blum boys, slipping quietly through the timber in search of rabbits, came upon the empty cutter standing in the brush, and near it the two ponies, stamping impatiently where they were tied. [P. 66]

It is by means of such a rhythm that we are introduced to the particular atmosphere which permeates the events that follow. It is the rhythm that anticipates the most intense moments of the novel. Such a rhythm offers premonitory hints that can leave time for meditation on the facts and yet it also lessens the tensions present in the same facts.

Because of her tendency to lyricism Willa Cather, more than other prose writers, can also stand up to a physical analysis of her linguistic devices. It is not difficult to evince samples of phonic iterations and other rhetorical figures and correspondences.

What is shown here is that her linguistic devices are constructed according to a harmony, in a clearly established order. Willa Cather's world view is both ordered and harmonious. Man's life must turn out to be harmonious, and so must the relations between men and peoples. As some critics might put it, the linguistic microstructures have their place within the macrostructures, where harmony and order are taken up as a way of life on both an individual and a collective level. Just as the harmony of language is the basis of the harmony of facts, so exterior harmony is a proof of spiritual harmony. Order and harmony equal beauty: whoever has harmony and order in his heart is beautiful.

Harmony and order constitute the central myth of Willa Cather's work; the garden of Eden, the Golden Age, her great metaphors. In correspondence with order and harmony we have their rupture, with a parallelism for opposition. But a salient characteristic of her work is also to be found in the progression by parallelisms and oppositions on an obviously binary construction. Thematic oppositions of the following sort are always easy to find: past/present; old world/new world; land-country/town; man/earth; garden/machine; civilization/ barbarism; and so on down a long list. Also easy to find are the ideological oppositions such as faith/agnosticism; idealism/materialism; will/acceptance; and many other oppositions such as those of characters: conquerors/conquered; winners/defeated; dreamers/doers.

One of the oppositions that we encounter on all levels in Cather's narrative is that which opposes the norm to deviation from the norm. In her writings a code is constructed which centers on the norm; its meaning operates by discarding above and below the established norm. For example, we have on the one hand the heroes of her stories who stand out because they are above the norm, they come out of it; and on the other hand one can hear the voices of the others, of those who make up the norm, the majority of mediocre people. The norm can be exceeded in excess (see, for example, Marie in *O Pioneers!*), but then one comes up against a punitive nemesis. The quality of her heroes, Willa Cather tells us, consists of building up their own codes. Likewise we find in her novels a norm of linguistic expression, a norm of behavior, a norm of the emotions. However, the demarcation line of the norm in her narrative seems to rotate on itself; and what appears on the denotative plane seems to take on a different meaning on the connotative level. The moment of conquest, the realization of one's individual ego, is no longer the overcoming of the norm but the adhesion to another norm—the norm of an elite with its view of the world, its ideological position, its behavioral code.

The complexity of Willa Cather's writings offers us many other dimensions. I will point out two more as hypotheses of a very different order.

We know how strongly the archetypal dimension is present in her writings. We may recall the initiation voyage—Thea Kronborg at Panther Canyon, Tom Outland at the Blue Mesa, Claude Wheeler in France. Youth in general is shown in its initiatory moment; "the best years" of her books can be seen as the years of initiation. We may remember the conquest or the rebuilding of the earthly Paradise, the expulsion of Adam, and so on. Once the archetypal substrata that underly her characters and the essential patterns of her stories have been shown, a fable-like dimension is revealed. Generally, Willa Cather's novels present a central presiding character (the very titles of her books are indicative of the fact) around whom and for whom the other characters move, in harmony with him or in conflict with him. Thus, taking *O Pioneers!* as an example, one may find the presence of the "goddess-mother"; the despotic queen; the good, wise, old man; the wandering knight; the bad brothers; the prince charming; the woman of fate; the victim of love. Like fables, Willa Cather's tales and novels are based on essential situations, and in them one can discover an implicit system of unity and discrete rules of codification.

In addition, her mode of narration includes a frequent use of anticipation. The anticipations in her stories re-echo until they develop and transform themselves to the point of becoming essential to the understanding of the whole on their own level, as well as on others. Again taking *O Pioneers!* as an example, from the beginning we have the first seeds of anticipation of the kind of communication that will be established between Alexandra and Carl: "The two friends had less to say to each other than usual" (p. 15). A few pages earlier we had, metaphorically, the first anticipation of the destiny that awaits them throughout their lives: "The two friends stood for a few moments on the windy street corner, not speaking a word, as two travelers, who have lost their way, sometimes stand and admit their perplexity in silence" (pp. 10–11). Such anticipations have their share in the metaphorical-metonymic interplay of the novels.

Like the folk tale, Willa Cather's novels have the recurrent process of elaborating common material in a multi-dimensional context. On the other hand, actions in her novels may become emotions and produce an atmosphere which can ensnare the reader as well as the characters in the book. It is sometimes difficult to describe Willa Cather's plots in the Aristotelian sense of "men in action," because her stories are distinguished by their emphasis on a situation more than on an action, as in the old German epic tales. As in the old saga, the characters in her stories may be better defined as men in tension who become more interesting for the psychological problems arising out of their situations than for what they seem actually to be doing. It is not, in fact, a single event which counts but the interaction of several events and the way they are conditioned by all the other elements of the narration. Of great relevance, once again, is the dialogue. And Willa Cather has a bent for dialogue, to the point of establishing an indirect dialogue between the narrator and the reader. This is particularly the result of the tone of voice in which the narrator speaks.

My second hypothesis derives from the observation that the compositional patterns, at least in some of Willa Cather's books, recall the patterns of melodrama. First of all, one notices that there are cases in which her characters seem to act like actors. In *A Lost Lady* Mrs. Forrester, for example, is given a role, and it is within the sphere of this role that she is known, respected, loved, admired, betrayed, scorned. Willa Cather reveals to us that she saw Mrs. Forrester in the role she was acting: "She was still her indomitable self, going through her old part,—but only the stage-hands were left to listen to her" (pp. 166–67). Indeed, at the very beginning we are given such a presentation of her: "In [Cyrus Dalzell's] eyes, and in the eyes of the admiring middle-aged men who visited there, whatever Mrs. Forrester chose to do was 'lady-like' because she did it" (p. 13). The place in which Mrs. Forrester's fate is decided is a décor, a formality; according to principles established a priori, it is a stage setting:

> The Forrester place, as everyone called it, was not at all remarkable; the people who lived there made it seem much larger and finer than it was. . . . Stripped of its vines and denuded of its shrubbery, the house would probably have been ugly enough. [Pp. 10–11]

116

Aldo Celli

We may read in this light the passage in which we are told how Niel learns about Mrs. Forrester's end. The scene takes place at a Chicago hotel, and it all proceeds at a theatrical rhythm and pace; one is really in front of a stage. The movement, the dialogue, the gestures are all theatrical: a chance encounter, a physical arrangement so that the actors do not go out of the spectator's sight, a more than noncommittal setting, an unreal detachment:

> "I'm Ed Elliott, and I thought it must be you. Could we take a table together? I promised an old friend of yours to give you a message, if I ever ran across you. You remember Mrs. Forrester? Well, I saw her again, twelve years after she left Sweet Water,—down in Buenos Ayres." They sat down and ordered dinner. [P. 172]

In Willa Cather's novels there are gestures that reply to gestures, and are repeated; there is a dialogue at a distance that re-echoes, thus establishing certain norms that, from one time to the next, support each other or clash with each other. Actions are dilated and diluted. At the same time, one cannot avoid noticing the emphasis on seductions, adulteries, domestic hostilities, trivial deceptions, petty jealousies, grotesque deaths, irresponsible cruelties, and so on. Willa Cather's lexical predilections are also very significant in this connection. Among the words most frequently used in her writings are: *yearning, desire, virtue, soul, feeling, devotion, immeasurable, spirit,* and *spiritual.* The linguistic instrument itself explodes under the melodramatic thrust; the rhetoric of melodrama breaks the natural fluidity of speech that loses its personal nature without maintaining a social typology. In *My Ántonia* Jim Burden, telling of an event of his boyhood, says, "I felt a considerable extension of power and authority, and was anxious to acquit myself creditably" (p. 100), and this is a voice that is neither his nor that of his memory. Alternatively, the word can become a mimic gesture, almost a shout, rhapsodical, as in *The Song of the Lark*: "O eagle of eagles! Endeavour, achievement, desire, glorious striving of human art!" (p. 399).

These and other dimensions perhaps may be considered in Willa Cather's writings, and yet one cannot avoid seeing them in the paradigmatic perspective of a phase of American culture, and noticing that their elements surface and become historically concrete, linking themselves to a precise cultural circumstance. And so there are other fields to be explored.

Though her works do not offer the tortuous, mysterious sounding of the deep as some criticism understands it, they obviously have their depth. But what seems to be of greater importance is that Willa Cather's work and art give rise to problems even today and continue to set questions to which one attempts to offer an answer, and usually finds more than one.

[*Reference notes appear on page 262.*]

COMMENT

In the discussion, more illustrations of "horizontal" and "vertical" lines were tested. Matters of style—the relation to poetry, linguistic devices—were also touched on.

RICHARD GIANNONE: It seems to me that what you're after is a phenomenology of Willa Cather's fiction. We are reminded that words not only represent life but have a life of their own. . . . It seems very much what Willa Cather felt about the life of language, that is, words not only represent a world but make a world. I think you were right also in emphasizing artifice and being dissatisfied with the word "novel," because fiction—it's always astonishing to realize that the novel is made of merely words. . . . And I wonder if you would go on to say that these are fictions that deliberately deny action in order to create a form of effect. Because that, it seems to me, is the way I can participate in the novel—not to think of Ántonia as a friend or Ivar as someone I might like to know, because those things seem to violate what the fiction is, that is, the effects through words. I thought it was marvelous, about melodrama, and having a part. This is a kind of Fellini sense of control that the narrator has. A number of people have said this, though I just learned it this year, that Niel Herbert's point of view is given to us in order to be rejected. It's inadequate. She's much larger than he is.

The organic nature of fiction that emerges from serious esthetic and human concern justifies Professor Celli's rejection of the exclusively thematic or of the exclusively symbolic critic. The argument against reading for theme primarily is by now too well established to invite

118

further discussion here. Ordinarily, further, we would also turn away from predominantly symbolic readings that have made criticism a burdensome exercise in obscurantism. Although we sympathize with the desire to avoid symbol-hunting, we at the same time wish to emphasize the fairly obvious consideration that Professor Celli's stricture tends to underrate: that is, symbols appropriately intermingled with the details of a central text and kept under scrupulous control are not only useful but artistically inevitable. Now this truth has not been denied by the author of "Italian Perspectives" but it is in danger of being brushed aside by anyone using his cautious distrust of symbol-hunting as an excuse for literalizing the act of imagination. In order to avoid an admittedly frail *ignis fatuus* of symbolic pursuit, Professor Celli has provided a substitute, albeit a subtle one, by a relocation of options. Thus he has resorted to an almost uncomfortably austere strategy, the intersection of the syntagmatic and paradigmatic axes.

For one thing, as it seems to us, the substitution is of one kind of search for another: the conjunction of narrative ways and means for the fusion of symbolic (or thematic also, for that matter) interstices. The new language proposed, further, is at odds with the fluid narrative style and language of Willa Cather. If *symbol* misused can be an irritatingly tenuous concept, it still has a closer correspondence with Miss Cather's achievement than the geometrically suggestive *axis*. But we do not wish to become embroiled in semantic niceties or to underestimate Professor Celli's informed, sensitive analysis. Our aim in these brief comments, rather, is to suggest an accommodation of his rather formalized approach within a freer symbolic outer structure. Toward this end we venture to recommend the valuable distinctions of John Crowe Ransom between *texture* and *structure*. He was, of course, talking about poetry: the relevance of poetic criticism will require little justification when applied to a prose style as rhythmic and lambent as Willa Cather's. "The texture of a poem," he said, "is constituted of its rich local values, the quality of things in their 'thingness.' The structure is the 'argument' of the poem. It gives the poem such shape as it has; it regulates the assemblage of sensory data, providing order and direction. . . . A poem . . . has a texture *and* a structure. Though the texture is strictly irrelevant to the logic of the poem, yet it does after all affect the shape of the poem; it does so by *impeding* the argument. The very irrelevance of the texture is thus important. Because of its presence we get, not a streamlined argument, but an argument that has been complicated through having been hindered and diverted." (As interpreted by W. K. Wimsatt, Jr. and Cleanth Brooks, *Literary Criticism: A Short History* [New York: Alfred A. Knopf, 1957], p. 627. See also E. A. Bloom, *The Order of Fiction* [New York: Odyssey Press, 1964], pp. 213–15.)

Reduced to even simpler terms, the structure is the totality of the novel—the plot or outward shape—and insofar as the totality is not a rendering of literal truth but a refined, envisioned representation of general truth, that structural totality is symbolic: it "stands for" something other than itself. Simultaneously the story contained within itself what Ransom once called a "fringe of feeling," or "local excitement" of texture (the interior, heterogeneous details of feeling and meaning). Plainly the critic is obliged to isolate for analysis only what is there. He must observe the contextual limits of the novel with which he is working and avoid irrelevant symbol-hunts or assertions of complexity that do not exist. Through his own kind of alchemy, then, the critic is left with only what is real in the context of the novel. Within the large, structural symbolism of plot and meaning, that is, he may be able to disclose textural truth—symbols, if we insist—that help to illuminate and vivify the structural.

The plow against the sun is just such a textural detail—it is one of the feeling, local means by which Willa Cather asserts the infinitely larger, more significant truths of her novel. As a particular, it is not important in and of itself, any more than the shifting seasons of the prairie, or any more than the cruelty of Ivy Peters blinding the bird. How Willa Cather arrived at these textural details is unimportant, even if we had access to that information. What are important are the shape of the novel and the details relevant to its growth: the structure and the organic texture.

If, then, we correctly read Professor Celli's intersection of the syntagmatic and paradigmatic axes, we share his broad view of the way in which Miss Cather constructed her novels and his admiration for the way in which she manipulated affective response. A symbolic strategy, we agree, must not overwhelm the reader, but neither must it be denied when it is practiced so meticulously by Willa Cather, whether in relation to the pioneer at his apex or in his decline, whether to the artist enthralled, or to the residue of "machine-made materialism." Professor Celli has important things to say about the structure, language, and rhythm of Miss Cather's novels. Indeed in his formula of the crossed axes he implies the presence of the symbolic data that we have barely touched upon. The critical approach that we suggest would make full use of Professor Celli's horizontal findings, but then go much deeper—symbolically—toward the discovery of truths which are no longer dependent on the overt assumptions of language, place, and time.

LILLIAN D. BLOOM and EDWARD A. BLOOM

Willa Cather
and the Art of Fiction

James E. Miller, Jr.

It is difficult to remember that Willa Cather was born as recently as 1873, that she died only twenty-five years ago, in 1947, and that her most impressive period of achievement was the 1920s. She seems far more distant from us now than all these dates testify. In our memory she belongs to a vanished age which she herself glimpsed and touched but which we did not—except through the vision of her work. Even in the 1920s, when she was producing her finest novels, she must have seemed an anachronism to many alongside the makers and shakers of the time—T. S. Eliot, James Joyce, Ernest Hemingway, William Faulkner. And when we turn to her today, fresh from the astonishingly overstuffed rooms of such recent remarkable novels as Joseph Heller's *Catch-22*, or John Barth's *Giles Goat-Boy*, or Thomas Pynchon's *Gravity's Rainbow*, we feel more than ever the remoteness of her fiction and its world. The superficial view might well insinuate itself that Willa Cather, in 1973, is obsolete. But it takes no very deep digging to discover that this view *is* superficial, and that Willa Cather took out some critical insurance policies that protected the life of her fiction through the 1920s and 1930s, and that extend to the present time and into the future: these policies were issued by the "kingdom of art," to which Miss Cather paid her costly premiums faithfully throughout her career.

In this reassessment, my aim has been to focus on the art of

Willa Cather's fiction. But for such a focus, I have felt the need for a frame to hold the glass as it moves over the work. For this frame I have, as my title might have intimated, adopted the theory of fiction of Henry James. There are at least two good reasons for using James to see Cather more clearly. The first is that James's essays, prefaces, letters, and stories yield perhaps the greatest body of fictional theory yet produced by a writer in English, and I have recently gone through all his work to systematize the theory in the recently published *Theory of Fiction: Henry James* (1972). In brief, James's conceptions might well be used to take the measure of any serious novelist. The second reason is perhaps more persuasive: as nearly all of Willa Cather's critics have testified, James was a major influence on her work, rendering some of her early stories more Jamesian than the Master's own; and she herself made a number of evaluative comments on James that indicate the depth of her appreciation. Moreover, Bernice Slote, in her essay in *Sixteen Modern American Authors* (1969, 1973), observed that in the early Cather criticism, " 'Jamesian' became a cant word to describe almost anything she wrote. Yet there has been no real account of exactly what that relationship might be."[1] All of these considerations lie behind my use of James as a frame for my reassessment of Willa Cather, but I have certainly not intended to write a study ferreting out all the influences of James on Cather. Rather, I have meant to suggest lines of relationship, many quite obviously unconscious, and to point to some subtle vibrations, some faint resonances, that are more suggestive than conclusive.

I

The body of Willa Cather's essays relating to fictional theory is not large, filling only two slender books and even there somewhat duplicative. One of these Willa Cather put together herself, under the title *Not Under Forty*, in 1936. The other was assembled by an English writer, Stephen Tennant, after Willa Cather's death, with the title *Willa Cather on Writing* (1949). In addition to these, however, there are her stories of artists, who interested her almost as much as they did Henry James as subjects for fiction.[2] And perhaps even more important than these are the great bulk of Willa Cather's early newspaper columns, reviews, and essays, written in the 1890s, and brought together, sifted, systematized, and superbly edited by Bernice Slote in 1966 in *The Kingdom of Art.* In her introductory essays to that volume, especially in "First Principles: The Kingdom of Art," Miss Slote has demonstrated amply and persuasively that long before she had launched her career as a novelist, Willa Cather had found her way to some fairly sophisticated, even profound, beliefs about art, and held in embryonic form most of the basic principles that were not to find mature statement and affirmation until around a quarter-century later.

There is no need to recapitulate here Willa Cather's many laudatory references to Henry James scattered throughout those early reviews gathered into *The Kingdom of Art;* it will suffice to point to Bernice Slote's listing of James among the early influences on her, detecting in these early pieces, as she says, the echoes of "the judgments and spirit of Henry James (especially in *French Poets and Novelists* [1878] and *The Art of Fiction* [1884])."[3] It is perhaps worthy of note that one of Willa Cather's short essays which Stephen Tennant collected in *Willa Cather on Writing* is entitled "On the Art of Fiction" (first published in 1920). Typical of Willa Cather's references to James is the following found in her 1936 revision of her 1925 essay on Sarah Orne Jewett: "At that time [the time of Miss Jewett's development] Henry James was the commanding figure in American letters, and his was surely the keenest mind any American ever devoted to the art of fiction."[4]

The phrase—*the art of fiction*—clearly and easily and early found a life of its own in Willa Cather's critical vocabulary because it summed up for her the basic principle of her theory of fiction. It is perhaps easy to forget that in Cather's day as well as in James's, the phrase was in dispute. Fiction might be many things other than art—an elaborate filler for the leisure of young girls, for instance, or simply a form of journalism. The youthful Willa Cather wrote in 1894, "In a work of art intrinsic beauty is the *raison d'être.* Any piece of art is its own excuse for being. . . . No man, or woman, is ever justified in making a book to preach a sermon. It is a degradation of art. . . . An artist should have no moral purpose in mind other than just his art."[5] In "The Art of Fiction," James had written in response to Walter

Besant's demand for a "conscious moral purpose": "To what degree a purpose in a work of art is a source of corruption I shall not attempt to inquire; the one that seems to me least dangerous is the purpose of making a perfect work."[6] In Willa Cather's 1920 essay "On the Art of Fiction," she wrote: "Writing ought either to be the manufacture of stories for which there is a market demand—a business as safe and commendable as making soap or breakfast foods—or it should be an art, which is always a search for something for which there is no market demand, something new and untried, where the values are intrinsic and have nothing to do with standardized values."[7] In "The Novel Démeublé" (1922) she wrote: "If the novel is a form of imaginative art, it cannot be at the same time a vivid and brilliant form of journalism."[8]

Although Willa Cather's insistence on fiction as art was fundamental to her conception of the novel, her most famous principle of fictional theory was embraced in the title of her most influential essay, "The Novel Démeublé": "How wonderful it would be if we could throw all the furniture out of the window; and along with it, all the meaningless reiterations concerning physical sensations, all the tiresome old patterns, and leave the room as bare as the stage of a Greek theatre, or as that house into which the glory of Pentecost descended; leave the scene bare for the play of emotions, great and little—for the nursery tale, no less than the tragedy, is killed by tasteless amplitude."[9] It is surely significant that this oft-cited essay takes as its guiding metaphor the conception of fiction as a house, strongly echoing that famous passage in Henry James's Preface to *The Portrait of a Lady:* "The house of fiction has in short not one window, but a million—a number of possible windows not to be reckoned, rather; every one of which has been pierced, or is still pierceable, in its vast front, by the need of the individual vision and by the pressure of the individual will" (p. 313). However varied in shape the windows in the house of fiction, Willa Cather would find them large enough to use for heaving out the furniture from any of the overstuffed rooms. In stationing his novelists at the windows, James of course was suggesting something of the form which the artist imposed on the range of his vision as it focused on some corner of life. Willa Cather, too, in throwing the furniture out the window, was suggesting something of the necessity for spareness, for severe selection, in the novelistic form as it related to the abundance offered by life itself.

A number of critics in search of a theoretical base for what they conceive to be a weakness in her novels have seized upon "The Novel Démeublé" for attack. Indeed, Lionel Trilling has made this essay the focal point of his general condemnation in his 1937 evaluation published in *After the Genteel Tradition*. He begins: "In 1922 Willa Cather wrote an essay called 'The Novel Démeublé' in which she pleaded for a movement to throw the 'furniture' out of the novel—to get rid, that is, of all the social fact that Balzac and other realists had felt to be so necessary for the understanding of modern character." Trilling uses this aspect of Willa Cather's theory of fiction as a key to the recurrent deficiencies in her novels, for, he asserts, "this technical method is not merely a literary manner but the expression of a point of view toward which Miss Cather had always been moving—with results that, to many of her readers, can only indicate the subtle failure of her admirable talent."[10]

Whatever the merits of Trilling's value judgments of Willa Cather's novels, his misconception and misrepresentation of her fictional theory appear astonishing. In "The Novel Démeublé," Willa Cather was formulating in her own terms a set of principles that Henry James before her had worked out with considerable elaboration. She wrote: "There is a popular superstition that 'realism' asserts itself in the cataloguing of a great number of material objects, in explaining mechanical processes, the methods of operating manufactories and trades, and in minutely and unsparingly describing physical sensations. But is not realism, more than it is anything else, an attitude of mind on the part of the writer toward his material, a vague indication of the sympathy and candour with which he accepts, rather than chooses, his theme?"[11] In "The Art of Fiction," James wrote: "It goes without saying that you will not write a good novel unless you possess the sense of reality; but it will be difficult to give you a recipe for calling that sense into being. Humanity is immense, and reality has a myriad forms; the most one can affirm is that some of the flowers of fiction have the odor of it, and others have not." To produce the "illusion of life," James continued, requires application of "this exquisite process" that is the "art of the novelist"—the novelist's "attempt to render the look of things, the look that conveys their meaning, to catch the color, the relief, the expression, the surface, the substance of the human spectacle. . . . All life solicits him [the novelist], and to 'render' the simplest surface, to produce the most momentary illusion, is a very complicated business" (pp. 34, 36). A key term for James throughout his critical essays was "selection," which he called more than once the essence of art and which he posed over against the "saturation" which he found the essence of the big, sprawling, naturalistic and generally artless novel, sometimes self-styled a "slice-of-life."[12]

In "The Novel Démeublé," Willa Cather wrote: "Out of the teeming, gleaming stream of the present it [the novel] must select the eternal material of art. There are hopeful signs that some of the younger writers are trying to break away from mere verisimilitude, and, following the development of modern painting, to interpret imaginatively the material and social investiture of their characters; to present their scene by suggestion rather than by enumeration."[13] Like James, Willa Cather frequently pointed to the analogy between fiction and painting, stressing that certain principles governed both, and that the technique of the one art might well have its relevance to the other. In "My First Novels" (1931), she wrote: "Too much detail is apt, like any other form of extravagance, to become slightly vulgar; and it quite destroys in a book a very satisfying element analogous to what painters call 'composition.' "[14]

Willa Cather was, in a sense, following James's example in taking over critical terms from painting. James apparently took "rendering" from the one art to apply to the other, and he also adopted from painting the term for one of his favorite and most challenging concepts, "foreshortening." A close examination of what James meant by foreshortening reveals that it resembles very closely, perhaps duplicates, what Willa Cather was getting at in proposing to "unfurnish" the novel. In "The Lesson of Balzac" (1905), he referred to a basic and difficult element of art as "that mystery of the foreshortened procession of facts and figures, of appearances of whatever sort, which is in some lights but another name for the picture governed by the principle of composition" (p. 188). In his Preface to *The Tragic Muse*, James gave his fullest definition of foreshortening: "To put all that is possible of one's idea into a form and compass that contain and express it only by delicate adjustments and an exquisite chemistry, so that there will at the end be neither a drop of one's liquor left nor a hair's breadth of the rim of one's glass to spare—every artist will remember how often that sort of necessity has carried with it its particular inspiration. Therein lies the secret of the appeal, to his mind, of the successfully *foreshortened* thing, where representation is arrived at, as I have already elsewhere had occasion to urge, not by the addition of items (a light that has for its attendant shadow a possible dryness) but by the art of figuring synthetically, a compactness into which the imagination may cut thick, as into the rich density of a wedding-cake" (pp. 192–93).

The avoidance of the "addition of items" by the art of foreshortening, by figuring synthetically, was surely in some sense what Willa Cather meant when she called on the novelist to desist relying on lists and catalogues, on crowded and over-stuffed rooms, and to "present their scene by suggestion rather than by enumeration": "Whatever is felt upon the page without being specifically named there—that, one might say, is created. It is the inexplicable presence of the thing not named, of the overtone divined by the ear but not heard by it, the verbal mood, the emotional aura of the fact or the thing or the deed, that gives high quality to the novel or the drama, as well as to poetry itself."[15] In her repeated references to the principle of what James called "foreshortening" and she called "composition," Willa Cather always put the emphasis on spareness, sparseness, as, for example, in "On the Art of Fiction": "Art, it seems to me, should simplify. That, indeed, is very nearly the whole of the higher artistic process; finding what conventions of form and what detail one can do without and yet preserve the spirit of the whole—so that all that one has suppressed and cut away is there to the reader's consciousness as much as if it were in type on the page."[16] It may seem paradoxical that the same fictional principle of foreshortening lies behind James's fat novels and Cather's lean ones, but it must be stressed that the principle in its basic sense has not so much to do with a novel's length as with the construction and presentation of its scenes. James could abide by the principle even in the prodigality of his prolific imagination. It seems likely that Willa Cather came to think of the principle as controlling and compressing the very magnitude, the scope, of the novel itself.

II

From a fresh reading of Willa Cather's twelve novels, and a substantial immersion in her short fiction and in the essays by and about her, I have come away with a deepened respect for her scope and range and a personal conviction that the work classifies itself in accord with her achievement in technique. As she herself has suggested, her first three novels (*Alexander's Bridge* [1912]; *O Pioneers!* [1913]; *The Song of the Lark* [1915]) constitute her apprenticeship, the novels displaying great talent at the same time that they reveal serious flaws. The great period of sustained achievement runs, I believe, from *My Ántonia* in 1918 through *My Mortal Enemy* in 1926, and includes the controversial *One of Ours* (1922), the deceptively simple *A Lost Lady* (1923), and the puzzlingly complex *The Professor's House* (1925). The last period, though it begins with an experimental work widely admired and skillfully constructed, *Death Comes for the Archbishop* (1927), appears to me to trace a downward curve, which, though relatively undetectable at first in *Shadows on the Rock* (1931), becomes unavoidably noticeable in the last works, *Lucy Gayheart* (1935) and *Sapphira and the Slave Girl* (1940). These three periods are distinguished, I believe, by developments or shifts in fictional technique or experimentation, by changes in artistic awareness or aim: they are best defined by their technical or artistic achievement.

When, in a 1922 preface and later in an essay ("My First Novels" [1931]), Willa Cather looked back on her first novel, she had very little good to say about *Alexander's Bridge*. She wrote, "The impressions I tried to communicate on paper were genuine, but they were very shallow."[17] Such remarks were to set the tone of Cather criticism of *Alexander's Bridge* for a long time to come, and it has become standard judgment that the book failed because Willa Cather was trying to write about an Eastern and London life quite foreign to her Midwestern experience. Perhaps. There is no doubt that the novel bears the marks of Henry James's influence. But it is possible that the real failure of the fiction is not the foreignness of experience depicted so much as a failure in craft stemming from a failure in vision. The novel is Jamesian, but perhaps not Jamesian enough. Bartley Alexander, bridge-builder, one of the makers and movers of the earth, finds himself in middle-age grown restless in a marriage gone stale, and strongly attracted to a London actress who had been his first youthful love years before in Paris. The focus of the novel is not on exterior events but on the developing awareness in Bartley Alexander, a Midwesterner turned Bostonian, that "he found himself living exactly the kind of life he had determined to escape" (p. 32). Thus the novel is related from his point of view, and becomes a kind of drama of his consciousness—a middle-aged awakening to loss not unlike that of Strether in *The Ambassadors*, though there is in Alexander an emotional deadness that he has mistaken for life for many years. At the opening and close of the novel, we view the action and characters through the eyes of Alexander's old professor, who "frames" the action by his opening conversation with Mrs. Alexander and a closing conversation with Alexander's mistress. The international scenes seem to be handled with great deftness, and the fault of the novel lies, perhaps, not in them but in the drama of Alexander's consciousness, where the newly awakened striving toward freedom wars with the deeply rooted impulse pulling toward respectability and spiritual death.

Just as Alexander has reached a peak of conflict in himself, and has written a letter to his wife making a clean break with all his imprisoning entanglements, but has failed to mail the letter because he envisions with some fright, if not horror, the drifting, restless life that might lie ahead—at this critical moment he is called to examine the weakness in the greatest of his creations, a Canadian bridge under construction, and he happens to be standing on the partially completed bridge just as it falls into the river, carrying him to his death.

It is difficult not to see this melodramatic, arbitrarily symbolic ending as an evasion. At the moment of his death, when there seems to have been critical preparation for some kind of epiphany or expanded awareness that might resolve, at least in vision, the internal conflict in Alexander, he instead imagines the fantasmic presence of his wife in the water near him, "telling him to keep his head" (p. 102). Perhaps more than Alexander is of divided mind in the novel. Is it possible that Willa Cather was writing against the current of her own deepest impulses when she gave Alexander over to his wife at the moment of his death? The emotional weight of the novel is clearly on the side of Alexander's awakening to life, to the warmth of a renewed love. Alexander was a flawed character, as his friend Professor Wilson perceived, but it is possible that Cather began the novel seeing his flaw as his yearning for a different life, and ended up seeing the flaw as his inability to break away from the old, dead ties. In any event, the novel seems to blur at the very moment that seems prepared for clarity.

A major part of the technical problem in *Alexander's Bridge* was that the fall of the bridge seemed *arbitrarily* yoked to the moral-spiritual fall of Alexander, builder of the bridge. A similar problem appears to exist in *O Pioneers!*. A melodramatic if not shopworn plot of a hotheaded husband killing his young wife in the arms of her young lover stands out in bold relief in the foreground of the novel, and appears, finally, to remain emotionally unintegrated into the rich texture of feeling in the novel, falling into no natural relationship to the thematic overtones and undertones of the work. By assuming the role of narrator in the novel, Willa Cather found herself forced to invest her feelings directly in the prairies and farms, in the struggling men and women, in the sunsets and seasons, as, for example, in the conclusion of the novel, where there is a felt need for a strong affirmation that should come surging up from the novelistic material itself. The author's only recourse by this time is direct entry and comment: "Fortunate country, that is one day to receive hearts like Alexandra's into its bosom, to give them out again in the yellow wheat, in the rustling corn, in the shining eyes of youth!" (p. 309). The reader grows uncomfortable and perhaps even resistant in the realization that this feeling might best have been evoked by the author in aroused responses to the strategies of the fiction. The author's direct intervention suggests a recognition of subtle failures in craft.

The Song of the Lark was the most troublesomely long of Willa Cather's apprentice novels, and she came to believe that she knew what the fictional problems were. It is the only one of her novels that she put through extensive revision after publication, cutting it back in length considerably when it was reissued in a 1932 edition, and adding a preface which, though brief, has some of the aspects of a Henry James preface revealing a novel's weaknesses and strengths. The book might be looked upon as her *Portrait of the Artist as a Young Woman*, and one wonders what might have happened had she put the novel through the same rigorous revision that James Joyce put his voluminously meandering *Stephen Hero* through to make, finally, *The Portrait of the Artist as a Young Man*. The implied comparisons here have some value, I believe, because Willa Cather's novel traces the developing artistic consciousness of her Thea Kronborg from her youth in a small Colorado town through music training (piano and, ultimately, voice) in Chicago, to her discovery of her fate and her life's determining center in an interlude among the ancient cliff dwellings and broken pottery of Panther Canyon in northern Arizona. There, as she is bathing in a stream one morning, she has her epiphany, toward which the foregoing parts of the novel have built (or ought to have built), and from which the remainder of the novel must flow (and perhaps rapidly): "The stream and the broken pottery: what was any art but an effort to make a sheath, a mould in which to imprison for a moment the shining, elusive element which is life itself—life hurrying past us and running away, too strong to stop, too sweet to lose? The Indian women had held it in their jars. In the sculpture she had seen in the Art Institute, it had been caught in a flash of arrested motion. In singing, one made a vessel of one's throat and nostrils and held it on one's breath, caught the stream in a scale of natural intervals" (p. 378).

The epiphany here, the awareness of her destiny that comes to Thea, might be compared to the awareness involving both the nature of art and his destiny that comes to Stephen at the end of Joyce's *Portrait*. But while Joyce's book concludes at this point, *The Song of the Lark* goes on for two more books covering many more pages. Willa Cather pruned her book, but did not, as did Joyce with *Stephen Hero*, apply radical surgery. She later realized that the book suffered from two major defects. One of these she was to explain at length in "The Novel Démeublé": the novel groans with the weight of its overstuffed rooms, and though the center of the novel can support much of this weight (or at least decrease its heaviness) up to the climactic epiphany, after the Panther Canyon episodes the weight becomes deadweight indeed. The second criticism that Willa Cather levelled at her book focuses on the latter part; she observed that "the life of a successful artist in the full tide of achievement is not so interesting as the life of a talented young girl 'fighting her way' " (p. v). In making this observation she was echoing a criticism that Henry James made of his own *The Tragic Muse* (a novel, incidentally, that Willa Cather had. earlier [1896] deeply appreciated: "It is a great novel, that book of the master's").[18] In his Preface to *The Tragic Muse* (1908), James saw the problem pretty much as Willa Cather was later to see hers. He wrote: "Any presentation of the artist *in triumph* must be flat in proportion as it really sticks to its subject—it can only smuggle in relief and variety. For, to put the matter in an image, all we then—in triumph—see of the charm-compeller is the back he turns to us as he bends over his work" (p. 222). Willa Cather wrote, in her 1932 preface to *The Song of the Lark*: "The interesting and important fact that, in an artist of the type I chose, personal life becomes paler as the imaginative life becomes richer, does not, however excuse my story for becoming paler" (p. vi).

III

In *Willa Cather: A Memoir*, Elizabeth Shepley Sergeant recalls how, in 1916, Willa Cather sat in her apartment musing over some of the elaborate sentences of Henry James's *Notes on Novelists*, and how from it she was moved to describe her next novel by setting an "old Sicilian apothecary jar" in the middle of an antique table, commenting: " 'I want my new heroine to be like this—like a rare object in the middle of a table, which one may examine from all sides.' "[19] We might take this incident as indicating, not literally but symbolically, Willa Cather's determination to apply Jamesian principles of craft to her own non-Jamesian material and experience. In any event, in her next five novels published over a period from 1918 to 1926, Willa Cather discovered herself possessed with an artful artlessness that worked with a kind of magic on materials she could mine from her memory. In his extensive treatment of the subject of fictional point of view in his Preface (1908) to *The Princess Casamassima*, Henry James had written, "I confess I never see the *leading* interest of any human hazard but in a consciousness (on the part of the moved and moving creature) subject to fine intensification and wide enlargement" (p. 239). On the evi-

James E. Miller, Jr.

dence of her work beginning with *My Ántonia*, Willa Cather might well confess a similar concern. When she put that apothecary jar in the middle of the table, she was creating a metaphor for the nature and possibilities of point of view that James himself would have been pleased to adopt: the isolated jar might be examined from all sides, and the job of the novelist is to create the reflectors or registers to embody the examination.

Willa Cather's next five novels alternate between novels using registers and novels presenting a central presiding consciousness. Clearly she was not rigidly committed to a single method, but worked from the principle that the subject and material itself should determine and dictate the method. Henry James before her, contrary to popular belief, varied his techniques radically in accord with the demands of his subject. Sometimes he used reflectors and registers, and sometimes he found the center of his interest in the drama of a consciousness. In *My Ántonia, A Lost Lady*, and *My Mortal Enemy*, Willa Cather found her subject most effectively illuminated by a series of observers—Jim Burden, Niel Herbert, and Nellie Birdseye, with Jim and Nellie acting as their own narrators in their novels, and Niel used as a reflecting consciousness in his. The drama of the heroines—Ántonia Shimerda, Marian Forrester, Myra Henshawe—is a drama whose meaning is best revealed in external relationships, in observable developments and significant encounters: were we confined to the limitations of their own awareness or to their limited perspectives, their stories might well lose most of the meaning they now have. On the other hand *One of Ours* and *The Professor's House* are clearly dramas of consciousness, in the Jamesian sense. In both instances the heroes—Claude Wheeler and Professor St. Peter—gradually develop an understanding of their own beings, and undergo what can only be called epiphanies, and it is this internal drama of expanding and expanded awareness that is the subject of each of the novels. And in all these novels, Willa Cather abides by principles of selection rather than saturation (or, to use her term, tosses the excess furniture out the window), and foreshortens, sometimes severely, but always with the aim of evoking (by "figuring synthetically") what is not specifically named or enumerated on the page.

It is of some interest to examine briefly *My Ántonia, A Lost*

133

Lady, and *My Mortal Enemy* in conjunction with each other, inasmuch as they have similar techniques and structures, but fundamentally different effects. Ántonia Shimerda, Marian Forrester, and Myra Henshawe are all women of innate qualities that shine through and out on the worlds they inhabit. But in character and fate they are basically different. In spite of the hardships that might have brutalized her, Ántonia remains free and open to life and appears fulfilled even with the meager share of material abundance that experience finally metes out to her. Although granted a higher social status that enables her to live a life of grace and ease never dreamed of by Ántonia, Marian Forrester seeks restlessly, and in ever more vulgar directions, for a fulfillment that appears to elude her. And Myra Henshawe, who throws over the immense family wealth to marry romantically and impetuously beneath her economic status, finds not fulfillment but petty bickering, and finally poverty, and remains yoked even in the indignity of dying to what she ambiguously terms her "mortal enemy." It is surely clear from these skeletal outlines of the actions of these three works that in less skillful hands their stories could easily be reduced to soap opera or popular-magazine level, with sensational emphasis on seductions, adulteries, and domestic hostilities. But it was Willa Cather's genius to invest the stories with meaning and mystery by her introduction of her registers and reflectors.

Jim Burden, Niel Herbert, and Nellie Birdseye all share an openness and innocence, and all are in quest of a dream that seems always elusive and illusory. It is only their fine consciousnesses that redeem the lives of their women—their heroines—from meaninglessness, or vulgarity, or triviality. It is, after all, *Jim Burden's* Ántonia, *Niel Herbert's* lost lady and *Nellie Birdseye's* Myra Henshawe that we witness in these novels, and no other. They thus provide not only the points of view of these fictional works, but their very life: these novels could not exist with any of their present significance without these characters as observers and narrators; the stories of the ladies' lives take on meaning only as those lives are filtered through the sensitive consciousnesses of the reflectors. They represent thus not only technical decisions in the handling of material, but the principal means of rendering the material in coherent patterns of meaning and theme.

In each of these novels the observer or narrator is in quest of a symbol that might lend significance to his life. At the end of *My Ántonia*, a weary, disillusioned Jim Burden returns from his successful but emotionally empty life in the East to find Ántonia on the prairie, full of vitality and total commitment to experience, surrounded by the explosive life of her large family; he finds with her, in their final moment together, that, whatever they had missed, they "possessed together the precious, the incommunicable past" (p. 372). But if Ántonia offers Jim a renewal or a renewed glimpse of innocence, the lost lady, Marian Forrester, offers Niel Herbert, in the narrative of her fall into one sordid affair after another, only disillusion and loss of innocence; he comes to appreciate that she had "a hand in breaking him in to life," but deep down he resents her for her unwillingness "to immolate herself . . . with the pioneer period to which she belonged": "she preferred life on any terms."[20] For Nellie Birdseye, Myra Henshawe begins as a romantic illusion, having thrown over her immense inheritance to marry her poor lover and then set out with perfect freedom to live happily ever after; but, alas, as Nellie discovers, even the romantic life is filled with daily bickering, trivial deceptions, petty jealousies; and even the romantic death—as it comes years later to Myra Henshawe—brings not peace of fulfillment but agony at some obscure betrayal in life, the cry from the soul: "Why must I die like this, alone with my mortal enemy?"[21] For Nellie the vision of life's promise of beauty and fulfillment is forever after haunted by the invisible and lurking presence of the "mortal enemy."[22]

Unlike these novels, *One of Ours* and *The Professor's House* utilize no reporters or observers, primarily because they are novels of interior action, or dramas of consciousness, in which the protagonists grow into some kind of critical knowledge about their lives and experiences. *One of Ours* has been much maligned because it has been mistaken for a novel about World War I, and many a male critic (including Ernest Hemingway) has snorted at the temerity of a female novelist attempting to recreate wartime experiences.[23] But of course, Willa Cather's subject is not the war, but the developing consciousness of Claude Wheeler, son of the Nebraska farmlands, who seems fated to live his life in quiet desperation on the Nebraska prairie married to a vacuous wife devoting what little energy she has to neurotic religious and temperance causes and surrounded by family and friends increasingly devoted to the acquisition of things and the accumulation of wealth. By an accident of fate, the war picks Claude up off the prairie out of his meaningless life and carries him across the seas to France and the battlefields, where he discovers not only the horrors of war, but also a redeeming purpose to his life. Willa Cather handles the awakening of Claude with great skill and subtlety, with the bulk of the novel devoted to Claude's life in Nebraska. When she follows him overseas on a ship devastated by the influenza epidemic, and into France and the battlefield, she has clearly researched her material carefully to give it as much authenticity as possible—indeed, some of the scenes of grotesque mutilation and death are handled with a keen sense of the "banality" of horror.

But when Willa Cather introduces the war scenes into her novel, it is not to dramatize the war for its own sake or to make an elaborate moral commentary on the war, but to show its impact on her central subject—Claude's developing consciousness about life and experience. As a matter of fact, Cather goes to great pains in the closing pages of the novel to show the reader that whatever the war meant to Claude in his small but critical experience of it, the war as it really was in its totality was something quite different from his perception. But this fact made the importance of the war to the growth of his consciousness no less critical. In a climactic scene near the end of the novel, he has his epiphany: "The sound of the guns had from the first been pleasant to him, had given him a feeling of confidence and safety; tonight he knew why. What they said was, that men could still die for an idea; and would burn all they had made to keep their dreams." To Claude, the war represents the alternative to the life he has witnessed with intense distaste, in which the "world seemed like a business proposition" under the control of the unrelenting materialists and acquisitors like his brother Bayliss. The war affirmed that "ideals were not archaic things, beautiful and impotent; they were the real sources of power among men" (p. 357). Of course as we read these lines, we know, and we realize that Willa Cather knows, that World War I was entirely unworthy of the idealism with which Claude surrounds and invests it. And when we later see him die as he leads his men into the fire of the enemy, we know that he dies with an illusion. As with Jay Gatsby and Daisy Buchanan in *The Great Gatsby*, Claude's ideal or dream transcends the unworthy object that gives it birth and being, and the very transcendence lends it passionate reality that is undeniable. At the end, Claude's mother meditates on her son's fate: "He died believing his own country better than it is, and France better than any country can ever be" (p. 390). And as the last page of the novel details the numerous suicides of the war's survivors, we realize that had Claude not died in battle in the fullness of illusion, he might well have died by his own hand in the fullness of disillusion that came after the war. Claude's perception that the world he had known "seemed like a business proposition" was no illusion, after all; to discover that the war was perhaps even more of a business proposition, only infinitely more sordid, would surely have broken the strongest spirit.

In the struggle to understand his own deeply disappointing experience back in Nebraska, Claude Wheeler comes to the view that people imprison another self inside themselves: "Inside of living people . . . captives languished. Yes, inside of people who walked and worked in the broad sun, there were captives dwelling in darkness,—never seen from birth to death" (p. 178). In some ways, *The Professor's House* relates the story of the release of such a captive. Professor St. Peter has reached a critical point in his career at which he has completed his life's work, a multi-volume history of the Conquistadores, and at which his affluent family insist on living up to the status of their new wealth by moving to a more expensive, more luxurious house. But Professor St. Peter is reluctant to leave the attic-study of the old house where he has spent so many hours and years at his intellectual labors. He is, moreover, repelled by the crass materialism of the various members of his family as they bicker and scheme for advantage and money. He is even moved at one point (citing the example of an incident in Henry James's *The American*) to apologize to one son-in-law for the mean behavior of other members of his family.[24] It is this son-in-law, Louie Marsellus, who has built up a tidy fortune from an invention willed to his wife by Tom Outland, her fiancé killed in World War I. Louie wants to take his wife's parents on a trip to Europe, but the Professor begs off and is relieved to see the others away and himself alone for a time to examine his own life and feelings. That life is bound up in a strange way with Tom Outland, whose diary the Professor wants to edit and publish. Tom had appeared out of the West at the Professor's college in a small Michigan town, and had strangely affected all their lives. As the Professor turns to meditate on Outland's life, Willa Cather inserts "Tom Outland's Story" in its entirety as Book II in the novel, in the version that St. Peter had once, earlier, heard from his own lips. This technique makes Tom Outland a living presence in the novel just at the moment that Professor St. Peter falls more and more under the influence of his memory. The essence of Tom's story is that he is the discoverer of cliff dwellings in New Mexico, that in spite of his energetic efforts the cliff dwellings have been plundered for their spoils, and an indifferent government in Washington, D.C., has refused to listen to his pleas for preservation of the valuable sites and relics. He subsequently (and belatedly) came to college where he was a brilliant student of physics, casually conducting experiments that led to the invention that had become so valuable after his death.

Remembering and reliving the life of Tom Outland, who because of his early death has been preserved in vivid memory in all his freshness, frankness, openness, idealism, Professor St. Peter reaches a critical juncture in his paralysis of spirit, the paralysis that will not allow him to move out of his old attic into the new house: those ancient cliff dwellings in their simple, austere purity reenforce his attachment to the attic, increase his revulsion for the expensively overstuffed new house awaiting him. In reviewing Tom's life, the Professor is forced to review his own, and he discovers inside of himself an imprisoned captive of the kind that Claude Wheeler imagined lurking within all people (a counterpart to the youthful self that began to shadow Bartley Alexander in *Alexander's Bridge*). This "captive" is none other than the boy Godfrey St. Peter of Kansas, that the Professor thought he had long left behind, a boy that might have had a life like that of Tom Outland. Suddenly St. Peter confronts the events of his life like a fresh revelation: "His career, his wife, his family, were not his life at all, but a chain of events which had happened to him." He followed the chain with the shock of unpleasant discovery: "Because there was Lillian [his wife], there must be marriage and a salary. Because there was marriage, there were children. Because there were children, and fervour in the blood and brain, books were born as well as daughters. His histories, he was convinced, had no more to do with his original ego than his daughters had; they were a result of the high pressure of young manhood" (pp. 264–65). That original ego—the boy Godfrey St. Peter—had remained solitary, isolated, "terribly wise" in the primitive wisdom of the earth. In Professor St. Peter's vision, that boy peers out from his imprisonment inside the Professor, and renders him indifferent to his life, unwilling to confront his family, now on the point of returning from Europe: he feels all his relationships have sharply changed. And one night he drifts to the verge of semi-conscious suicide in his old attic filling with gas from the defective stove. Saved at the last moment, he feels like one brought back from the dead: "He had let something go —and it was gone: something very precious, that he could not consciously have relinquished, probably" (p. 282). Can there be any doubt that the poisonous gas has succeeded in taking a life—the life of that imprisoned captive that had been summoned from within by the vivid recollection of the Tom Outland story: the "original, unmodified Godfrey St. Peter"? Professor St. Peter had let go of an inner connection, an obscure identity, that he had maintained, however unconsciously, with the kind of idealism, frankness, primitive wisdom represented so brilliantly in the short life of Tom Outland. What remained in the hollow within was indifference, apathy, which his self-centered family would never detect. His radical transfiguration would remain his secret, out of sight.

I believe that, within the total body of Willa Cather's work, *The Professor's House* together with *My Ántonia* comprise her two greatest novels. It is perhaps significant that she saw these particular works as analogous to works of art in other materials. We have already noted her viewing *My Ántonia* as a Sicilian apothecary jar sitting in the middle of a table. She remarked of the Tom Outland story set in the middle of *The Professor's House* that she had intended it to resemble the square window found in so many paintings of Dutch interiors; in the novel's "overcrowded and stuffy" house, filled with "American proprieties, clothes, furs, petty ambitions, quivering jealousies," she wanted to open a window to "let in the fresh air that blew off [Tom Outland's] Blue Mesa."[25] In moving from her apprentice work to these impressive works, Willa Cather discovered the techniques that would reveal the meanings, the ambiguities, the mysteries that existed in the sometimes inert, sometimes diffuse material. By the use of Jim Burden as narrator in *My Ántonia*, and by using interior drama (drama of consciousness) but boldly suspending it for Tom Outland's first-person narrative in *The Professor's House*, she showed herself in supreme command of the techniques necessary to the practice of the art of fiction.

IV

Beginning in 1927 with *Death Comes for the Archbishop*, Willa Cather's novels underwent a radical change, almost as though she had decided that, now that she had mastered the technique of the traditional novel, she would go on to new materials and experimental forms. She was amused by the fact that reviewers did not know how to classify *Death Comes for the Archbishop*, and said that she herself would prefer the term "narrative" to "novel." But even the term narrative needs the qualifications she gave it to describe the nature of this "story of the Catholic Church" (her own characterization) in the American Southwest during the pioneer period of the mid-nineteenth century.[26]

In a letter to the *Commonweal* in 1927, she wrote: "I had all my life wanted to do something in the style of legend, which is absolutely the reverse of dramatic treatment. Since I first saw the Puvis de Chavannes frescoes of the life of Saint Geneviève in my student days, I have wished that I could try something a little like that in prose; something without accent, with none of the artificial elements of composition. . . . The essence of such writing is not to hold the note, not to use an incident for all there is in it—but to touch and pass on."[27] Immediately on reading her remark, the reader senses the aptness of her use of the fresco analogy with *Death Comes for the Archbishop*. She has used a kind of fresco or tapestry method in prose, and has deftly painted or woven a series of pictures that relate a story of a life,

140

a narrative of a period. In adopting this method, she has not avoided the problems of craft. As never before, she clearly has had to select and arrange, to compose and foreshorten on a broad scale: to sustain her mood not by the mere "addition of items" but "by the art of figuring synthetically."

She was to try the fresco method in other fictions, but never with the success achieved in *Death Comes for the Archbishop*. *Shadows on the Rock* (1931), set in Quebec in the late seventeenth century ("Quebec is . . . a stronghold on which many strange figures have for a little time cast a shadow in the sun"), represented an attempt to capture a subject even more elusive than that of *Death Comes for the Archbishop*—a "feeling about life and human fate . . . . more like an old song, incomplete but uncorrupted, than like a legend." In attempting to capture that subject, she tried a method analogous to both music and painting: "I took the incomplete air and tried to give it what would correspond to a sympathetic musical setting; tried to develop it into a prose composition not too conclusive, not too definite; a series of pictures remembered rather than experienced; a kind of thinking, a mental complexion inherited, left over from the past, lacking in robustness and full of pious resignation." Willa Cather's description of her aim in *Shadows on the Rock* does get at a quality, a mood, a melancholy feeling that the reader surely feels or senses. But the reader cannot help feel, also, that the author's sureness of touch has slipped, that the method falls short, finally, of all the weight placed on it, that the subject remains as elusive of words ("it is hard to state that feeling in language") in the realized fiction as in later comment on the fiction.[28]

The slight falling off felt in *Shadows on the Rock* becomes sharp decline in Willa Cather's next novel, *Lucy Gayheart* (1935), which represents a return to her earlier Nebraska material but without a return to the techniques she had found so successful in her great period. It is a strangely thin, impatient book. She drowns her hero in Italy's Lake Como at the end of Book I, she drowns her heroine (who is also her point-of-view character) in a Nebraska river at the end of Book II, and she presents in Book III scenes set some twenty-five years after the previous episodes (but thankfully no more drownings). In her last novel, *Sapphira and the Slave Girl* (1940), she turns to the material of her Virginia past, going back to the pre-Civil War period and the legends and characters of her own family history, and even introducing near the end of the novel, during some postwar episodes, herself at the age of five. The novel takes on an eerie feeling, and the distant events of the past suddenly loom near at hand, when what has appeared to be an omniscient author carefully distanced from her material all at once becomes a first-person narrator, related to the characters we have now become involved with, and recollecting the earliest memories of her life which make up the closing events of the narrative. However interesting we may find these last two novels as semi-experimental in form, we sense that we are in the presence of an imagination that is flagging, of a talent that has lost its firm grasp on technique and craft.

V

In 1889 Henry James wrote in his letter to the students of the Deerfield Summer School: " 'Oh, do something from your point of view; an ounce of example is worth a ton of generalities; do something with the great art and the great form; do something with life. Any point of view is interesting that is a direct impression of life. You each have an impression colored by your individual conditions; make that into a picture, a picture framed by your own personal wisdom, your glimpse of the American world. The field is vast for freedom, for study, for observation, for satire, for truth' " (p. 94). In such statements as these, scattered the length and breadth of James's literary career, the master theorist made it quite clear that he was not seeking disciples who would write Jamesian stories using Jamesian materials. On the contrary, each writer had his own life, his own experience, his own conditions, his own impressions—and out of these he must frame his picture. In his Preface to *Lady Barbarina*, James affirmed: "One never really chooses one's general range of vision—the experience from which ideas and themes and suggestions spring. . . . The subject thus pressed upon the artist is the necessity of his case and the fruit of his consciousness. . . . The thing of profit is to *have* your experience—to recognise and understand it, and for this almost any will do; there being surely no absolute ideal about it beyond getting from it all it has to give" (p. 118).

Willa Cather's experience which became the subject of her fiction was, surely, the "necessity" of her case and the "fruit" of her consciousness. Nebraska was not her choice but her fate. Her genius lay in her coming to "recognise and understand" her experience in the West, and to mine it for her stories and novels. She herself has described with some poignancy her feelings of release when she discovered her true material. In "My First Novels" she gives an account of setting about to write *O Pioneers!*, her second novel: "When I got back to Pittsburgh I began to write a book entirely for myself; a story about some Scandinavians and Bohemians who had been neighbours of ours when I lived on a ranch in Nebraska, when I was eight or nine years old. . . . This was like taking a ride through a familiar country on a horse that knew the way, on a fine morning when you felt like riding. . . . Since I wrote this book for myself, I ignored all the situations and accents that were then generally thought to be necessary. The 'novel of the soil' had not then come into fashion in this country. The drawing-room was considered the proper setting for a novel, and the only characters worth reading about were smart people or clever people. . . . Henry James and Mrs. Wharton were our most interesting novelists, and most of the younger writers followed their manner, without having their qualifications."[29] In thus coming to reject James's subjects and settings, his characters and manners, Willa Cather was following a solid Jamesian principle of returning to and relying on her own "direct impression of life" and of embodying that impression in a "picture framed" by her own "personal wisdom" presenting her "glimpse of the American world."

If Willa Cather in the subjects of her fictions seems distant from James (yet a fulfillment of his theories), she also seems distant from him in her prose style. For a writer whose style has generated so much comment and controversy, James has had relatively little to say theoretically about style in fiction—nothing in "The Art of Fiction," and very little in his Prefaces. But he did comment on the style of other writers in his critical essays, and in these stray comments we are able to glimpse his basic principles. Here again he did not present his own fiction as a model, but pointed the writer back to his own resources, his own language and art. In his 1888 essay on Robert Louis Stevenson he reveals in one exclamatory aside the essence of his view of style: "How few they are in number and how soon we could name them, the writers of English prose, at the present moment, the quality of whose prose is personal, expressive, renewed at each attempt!" (p. 276). *Personal, expressive, renewed:* no writer could achieve the ideal suggested by these words by imitating another's style. Moreover, James asserted over and over again that subject and style are, finally, inseparable and indistinguishable. In his essay on *The Tempest* (1907), he cited Shakespeare as the best example we have of the close "relation of style to meaning": "the phrase, the cluster and order of terms, *is* the object and sense, in as close a compression as that of body and soul, so that any consideration of them as distinct, from the moment style is an active, applied force, becomes a gross stupidity" (p. 284).

Whatever else we might want to call Willa Cather's style in her greatest novels, we would also want to adopt James's terms—personal, expressive, renewed. We might even want to say of her what James said of Turgenev: "His first book [for Cather, read *My Ántonia*] was practically full of evidence of what, if we have to specify, is finest in him—the effect, for the commonest truth, of an exquisite envelope of poetry. In this medium of feeling—full, as it were, of all the echoes and shocks of the universal danger and need—everything in him goes on; the sense of fate and folly and pity and wonder and beauty" (p. 281). In this comment, James appears to be reading Turgenev's meanings in his style, as the contemporary critic might well seek to find Willa Cather's subject and significance in the rhythms of her sentences and the color and shape of her words. That she wanted it that way is strongly suggested by the planning and effort she put into the perfection of her style. For example, take *Death Comes for the Archbishop:* here is a glimpse Elizabeth Sergeant gives us of Cather writing this novel at the MacDowell Colony in Peterborough, New Hampshire: "An inveterate walker in her leisure hours, Willa soon knew all the paths and woodland lanes of the Colony, and was sometimes spied at the Pageant Theatre, an amphitheatre of stone, almost a cliff, surrounded by great pines. Standing against the grey rock, a tiny, determined figure, she read aloud the paragraphs and pages she had been working on—to see how they sounded. No wonder the prose is so bland and so sensuous."[30] In her later comment on this novel, in trying to describe what she had attempted, Willa Cather found most useful a musical metaphor—"The essence of such writing is not to hold the note"; "Some of those time-worn phrases I used as the note from the piano by which the violinist tunes his instrument. Not that there was much difficulty in keeping the pitch. I did not sit down to write the book until the feeling of it had so teased me that I could not get on with other things."[31] Clearly the *sounds* of the sentences in *Death Comes for the Archbishop* have been molded as fully as the sense to create the meaning of the fiction.

In comparing and contrasting Willa Cather's subjects and style with Henry James's, we are on fairly open ground, because their subjects are visible for all to see and their styles are there to be felt on every page. But when we come to *meaning* or *theme*, we enter a ground dense with thickets and shrubbery where vision is frequently obscured. James's work is still debated, and Willa Cather's has been characterized in multitudinous conflicting ways. James's best statement on morality and fiction appears in his Preface to *The Portrait of a Lady* (1908): "There is, I think, no more nutritive or suggestive truth . . . than that of the perfect dependence of the 'moral' sense of a work of art on the amount of felt life concerned in producing it. The question comes back thus, obviously, to the kind and the degree of the artist's prime sensibility, which is the soil out of which his subject springs. The quality and capacity of that soil, its ability to 'grow' with due freshness and straightness any vision of life, represents, strongly or weakly, the projected morality" (p. 313). It is perhaps likely that James had himself and his own work in mind when he portrayed the novelist in "The Figure in the Carpet" as persistently misunderstood and misinterpreted by his critics. The figure in the carpet, according to the novelist of the story, is "the thing that most makes him [the writer] apply himself, the thing without the effort to achieve which he wouldn't write at all, the very passion of his passion. . . ." It is the "primal plan; something like a complex figure in a Persian carpet" (p. 311–12).

Is there any way of approaching with some insight the "prime sensibility" of Willa Cather, of exploring with understanding the "primal plan" of her work? And is it even remotely possible that on these deepest levels of her art she is closer to

145

James than their surface differences suggest? I cannot attempt definitive answers to these questions, but I would like to throw out a few suggestions, worth, perhaps, further investigation.

First of all, the clichés that have long served as critical generalizations of Cather's work must be challenged. I have in mind the kind of phrase—"elegist of the past"—that filters through so much of Cather commentary. For example, in a recent review of the reissued *A Lost Lady* in *Time* magazine, Martha Duffy drops in a number of such phrases: "reverent regionalism"; "powerful nostalgia"; "a kind of rigid moral nostalgia."[32] Of course, if Cather were simply an elegist of the past, a historian of the pioneers, a reverent regionalist, a romantic escapist, we already have a fairly comprehensive delineation of the figure in her carpet. But it is difficult if not impossible to accept these generalizations after a fresh rereading of her work. Indeed, it is difficult to escape the conclusion that she has been served as badly by her reviewers and critics as James's Hugh Vereker in "The Figure in the Carpet."

In getting at Cather's "prime sensibility," in order to discover the basic pattern of the "primal plan" of her work, I would suggest that critics turn their attention from external matters, from chronological time (the past) and from geography (Nebraska and the West) and focus on internal matters, on states of feeling and awareness. The word that might best define this area—consciousness—is a word that became for James almost holy in its evocation of being and becoming, the key not only to the nature of fiction but to the nature of life itself and even of death (as, for example, in his essay, "Is There a Life After Death?").[33] In "The Art of Fiction," James described the "chamber of consciousness" as hung with a "kind of huge spider-web of the finest silken threads" which caught and converted, in an imaginative mind, the "very pulses of the air into revelations" (p. 35). In such catches and conversions from whatever experience fate awards him, a human being shapes his individuality and fashions his moral identity.

It is consciousness in some such meaning as this, I believe, that provides a central figure in the design of Cather's fictional carpet. She places her greatest value on the aware life lived in the fulness of its awareness. Her novels are filled with characters who live mean lives severely limited by consciousnesses

146

that seem to catch and convert nothing out of the riches of experiences, or so little that they remain parochial in vision and morality: Alexandra's brothers, for example, in *O Pioneers!*; or the town gossips and busybodies in a whole host of novels —*The Song of the Lark, My Ántonia,* or *One of Ours*; or the entire Professor's family in *The Professor's House.* These are the people whose limited consciousnesses lead them to believe that the meaning of life lies somehow in external materiality, in the acquisition of things, in the accumulation of objects.

Standing over against these characters who lead mean little lives are a number of characters, rich in range and variety, who encounter life with openness and freedom and strive to exploit experience not through the piling up of external things and objects but by discovering and expanding internal horizons. Notable examples of such characters are Ántonia Shimerda in *My Ántonia* and Claude Wheeler in *One of Ours*, one living on to fulfillment, the other cut off by death in war. But there are characters who seem somehow trapped by the meanness surrounding them or by the internal limitations or deceptions or compromises of consciousness. There are, for example, the somewhat complicated cases of Marian Forrester in *A Lost Lady* and Myra Henshawe in *My Mortal Enemy*, whose lives remain unfulfilled, and whose consciousnesses appear to fail them —perhaps because of the limitations of their own imaginations. Professor St. Peter in *The Professor's House* suffers a death of consciousness at the end of the novel, and therefore a kind of death of the self, as his re-visioning and reviewing of the life of Tom Outland brings to him his own awareness of self-betrayal. Tom Outland belongs, of course, in that small gallery of the totally aware, of the self-fulfilled; like Claude Wheeler, he is tragically cut off in the war. And as if to demonstrate that the fully conscious, morally aware individual need not either die young or compromise along the way, Willa Cather portrayed Jean Latour in *Death Comes for the Archbishop* living out his life to a rich old age of genuine fulfillment by means of a consciousness rich in aware feeling and finely attuned to the deepest vibrations of experience.

So far as we know, Henry James, who died in 1916, never read any of Willa Cather's work. Back in the early part of this century, Witter Bynner had sent him a copy of Cather's *The Troll Garden*, and James had replied (1905): "I find it the hardest thing in the world to read almost *any* new novel. Any is hard enough, but the hardest from the innocent hands of young females, young American females perhaps above all."[34] It is a pity that James did not live to read some of the work of the young American female who learned so much about her craft from him. He surely would have found her novels an interesting "case." On the surface, the body of her work appears radically different from James's. What she learned from him was, finally, independence, the self-reliance to use her own experience and find her own material, and to apply the artistry, the craft, the method that would discover and release its inherent meaning and significance. James would not have been much interested in those early stories that sounded like Henry James (such as "The Marriage of Phaedra" and "Eleanor's House" and *Alexander's Bridge*), but he certainly would have been interested in the great work that sounded so unlike James—even the flawed experiments. James's own theory of fiction was built not on a body of rules to follow but on a deep sense of and wonder at the freedom the novelist has in his art. He wrote, in 1899 in "The Future of the Novel," that the art of fiction "moves in a luxurious independence of rules and restrictions." And he affirmed with great passion: "The more we consider it the more we feel that the prose picture can never be at the end of its tether until it loses the sense of what it can do. It can do simply everything, and that is its strength and its life. Its plasticity, its elasticity are infinite; there is no color, no extension it may not take from the nature of its subject or the temper of its craftsman" (pp. 339–40). This, ultimately, must have been the great lesson that Willa Cather learned from the Master—and which any novelist today might still learn. It was surely this kind of passionate commitment to artistic freedom and independence that pervades all of James's writing about fiction that could cause Willa Cather to say, as she said in 1936, that Henry James's "was surely the keenest mind any American ever devoted to the art of fiction."

[*Reference notes appear on pages 262–63.*]

Willa Cather

This 1927 photograph by Edward Steichen is perhaps the best known of Miss Cather.

The Panel at the C

Left to right: Bruce P. Baker II, Leon Edel, Hiroko Sato, Donald Sutherland, Robert L. Hough, Eudora Welty, Bernice Slote,

Lucia Woods

ɔn of the Seminar

John W. Robinson, Aldo Celli, Marcus Cunliffe, Michel Gervaud, James E. Miller, Jr., James Woodress.

At Willa Cather's Childhood Home, Red Cloud, Nebraska

Left to right: Donald Sutherland, Aldo Celli, Ellen Moers, John Hinz, Eudora Welty, Alfred A. Knopf. They are shown in the room (recreated as described in "Old Mrs. Harris") which was occupied by Willa Cather's maternal grandmother, Mrs. Boak.

James E. Miller, Jr.

COMMENT

Some determined argument in the discussion centered on the use of the Jamesian frame of reference for Willa Cather, on the question of a "decline" in the later novels, and on whether Cather was an intuitive or a conscious artist.

LEON EDEL: . . . It is interesting to argue as Professor Miller has so brilliantly, from these very important and basic statements, the affinity or the relation to James; but in terms of craft, in terms of what Willa Cather, as I see her, did, one begins to see important, very significant differences. For instance, her constant use of narrators, which is un-Jamesian, totally un-Jamesian. . . . But this is where we are in *My Ántonia*. We have then a totally different approach to fiction, an approach which takes us back to older forms, earlier forms, to the happy course of the novel, very much the English novel where the novel is free to just tell stories and go off into digression. And this is very un-Jamesian, about as un-Jamesian as it could possibly be. Now, on the other side, I respond very warmly to Professor Miller's reference to consciousness, but I would apply it to the prime sensibility which is the sensibility which spins the story, the sensibility which expresses itself, which finds its personal solutions . . . in the kind of stories that are woven. In my lectures in the Library of Congress I tried to show that what we have to look at is the elegiac because it is a form in which she expressed a personal, a profound melancholy. . . . *The Professor's House*—yes, "death of consciousness," exactly. I think it's a very happy way of putting it. Something very profound then was going on inside Willa Cather, as something profound was going on in T. S. Eliot when he wrote *The Waste Land*. . . . I think Willa Cather wanted to die. The Professor almost died. I think by writing out that experience, she rescued herself. . . . If we talk about the forms of fiction, we see her seeking forms that were best expressed with personal melancholy, with state of being. Most of the great novelists reached moments of such crisis, and out of those moments came their best work. I think the supreme example would be Tolstoi, and *Anna Karenina*. . . . The prime sensibility must also be the personality of the artist.

JAMES E. MILLER, JR.: . . . James did use first-person narration brilliantly in "The Aspern Papers" and in "The Turn of the Screw" and the shorter works where he does not open himself to the kind of thing he warns himself about in the Preface to *The Ambassadors*. . . . I would not want to place my whole argument on the resemblances of James and Cather. I think the differences are what make Cather interesting. . . .

JOHN HINZ: I think James and the analogy to James is a very useful way of viewing Cather as a literary artist, and that has to be done

—how she handles materials, how she uses point of view, perspective. I found it immensely useful. . . .

JOHN MURPHY: You speak about a decline from the *Archbishop* on . . . . It seems to me that most of the disagreement on *The Professor's House* and *Shadows on the Rock* and perhaps the later books, too, is disagreement with what she has chosen to write about primarily. And I kind of object to that. . . .

BERNICE SLOTE: It seems to me sometimes that the books that are most openly admired are the ones that people have read most often. I wonder what would happen if we would read *Sapphira and the Slave Girl* as often as we read *My Ántonia*. I wrestled with *Lucy Gayheart* for a whole winter—and I think that is one of the most subtle, complicated pieces of artistry I've read lately. . . .

LEON EDEL: I would like to have Professor Miller comment on whether Willa Cather really had a theory of fiction—whether she didn't write a series of commentaries rather than offer a theory.

JAMES E. MILLER, JR.: I might argue that she had a theory and some of it got down on paper, but not all of it. She may well have taken a good deal of it unconsciously from her early readings of James and perhaps other writers. Some of her most useful comments, I think, come in response to her own work after she looks at it from a perspective in time. But there's certainly not a body that can be fleshed out in fullness. If you put her theory up against Henry James's it's very thin, because she simply did not make those kinds of statements.

VIRGINIA FAULKNER: It seems to me, Jim, that in a book I know you've read—*The Kingdom of Art*—Willa Cather makes a great many statements about theories of art—I'm not referring to the later collections. It was not programmatic, however. . . .

MARGARET O'CONNOR: On whether or not Cather has a theory of fiction—it's in one sense very different from, "Does she write about her theory of fiction?" We all assume, for instance, that she has a consistent pattern. It's not the same, perhaps, that she is consciously, in each one of her works, aware of the techniques that she was using, that she was really in control of her novels. Perhaps what Mr. Edel is suggesting is that her concept was not as clear to her as James's concept of the novel was to him.

LEON EDEL: I don't want to quibble. It seems to me that she had no theory of any kind. She wrote intuitively. She wanted to tell stories and she told them. She commented on theories. She was interested. But I don't think we can say it's a theory. It's really an artist talking very vividly about her work, which is not the same thing as having a theory of fiction.

150

James E. Miller, Jr.

WARREN FRENCH: I agree that she did not have what we commonly call a theory of fiction, but I definitely disagree that her writing was purely intuitive. I think she did have a program. It is the extraordinary relationship between Willa Cather's novels and painting, between art forms. The program that is realized through her fiction is closely related to problems that painters have faced. . . . But I don't think this is all intuitive. This is a very deliberate and conscious calculation, quite as conscious as Picasso's and Matisse's, for example. . . .

BLANCHE GELFANT: I want to suggest that it's a typical and recurring thing to say that a woman writer is intuitive. . . . If you approach a woman's work as you would the novel of a man writer and consider it an important work worth looking at, then you dismiss it by saying, well, she really didn't know what she was doing but somehow this surged up in her. . . .

LEON EDEL: I have written many times and am on the record as saying that Faulkner was one of our most intuitive novelists. I think "intuitive" is a good word, and I use it in a very special sense. . . .

BRUCE BAKER: I really don't see how we can consider her art intuitive if we look again at *The Kingdom of Art*, and see what is emerging. . . .

GEORGE GREENE: I'd like to suggest as a possible middle theory a phrase—that she was an artistic empiricist. She did say about 1920 that the greatest peril as she saw it in American fiction at that time was the enormous excess of reportage, in the more naturalistic sense. She mentions some of her tremendous admiration for an impressionist such as Stephen Crane. She speaks about her indebtedness to Hawthorne. She speaks about some of the things that she learned from Mérimée. These are all momentary; they're tactical approaches which she doesn't want to generalize too much. It is a reasoned and a consecutive assemblage, a dicta, if not a theory in the more classical sense.

RICHARD GIANNONE: It seems to me the paper was somewhat at cross purposes. On the one hand it sought to define Cather's style in terms of James and at the same time it sought to point out experimentation. What we end up with is a lot of Cather that is larger than James, and the very distinctive Cather seems to be beyond that. Perhaps that is where the word "intuitive" was going. . . .

JAMES E. MILLER, JR.: . . . I'm showing that she's Jamesian in a deeper sense in being independent of James and being experimental in her own art. . . . Within James's theory is the total freedom to experiment that he gives to the novelist, and this is what I finally decided about Cather, especially in that later period beginning with *Death Comes for the Archbishop*. Even in the middle period there's experimentation and movement away, too, but she's being Jamesian when she's being most un-Jamesian, if you could accept that paradox.

EDWARD BLOOM: . . . I wonder whether in stressing James so much through this paper you have not perhaps consciously tended to obscure all of those non-Jamesian echoes, if we go back to her early readings in *The Kingdom of Art* where she is obviously steeped in Keats, in Shelley, in Byron, and some of the Victorians. . . . The parallels are so very significant here that we have to talk about Keats and Shelley along with James and some of the later writers.

JAMES E. MILLER, JR.: . . . I didn't want to start out on a kind of influence study that tried to list all writers and ways. I really adopted James as a way of thinking about Willa Cather. . . .

BERNICE SLOTE: The emphasis on Henry James does hit a very important tradition that Willa Cather allied herself with—the tradition of the artist's freedom, the freedom to take his own material and do with it what he pleases.

I found myself in agreement with the author of this paper more frequently than not. However, I think he was wise to leave himself an out by stating, "These categories suggest division in her work deeper than I would want to affirm or defend." It is true that we must challenge the critical clichés. And I trust that Professor Miller's doing just that regarding *One of Ours* carries over to other critics' challenging of his "decline-falling off" cliché applied to Willa Cather's last three novels. Intensive study of one or more of those novels will yield a rich critical harvest, as many can testify.

Lucy Gayheart, according to my reading, is not "a strangely thin, impatient book." I must confess I did not find its dismissal by the author very amusing. . . . In a letter to Carrie Miner Sherwood, dated July 3, 1934, Willa Cather says that *Lucy Gayheart* is built in such a way that the first part does not mean very much until one gets to the last part (Archives, Red Cloud). She was right.

In the author's discussion of *The Professor's House*, he omits what I think is a basic consideration in the closing pages of the novel —Augusta. And what he [the Professor] "lets go," in my reading of these pages, is something a bit more complicated than what the author calls St. Peter's "imprisoned captive." He now feels "the ground under his feet," and a genuine Augusta is helping reinstate him in the human family, although his limited family—with its superficialities— draws from him no sense of obligation, at this time.

I see one very significant theme of *The Professor's House* relating to the largeness of "the country where love is lost" (Tom Outland and his need to forgive Rodney Blake for selling "the things," and the Professor and his need to include not only "a world full of Augustas" but

James E. Miller, Jr.

eventually his own family in his "house" of life). I see *Lucy Gayheart* in much the same way, with the main interest in the novel residing in Harry Gordon's growing realization of what it really means to love and forgive and transcend—on the long haul, so to speak.

Sister Lucy Schneider

Professor Miller sees the fall of the bridge in *Alexander's Bridge* as "*arbitrarily*" yoked to the moral-spiritual fall of Alexander." The collapse of Bartley Alexander's bridge at the end of the novel appears much less arbitrary if the book is viewed as a form of literary epic wherein the public view of the hero is as important as the personal or private one. The initial descriptions of Alexander (including of course the suggestion in his name) stress the heroic aspect of his physical stature and his extraordinary energies; throughout the book we glimpse him through the public eye (as a ship passenger of note, in newspaper accounts) and we are reminded that he is a builder of "bridges into the future, over which the feet of every one of us will go." In this light his public downfall, symbolized very naturally by the collapse of his most important bridge, is as significant as his personal disintegration. His wife embodies his epic ambitions, while Hilda Burgoyne embodies his desires for renewed youth and love. Professor Miller would like to see Alexander's conflict resolved—"at least in vision"—but surely no resolve is possible if Alexander's epic role, his career, is as important in the novel as his personal life.

David Stouck

Although the Jamesian "frame" provided by Professor Miller is useful for an approach to Willa Cather's fiction, it creates an illusion of critical rigidity in Part I which perhaps he did not intend and which she certainly did not practice. That she learned much about aspects of her craft from the Master we all agree, and the demonstration which constitutes a major portion of "Willa Cather and the Art of Fiction" helps to substantiate the assertion. It is more difficult, however, to be persuaded by Professor Miller's contention that James was such a dominant force in Willa Cather's development as theoretician. She was indeed little inclined toward theory except as matter for subjective relevance, and whatever critical attitudes she may have absorbed from James she blended inseparably with others that had contributed to her cultural and esthetic growth from the time that literature began to be the center of her life. James, as Professor Miller acknowledges, is "among the early literary influences," but presumably to enforce his thesis he omits all others from his discussion. This creates a curious, if not serious, disproportion when we recall that *among* those who figure in Professor Slote's edition of *The Kingdom of Art* are also Stevenson,

153

Dumas, Daudet, Thackeray, Keats, Shelley, Byron, Tennyson, Browning, the French Romantics.

The nineteenth-century writers mainly responsible for Willa Cather's formative literary tastes, according to Professor Slote— exclusive of James and Tolstoi—were the Romantics and some Victorians. And it is significant that a number of the critical attitudes placed by Professor Miller in a Jamesian context can be assigned with equal assurance to earlier writers very familiar to Willa Cather. It is altogether plausible, for example, that she shared with James a feeling that escapism is a valid release not from responsibility but, temporarily, from "the ache of the actual." But literature in this sense—as respite and restorative, as source of inner change—was surely a part of her youthful experience when she was reading the Romantic poets. Shelley's absorption in "the harmonious madness" of the skylark could have taught her as much about the parenthetic powers of literature as James's analogy with "dentist's ether." From Shelley's more rhapsodic prose, likewise, in *A Defence of Poetry*, she could have discovered a complementary truth that "all spirits on which [poetry] falls open themselves to receive the wisdom which is mingled with its delight."

Alluding to the design of Willa Cather's novels—or, more specifically, to point of view—Professor Miller makes an interesting connection with the apothecary's jar on the antique table as a fictional metaphor, Cather saying: "I want my heroine to be like this—like a rare object in the middle of a table, which one may examine from all sides." The parallelism with Jamesian point of view is valuable, but Professor Miller by limiting his own critical focus has also reduced the range of speculative possibility. The relationship between this jar and Keats's Grecian urn is equally worth noting, especially since Miss Cather appears in her action to provide a comprehensive point of view for herself even as Keats achieved a perspective from which he could observe the totality of the urn. The immediate question is not whether one influence or inspiration is better than the other. Both, it seems to us, work. But the Keatsian analogy has the added advantage of similitude which brings it closer to Willa Cather's symbolic intention than James's imagined correspondence. The visual, romanticized approach, incidentally, is characteristic of her ability to *see* stories. "Anyone," she wrote in the essay on escapism, "who looks over a collection of prehistoric Indian pottery dug up from old burial-mounds knows at once that the potters experimented with form and colour to gratify something that had no concern with food and shelter." What remains a bare hint here blossoms into evocative narrative only in the novels.

The special transmutation of scene into story is of course the Cather

James E. Miller, Jr.

idiograph, and it is one to which Professor Miller addresses himself near the end of his essay as part of his concern with point of view. As example, he introduces Willa Cather's analogy of *The Professor's House* with Dutch interiors, most of which have a square window affording a view of ships or the sea. Comparably she wanted the Tom Outland story to be like that square window "to let in the fresh air that blew off the Blue Mesa." Constrained again by the limits of his Jamesian tests, Professor Miller has to stop before he can make the more important point. The Outland story, it seems to us, is given only vague identification with angle of vision, and that in any event would be far less significant than the romantic coloration of the episode or scenes. In the interior story, as in Dutch interiors, the viewer is given an opportunity to look beyond the clutter and fasten his gaze on what is natural and good. He is allowed to stretch his sympathetic imagination as, say, Hazlitt would have had it. To see the atmosphere, in Hazlitt's idiom, is not enough; one must feel it. Miss Cather gives us something of that same compulsion when she writes of the remarkable "feeling of the sea that one got through those square windows," and even more when she has us look out over the Blue Mesa, oblivious now to "trivialities."

If Willa Cather's house of fiction, unlike James's, has only one window, it serves as well "the need of the individual vision and . . . will." She would have had little need to throw furniture out of her sparsely furnished rooms, but she—like James—would have used that window to best artistic advantage. And she would have been glad to have the company not only of Henry James but of a numerous body of nineteenth-century writers whose vision had long been congenial to her.

EDWARD A. BLOOM and LILLIAN D. BLOOM

Willa Cather:
The Classic Voice

Donald Sutherland

In the spring of 1901 Willa Cather taught a term of Latin in a Pittsburgh high school. By the end of the term she had lost twenty pounds. Or so she wrote to some friends.[1] Even if the twenty pounds are an exaggeration, that is how she felt about it. She could not bring herself without agony to a scholar's meticulous care for the details of Latin grammar, which verbs take the dative and so on. Toward people who devote their lives to that kind of thing her feeling is not amusement so much as dismay at the waste of precious time which might be spent on some larger or livelier purpose. Latin grammar was not only painful to her, it was nothing to her very large purposes as a writer of English, and her grasp of it remained weak.

In *The Song of the Lark* (1915), Fred Ottenburg says of Dr. Archie, *"Lupibus vivendi non lupus sum."** Though the meaning is apparent—"Living with wolves I am not myself a wolf"—it is somewhat beclouded by at least four mistakes in the first two words. Fred Ottenburg has been drinking, which might account for the state of his Latin, but I am afraid I think the Latin is Willa Cather's.

In *Death Comes for the Archbishop* (1927) she uses the motto

---

*1915 edition, p. 424. The Latin sentence is preceded by: " 'Living among wolves, you have not become one.' " Most of this speech, including the Latin, was cut in the 1937 revision. In the revised edition, the corresponding paragraph is the third on p. 512.

Donald Sutherland

Auspice Maria, which is good enough Latin, like the formula on Spanish coins, *Auspice Deo.* Grammatically it is a kind of ablative absolute, "with the verb understood," as they say, or two nouns in the ablative case in apposition, a construction altogether alien to English, but the sense is roughly "with Mary as favorer" or, less literally still, "by the favor of Mary." The motto is used as a chapter heading, and it sits handsomely, except for the exclamation point after it: *Auspice Maria!,* which seems an undue emphasis until, in the course of the chapter you find Father Joseph murmuring, *"Auspice,* comma, *Maria!* exclamation point!" (p. 255). Then it is clear that Willa Cather took *Auspice* for a verb in the imperative, *Maria* for a vocative, and the two words together to mean something like "Be auspicious, Mary!" or perhaps "Watch out for us, Mary!" I suspect she heard, unconsciously, the German word *aus* in *Auspice.*

In another story* she quotes the beginning of the Lord's prayer in Latin—*"Pater noster, qui in coelum est"*—which is pretty bad and I shall not dwell on it, nor shall I, on her centenary of all occasions, make a list of her mistakes, though it would not be long. These few are enough to show that her Latin was not scholarly. But they do not at all mean that her mind and style were not deeply influenced by Latin, by the language itself as well as by the literature, the content of which can be had in translation, and by the Latin mentality or temperament, which is not confined to the ancient Romans. It can be found alive in certain qualities of the French, the Italians, and the Spanish, all of whom she studied with care and wrote about, though primarily the French. Taking Latinity that generally, as a mentality distinct from the Gothic, the Anglo-Saxon, the Judaic, and even the Greek, one may say that while Latin grammar has something to do with its formation it is hardly the essential, and Willa Cather could largely do without it.

Her relation to music is comparable. She was not a musician and had little or no knowledge of counterpoint and the rest of it,

*"Peter," originally published in the *Mahogany Tree,* May 21, 1892; reprinted in *Collected Short Fiction, 1892–1912.* See p. 543. This was Willa Cather's first published story. In a revised version titled "Peter Sadelack, Father of Anton," *Library* 1 (July 21, 1900): 5, the Latin is changed to: *"Pater noster, qui es in coelis." (Editors' note)*

157

so to say the grammar of music, but, as Richard Giannone has abundantly and subtly shown in his book *Music in Willa Cather's Fiction*, her work is very frequently guided if not dominated by a kind of musicality, in style and sometimes in structural procedures, along with being so often about musicians. The results are ordinarily too splendid or too charming to be even slightly discredited by her lack of musicology.

The question of the Latin language itself, within her Latinity, is not quite so easy. If something very like the essential expression of an aria can be caught and strongly felt by a listener who has no idea of what key it is in, what metric, or what the intervals are, can the essential expression of a Latin poem be caught by a reader who has only an approximate knowledge of its grammar, upon which not only the literal meaning but the rhetorical effect greatly depends? A good deal is lost on him, of course, but perhaps not the essential expression; he misses many details of the style but perhaps not the style itself, the substance or hang of it.

Some properties of Latin which have little to do with grammar are clear to anybody: its sonority, and its solemnity, which make it so good for inscriptions on monuments or for the mass, and its concision, its way of formulating a great deal in a very few words, as in *suum cuique*, or *carpe diem*, or *lacrimae rerum*. Though Willa Cather's vocabulary is usually very plain English and sparing of all but the simplest Latin derivatives, those and other properties of the Latin language at large do appear frequently in her prose, especially the concision and a certain round finality of assertion. She is said to have been influenced by Virgil in particular, and I have no doubt she was, but the style of a particular author, the Virgilian style, or the Tibullan, or the Tacitean, is not easily apprehended by everybody, not even by scholars as such. It takes an acute literary sensibility to catch these rather irrational inflections and the precise "verbal mood"—as Willa Cather calls it—of an actual poem, and that sensibility can be disconcertingly inattentive to the grammar. The great example in our time was Ezra Pound, whose mistakes are more painful than those of Willa Cather because of his far more scholarly habit of mind, but who did catch the manner of Propertius, or something very close to it, I believe, more clearly than anyone had done for centuries. He did the same for our sense of many other authors, forcing upon us what was their modernity in their time. His defective Latin did not keep his general Latinity from being vast and aspiring even to a sort of imperial administration of a conglomerate world, its money as well as all its cultures and their history. I wish he had never written such a word as *opusculus*, but at least it startles an academic mind into looking beyond grammar to something more essential, if less articulate. One has to recognize that in many qualities of style and mind Willa Cather may quite well be as "steeped in the Classics" and as Virgilian, specifically, as she has been said to be.

If Latin grammar was even physically too much for her, how did the language get into her? The answer is simple, and much the same as for music: through her extremely attentive ears. When Latin is quoted or mentioned in her work it is, not always but ordinarily, being recited aloud rather than read in silence. It can be murmured, as by Father Joseph, and it can even be sung, as when in an early story (*A Son of the Celestial* [1893]) a white man is shipping the body of his Chinese crony back to China and sings—to what music I have no idea —part of an ode of Horace to his friend Maecenas.[2]

A more telling instance is Tom Outland, in *The Professor's House* (1925). When Tom is alone on his mesa he commits to memory "fifty lines or more" from the second book of the *Aeneid*, and recites them aloud to himself, in the high solitude of the Indian ruins. The lines are about the Trojan Horse, the beginning of the fall of Troy, and no doubt they enlarge his feeling, as well as the reader's, about the Indian ruins and the fall of that civilization. Later he recites the lines to the Professor with " 'a good pronunciation and good intonation' " (p. 113), but they are primarily inside Tom Outland, as they were first recited to himself alone, not for the Professor's ear. At this rate Latin is something assimilated into the organism, mentally by memory and physically by the muscles of the mouth and throat. The vocal performance for the Professor, however correct externally, belongs to a vital interior which has become somewhat Virgilian in feeling.

The voices of characters in Willa Cather's work, whether singing, speaking, or laughing, even snoring, are personal behavior and can characterize more intimately than gesture or action. This may also be the way with her own prose, in straight narrative, which would be, as much as dialogue, what she calls expression or utterance, something proceeding like a voice from an appreciable inside, outward.

This is all very easily said but not easily realized by people like myself, for whom writing, especially in the dead or foreign languages, is an existence in space, on the page, and though it takes time to read and is in sequence, one word after another, its existence is not primarily temporal, not vocal unless you happen to read it aloud. It is an objective continuity, a verbal object, and one need not feel there is a subjectivity out of which it is issuing. It just extends itself along its flat or two-dimensional space like a frieze or an inscription. This question, of the essentially written or inscribed word, as against the essentially spoken or sung word, cannot be settled in theory to anybody's satisfaction, certainly not in the case of the novel, whose theory is notoriously unsettled and which can ally itself with almost any other art it pleases, music, painting, drama, epic poetry or lyric, even letters. The problem is practical: how, if you are eye-minded, to learn to read works written primarily in a vocal mode. Or, how to apply the auditory imagination at least equally with the visual imagination. It is not a question of euphony, not even of rhythm, so much as of meanings and expression proceeding in time. Even at a particular tempo, if you please, as when the story "Uncle Valentine" (1925) has, under its title, the notation *adagio non troppo*.[3]

Willa Cather's attention to the expressive qualities of the voice going on was extraordinary, but not quite so extraordinary when you consider that her youth was spent in a terribly vocal era. It was the end of a great age of opera, there were the unbelievable divas and tenors and child prodigies, but the speaking voice too was having a great age, in the theatre and also in oratory. Sarah Bernhardt, one of Willa Cather's heroines and exemplars of a certain style, was, whatever else, a golden voice, and there is an interesting story about that. It was not a singing voice, though it behaved very like one, just as her style of acting was operatic but had to be confined to melodrama. She was the great star of *Tosca*, but when it was a play and not yet an opera. The limitation bothered her and she got the idea, which she proposed to Coquelin, another great speaking voice, of a *spoken* opera, presumably something with an orchestral score and all the other features of opera, except that the words would be spoken and not sung. It might have worked, with such voices. But Coquelin, though it was for him and his style of acting that the most operatic of melodramas, *Cyrano de Bergerac*, was written, did not think a spoken opera possible, so nothing came of it. You might say that *Pelléas and Mélisande* came of it, or from an idea very like it, but the point of the story in connection with Willa Cather is that at the time the speaking voice and the singing voice were nearly interchangeable, not quite, but so nearly as to be an open question. Willa Cather's remark that "singing is idealized speech"[4] may not have a very definite meaning now, but it would have been perfectly clear and irritating to Sarah Bernhardt.

Then there was oratory, and not only the golden voice of Sarah but the silver-tongued orator of the Platte was heard in the land. It was a great age of oratory, and the astonishing thing is that you could go to hear Bryan or Ingersoll and pay no attention to what they had to say about free silver or the existence of God, you listened to the rhetorical style of their speeches as you would to the negotiation of notes by the voices of great singers. The content was there, if you were interested, but it was mainly a pretext for virtuosity or style of expression. Listening to revivalists must have been much the same: there could have been nothing very novel in the content, but the expression of the voice could sweep the congregation into a paroxysm of interest. Like the orator, the revivalist was close to singing, at least to the hymnal, and both persons could be combined, as in Bryan.

In her story "Two Friends" (1932) Willa Cather describes the style of one of the friends thus: "Every sentence he uttered was alive, never languid, perfunctory, slovenly, unaccented."[5] That could be a description of oratory, or of her own prose, but it happens to be of a conversational manner merely, even if the conversationalist is imbued with the manner of his idol, William Jennings Bryan. His manner has virtues in common with oratory—aliveness, energy, intention, precision, and accentuation—which are also virtues in the rendering of musical phrases, not only of sentences. Today, in listening to conversation, our attention is certainly not on the sentences and

161

the way they are delivered, and insofar as we listen to oratory our attention is toward whatever information may or may not be forthcoming, not on the expression or execution. But in those days oratory was a major art and conversation was a concomitant minor one at least. Good pronunciation and intonation were accomplishments anybody at all ought to have, whatever he might be uttering. All the vocal arts were so closely related, all being utterance, that they could involve or imply each other. The simplest word of prose, spoken or written, not only of poetry, could at least approximate the emotional vibration of a word sung.

Here is a small example. In *My Ántonia*, Lena Lingard says to Jim Burden, who has to leave her and the University of Nebraska for higher things, as it were, at Harvard: " 'You are going, but you haven't gone yet, have you?' "(pp. 293–94). That is excellent Ovid if you like or, if you do not, an excellent line for an actress to deliver in a play by someone like Musset. But you may hear it as more poignant. To my ear, which is not a good one and I may be straining it, the voice could be the voice of Manon or of Marguerite Gautier, though the speaker is a very Norwegian seamstress. Ultimately I suppose it might echo the divine voice of Calypso speaking to Odysseus: "You are going, but you haven't gone yet, have you?" Is one to hear a whole chorus of traditional temptresses backing up Lena's voice or is one to hear a single voice? And is it Lena's only, or is it also the essential expression of an archetype, the Delaying Temptress, which need not suggest any particular temptress of tradition, but is at least a universal in excess of the particular dalliance in Lincoln. Willa Cather did believe in universals, and she heard single voices, melodies or songs, more than accompaniments and orchestrations, and that much would be properly classical of her, but it hardly settles the sonority of Lena's voice, which may just possibly be Wagnerian, though I hate to think so. I shall come back to these uncertainties shortly, but just now let me call them the hazards of the vocal mode and note that they help to make Willa Cather what she is called—elusive.

Along with intoning Virgil to himself, Tom Outland wrote an account of his excavations among the Indian ruins. The style was appropriately dry and factual. "Yet," says Willa Cather, "through this austerity one felt the kindling imagination, the

162

ardour and excitement of the boy, like the vibration in a voice when the speaker strives to conceal his emotion by using only conventional phrases'' (pp. 262–63).

That effect, of passion conveyed through a dry or plain style, as dry as archeological notes, was, in 1925, the time of *The Professor's House*, moving into fashion and was to make Ernest Hemingway's fortune, but it has another connection, more to my purpose, with the voice and vocabulary of Virgil himself, which seem to have got into Tom Outland. In his own time a rather harsh critic said Virgil was the inventor of a new kind of mannerism (*cacozelia*), neither inflated nor thin, but made of ordinary words—*communibus verbis*—and thus not apparent.

That style, mannered or not, was at least highly cultivated and would correspond, in English, to that of Dryden or Pope, which is neither inflated like Milton nor thin like Defoe, but made of ordinary words, about as ordinary as "You are going, but you haven't gone yet, have you?" The style is, I believe, known in the schools as the Augustan style, and the question about it is and has been, do you hear the vibration of any emotion in it? Sometimes you do and sometimes you do not. It is difficult now for the general reader to make out anything stirring under the perfection of Pope except the quick intelligence, but once in a while a vibration of great violence will come through. The very clever portrait of Atticus can suddenly seem heartbroken, even hysterical; other satires seem to have a cold fury under the mere spitefulness; and it was Pope, not Byron or Heine, who said, "This long disease, my life." But most of the time one feels the classical restraint is not restraining anything hard to restrain.

In Virgil's case, some of the inner vibration was lost even in his own time. A contemporary critic said he would find fault with certain things in Virgil if he could only find fault also with Virgil's voice, and facial expression, and impersonation, because the same verses, when Virgil was reciting them, sounded well, but without him they were empty and mute. It is well to remember that Virgil composed his poetry less for the page than for the voice, and apparently too much for his own voice, which was a peculiar one. It was too weak for oratory, which, in Virgil's youth, the age of Cicero, certainly had to be loud, so he gave it up after pleading one case. He also had something like

asthma, so the voice was probably wheezy or rich with overtones and its natural projection would have been *en sourdine.*
But he could manipulate it very effectively in recitation; it is
said to have been sweet or delightful (*suavitate*) and full of
wonderful allurements (*lenociniis*). This may help to explain the
troublesome remark of Horace, that Virgil's work was soft and
clever. Perhaps the expression of the voice, under the formal
versification and plain wording, was soft and charming, suave
and seductive, though it of course had to vary for the speeches
of his characters, which are sometimes vehement, and with his
subjects, from moonlight scenes to storms and battles. Well, the
voice is gone and we cannot hope to know exactly how it went,
how it enlivened passages that now seem empty and mute, but
Willa Cather was right in taking the poetry as essentially vocal
and if she recited much of it aloud herself she no doubt got
closer to the original vibration of the utterance than more scholarship of the silent kind would have brought her. To a literary
scholar it is an incredible fact, though probably a fact, that the
Eclogues of Virgil were staged and sung or chanted, but with
her addiction to opera and the approximations to it in her work
Willa Cather would have had little trouble recognizing that the
poetry of Virgil was not only vocal but for a kind of histrionic
performance, by himself and others, and potentially even
operatic. When he says "I sing of arms and the man" he may
almost mean it.

In *My Ántonia* there is an odd instance of someone reading
Virgil in silence—Jim Burden studying the *Georgics.* But even in
silence the voice of his friend and teacher, Gaston Cleric, returns to him, and he says, "as I sat staring at my book, the
fervour of his voice stirred through the quantities on the page
before me" (p. 265). The quantities are of course the long and
short syllables of Classical metrics, and it is typical of Willa
Cather's vocal approach that it is not so much the words or their
meanings that the fervor stirs through as it is their metrical
value, syllable by syllable. Elsewhere Jim Burden does not *read*
the *Aeneid* aloud, he *scans* it aloud. His mind is on the duration
of syllables as a singer's would be on the duration of notes.
What this can mean for readers of Willa Cather's prose is, I
think, that not only every word counts, but every syllable
counts, as in a poem. Though there is no metric to her prose,
however rhythmical it may be, and cadenced, one should at-

Donald Sutherland

tend to the syllabification, to the cunning use of words of one syllable, or a few, or many, which has its effect. *My Ántonia* ends with these words: "the precious, the incommunicable past," where the word *precious*, of two syllables or almost three, is succeeded and as it were augmented by the six syllables of *incommunicable*, which in turn introduces the final monosyllable, *past*. So introduced, the monosyllable gains an enormous emphasis, and surely anyone can hear the fervor stirring in it. The device is Virgilian, perhaps too recognizably so, though it remains, I think, moving, and makes a fine close to the book.

There is something like it in a passage of the *Georgics*, where Virgil is apparently tiring of a topic and says he is wasting precious time on details. But this bit of Romantic irony turns into the line "*Sed fugit interea, fugit inreparabile tempus,*" which means "But it flies meanwhile, it flies, unrecoverable time" and has an eloquence far beyond the occasion. The line is clever, in the manipulation of long and short words and long and short syllables, but I think it is also irresistible. It is very simple, in thought, rhetoric, and diction, and that could be a mannerism, as the critic said, or it could be the appropriate vehicle for a quite basic and universal emotion. Is there any fervor stirring in it, or any ardor, as in Tom Outland's archeological notes? What is commonly heard in Virgil is melancholy, of no great energy compared to tragic passages in, say, Homer, and the fervor Jim Burden feels in reading the *Georgics* may be gratuitously supplied by Gaston Cleric's voice and wide of Virgil's original expression.

But probably not. Virgil was a very popular poet in his time, with a public of Romans, who liked their strong passions as well as their ceremonies, their gladiators as well as their financiers. Once, when he entered a theatre the whole audience rose to greet him, an honor usually reserved for the emperor himself. A merely sad, gentle, and clever poet would scarcely command so enthusiastic a response in that public at large. Fervor and ardor and the like there must have been, even combined with melancholy. The combination, a note of fervid melancholy or melancholy fervor, is more vividly expressed no doubt in such disciples of Virgil as Dante and Tasso, but very likely they got it from Virgil. At any rate, for Willa Cather he was a model, and as she had a virtual dogma that great art is based on strong passions and the strongest passions are mainly the savage and

165

barbaric ones she must have found something of the kind in Virgil, and generally, not only when his subject is a nominal barbarian like Dido or Turnus or Megentius. And all that under a quiet or veiled voice. There are other sources for her own manner, naturally, but what she thought was the "perfect utterance" of the *Georgics* must have been a major one.

There is a magnificently exaggerated description of that kind of expression in a work which seems very remote but may easily have helped to determine her manner, Edgar Allan Poe's* quite unclassical and Gothic story, "Ligeia." "Of all the women whom I have ever known," says the narrator, "she, the outwardly calm, the ever-placid Ligeia, was the most violently a prey to the tumultuous vultures of stern passion. And of such passion I could form no estimate, save by the miraculous expansion of those eyes which at once so delighted and appalled me,—by the almost magical melody, modulation, distinctness, and placidity of her very low voice,—and by the fierce energy (rendered doubly effective by contrast with her manner of utterance) of the wild words which she habitually uttered." Later, as things get worse, we find: "Yet not until the last instance, amid the most convulsive writhings of her fierce spirit, was shaken the external placidity of her demeanor. Her voice grew more gentle—grew more low—yet I would not wish to dwell upon the wild meaning of the quietly uttered words."[6]

What Ligeia is going on about is of course universal death, as in what is supposed, in the story, to be her poem, "The Conqueror Worm," a very tortuous little poem in form and ghastly in content. In the event of tumultuous vultures or convulsive writhings of spirit there are naturally two manners of utterance but, to my knowledge, there are no dignified terms for them. The best I find come from popular singing, to belt it out and to cool it. That would hardly be Willa Cather's terminology. For her the alternatives were clear very early, not in words but in the styles of two great rival actresses, Sarah Bernhardt, who certainly belted it out, and Eleanora Duse, who certainly cooled it, if not to redoubled effect like Ligeia, at least

---

*Willa Cather wrote an extremely laudatory essay on Poe as an artist in the [Lincoln] *Courier*, October 12, 1895; reprinted in *The Kingdom of Art*. "With the exception of Henry James and Hawthorne," she said, "Poe is our only master of pure prose" (p. 382). The essay shows she had studied his verbal techniques, down to the effects of parts of speech, very closely.

with equal power. Willa Cather called Sarah's art one of color and the Duse's an art of marble. Though she could sometimes write with the overt vehemence, the full color, of Sarah, she ordinarily keeps to the more reserved or marmoreal style of the Duse, but in either manner the tumultuous vultures of stern passion are pretty constantly there.

The association of the Classics and classicism in general with white marble is fairly constant in the cultural world and not foolish, however gaudy and coloristic antiquity could in fact sometimes be. Willa Cather surely visualized what she calls "the drama of antique life" as she says Gaston Cleric did, as "white figures against blue backgrounds."[7] That may be an impression of the Parthenon pediments against the blue sky, or of the Portland vase, which was once admired as the essence of antiquity, though now it is an atypical piece of rather decadent bric-à-brac. Be that as it may, white was important in Willa Cather's youth, and it was not altogether a sign of purity. It had an erotic content, as the complexions of women were most attractive if kept very white, not bronzed or tan. What makes Lena Lingard particularly dangerous is the fact that even out tending the cattle all day, "her legs and arms, curiously enough, in spite of constant exposure to the sun, kept a miraculous whiteness which somehow made her seem more undressed than other girls who went scantily clad."[8] So white was a kind of nakedness, any way you looked at it.

With white went a passionate paleness, no doubt left over from the great Romantics, and the painting of the period was full of it, what with the Pre-Raphaelites, Whistler, Corot, Puvis de Chavannes. In 1903 Willa Cather could call her book of poems *April Twilights*, with full confidence that the incipient colors of April—as against the full colors of May or June—and twilights, as against the extreme chiaroscuro of noon or midnight, would have as much or more power. The pallor was not weakness at all, and could be stark, as she calls a painting by Burne-Jones, and in her own prose it is sometimes rendered in terms of hard materials, as in this passage from *Shadows on the Rock:* "A bright rain-grey light, silver and cut steel and pearl on the grey roofs and walls" (p. 70). We may not respond immediately to that tonality now, but it was real and forcible at the time and may be so again.

It was also a matter of good taste. Her own taste in dress was more an appetite than taste for loud colors, but she knew from her elegant mother and from fashion generally that loud colors should be used with great care, only in telling little touches or on special occasions. Her taste in jewels, as they appear in her work at least, is not for the saturated colors of rubies, emeralds, and sapphires, or the brilliance of diamonds, so much as for the paler and less aggressive colors of tiger-eyes, turquoises, and topazes. Whiteness and pallor were no doubt associated in her mind with classical austerity, and those qualities in her descriptive passages correspond to qualities in her vocabulary and rhetoric, colorless if you like, but hard, precise, and passionate.

Her prose, at least in her mature works, is also without brilliance, avoiding epigrams, witticisms, and paradox. It rarely so much as indulges in general ideas. William Dean Howells had worked out a similar prose, and she most probably learned much from him, though she had a revulsion of her own against the glittering manner of Wilde. But Howells, when he struck out all the witty things in his work, got a merely *mild* result—or so she thought—and mildness was the last thing Willa Cather wanted. The problem for her was how to be colorless, how to keep a dull finish as she liked it on silver, and still be thrilling. One of her solutions, the most conspicuous one, was a frequent use of atrocity, both physical and moral. She had rather a fancy for dismemberment, for people being eaten alive by wolves or something, and for cannibals, what another critic than myself might call the basic Dionysiac material, but she renders them in a matter-of-fact and nearly casual way.

Here is a description of the carp being fed by Louis XIV at Fontainebleau. " 'The carp there are monsters, really. They came grunting and snorting like a thousand pigs. They piled up on each other in hills as high as the rim of the basin, with all their muzzles out; they caught a loaf and devoured it before it could touch the water. Not long before that, a care-taker's little girl fell into the pond, and the carp tore her to pieces while her father was running to the spot. Some of them are very old and have an individual renown. One old creature, red and rusty down to his belly, they call the Cardinal.' "9

One could hardly make less of the caretaker and his little girl, but the essential horror of the story, or rather of the moment, is intact, the more vivid for the lack of elaboration. That is the classic way, a reluctance to develop a theme beyond the bare statement. Indeed Willa Cather does not even make the running father the end of the paragraph, which would be a kind of emphasis, but goes calmly on with information about the carp, ending the paragraph with something of a flourish, a red one, the Cardinal. Typically, the full color is muted, or graduated from red to rusty down to the belly. You are free to surmise what is in that belly, but Willa Cather does not prompt you to. Ligeia herself was not quieter than that.

From a passage in the *Georgics*, which Jim Burden is studying, she drew the epigraph for *My Ántonia*, "*Optima dies . . . prima fugit,*" meaning approximately, "The best days are the first to flee," as she says. The four words extracted are much compressed, more peremptory and sculptural than the original text and making a better epigraph, but the text in full is even more expressive of Willa Cather's view of life, in *My Ántonia* and in most of her work. Three lines of it go like this:

> optima quaeque dies miseris mortalibus aevi
> prima fugit: subeunt morbi tristisque senectus
> et labor et durae rapit inclementia mortis,

which means

> And so, for each poor mortal creature the best time
> of life is first to go; diseases come along
> and sad old age, and things become laborious,
> and death, hard death, unsparingly takes us away.

That is a questionable translation, mine, but it presents plainly enough, several of Willa Cather's favorite themes, diseases and the increasing laboriousness of life, in addition to age and death. Other passages in the *Georgics* are as close to her sense of things. The poem is not about nature but about farming, quite a different matter. It is not idyllic, like the *Eclogues*, where you find the bland remark that love conquers all. In the *Georgics* it is brute labor which conquers all and does not by any means always conquer. It can only struggle against the fatal current of things toward the worse.*

Georgics 1.199. "*Sic omnia fatis / in peius ruere ac retro sublapsa referri.*"

That view of poor mortals struggling in a desperate universe reckons of course with death as a governing fact, as steadily as a Lucretius did or indeed a Ligeia, but it also dwells on temporality, seeing the course of a lifetime, from youth to decrepitude, as a long and gradual decline, relieved by fugitive moments of happiness or of hard-won success. You may think that temporality and processiveness are not classical, and in very strict theory they are not, but in classical literature there is a kind of secondary tradition, beginning with the *Odyssey*, in which the basis of composition is not action, as in the *Iliad*, so much as the passage of time, or of a lifetime. Most of Willa Cather's work is composed on that basis and she may have derived from the *Odyssey* many of her techniques, especially that of long sad retrospect, the motif of absence or exile, and her very frequent device of having a person return home and find things changed—an excellent device for realizing the passage of time experientially, not as a concept. At any rate, a vision of the world which supports that kind of composition is plainly formulated in the *Georgics*. Not that she got that vision from Virgil alone, but his formulations had her full sympathy and are simpler to deal with than the whole tradition of pessimism she had behind her, Flaubert, Poe, *The City of Dreadful Night*, Carlyle, and so on. Those few lines from the *Georgics* can help to mark off a great deal of what her fiction is from what it is not.

Certain kinds of novel cannot well be written in the Virgilian perspective. The society novel, or civilized novel, which can treat the texture of the present in a drawing room as if it were definitive, and human associations as if they were substantial, cannot often afford to see it all in the open, as precarious and transitory, exposed to a largely destructive natural universe. Willa Cather did not write society novels, though a story like "Flavia and Her Artists" (1905)[10] shows she might have done so and at least tried her hand at that genre, as at many others.

She wrote a powerful story about an industrial accident, "Behind the Singer Tower" (1912),[11] but she did not write social novels. It is rather surprising that she did not, since she knew the muckrakers, but no doubt she felt that such subjects did not suit her voice. She might find herself vociferating instead of singing or speaking. Nor would social subjects do very well under the Virgilian perspective, where kings and shepherds, friends and enemies, empires and individuals, are equally doomed and leave little behind them but the land. With luck, a memory. Then social novels tend to be progressive, whatever horrors they may describe in the present state of things, but for Virgil and for Willa Cather the golden age is in the past. In Virgil there is some hope for its return, but his settled perspective is backward, like Willa Cather's. Marxist or even liberal criticism cannot do much with either of them, except perhaps to resign themselves to the existence of masterpieces somewhat to the right of center.

Nor did she write psychological novels, though here and there she finds a use for the stream-of-consciousness technique, in reveries and dreams, and so on, the passing thought. She had the notion, quite early, that "our psychologies" as she called them, are an excessive refinement, to be swept away by barbarian invasions, which would bring us back to hard and healthy work on the land. The notion is naturally not articulate in Virgil, though the nostalgia for the land is certainly there, even in the *Aeneid*. In Willa Cather the nostalgia for the farm is persistent and also for the frontier and the wilderness, for savage conditions as well as laborious ones. There is, under such conditions, no time for anything very subtle in the way of psychology. Her characters are so to say practical, having endurance and competence or not having them. They are brutal or delicate, energetic or lasting by immobility, like the Ácoma Indians in *Death Comes for the Archbishop*, who are compared to rock-turtles. Her characters have rudimentary passions, often ugly ones, but they do not have intricate states of mind. Some of them are indeed pathological cases, but they simply go crazy and are sent to an asylum or, if relatively harmless, are humorously tolerated, like Crazy Mary in *My Ántonia*. Then there are monsters, like Ivy Peters in *A Lost Lady*, or the unspeakable murderer in *Death Comes for the Archbishop*, but they are not analyzed or explained. The murderer is simply called degenerate and is hanged, which is rather summary but, I think, a mercy for the reader.

Nor did she write experimental novels. Under the Virgilian perspective the motive in writing is less to make something new than to make something as lasting as possible, more pe-

rennial than bronze, as Horace has it, and anyone can feel that a
work's chances of lasting are greater if it is based on what has
already lasted, that is, on long tradition, than if it is based on
novelty or contemporaneity. For a work to last, it had better
have some force of originality in it, but the originality may well
be in the spirit or in the content, as with Virgil, and not require
any radical break with traditional form. Willa Cather loosened
the conventions of, say, the *Woman's Home Companion*
considerably but she did not by any means scrap them. I am of
two minds or three about that, but I am told on good authority
that modernism is falling apart all over the place, and if so,
Willa Cather may already appear, not old-fashioned, which she
only is in her early work and in superficial detail, but permanent and universal as she meant to be.

Another kind of novel she did not write was the dramaturgical, that is, a novel built like a play, with a unified plot or action
to the casual continuity of which everything rigorously
contributes. That Aristotelian convention is all very well, but
under the Virgilian perspective, of the passage of lifetimes,
single dramatic actions appear as episodes, especially when
seen in retrospect, and are rarely rounded off with an exit
march. Ordinarily we outlive our dramas, dozens of them, as
Odysseus does his adventures and exploits, and we are not contained in any one of them. The novels of Willa Cather are made
up of episodes, even of little anecdotes, with characters who are
often arbitrary apparitions or disappearances, dramaturgically
useless enough, but like people who come to us and leave us in
life, moving in something experientially more terrible than almost any action, the passage of time and the dissolution of
things in it. The idea and the techniques for expressing it are to
some extent in Virgil, but, as I say, more evident in the
Odyssey. Just now, let me offer this essentially nondramaturgi-
cal tendency of Willa Cather as one among many reasons for her
forbidding the conversion of her novels into plays or movies.
The events in her novels are often dramatic, in a sense, even
melodramatic, but they are not put together to make a single
action or plot, as in a well-made play.

The kinds of novels she did not write, society, social,
psychological, and so on, were immensely in vogue in her time.
There were Proust, and Virginia Woolf, Joyce and Dos Passos,

Upton Sinclair, Faulkner and Hemingway, there was still Edith Wharton, and against all that elaboration and innovation she looks very simple. Indeed she is simple, or simplified, but not in any way naive, not even politically. She was after the practical essentials of survival, of getting something done, and of dying in the given world, finally between the land and the stars. Those essentials are quite simple, available to anyone by the age of fifteen, as she said her material had been to her. To keep them simple and present, however, to stay at the radical center of human being, takes a good deal of discipline and even strategy. It was not just an idiosyncrasy that she liked to write in a tent or that she built a cottage in so remote and primitive a place as Grand Manan. That closeness to the rudimentary world is in the *Georgics* and in the *Aeneid*, but is clearest perhaps in the *Odyssey*, where shelter and survival are great issues, and a bed of leaves can be a luxury.

The *Georgics*, as I said, are not idyllic. They are not about landscape but about the land. They are a farmer's almanac or handbook, based on such grim old authors as Hesiod and Cato the Censor. Natural beauty, general ideas, and Virgil's note of lofty or fervent melancholy, have to get into the *Georgics*, superinduced, as best they can. That handsome passage on deterioration and mortality in general happens to be brought in, rather arbitrarily, when his immediate topic is cattle-breeding. He has had to say which years in the early life of a cow are the best for breeding, and this prompts him to rise to a generality about all poor mortals. I think there is irony in Virgil's tone here, but perhaps not. Cows are in the world with us. At any rate, Willa Cather seems to have felt nothing captious in the transition. She speaks of "the perfect utterance of the 'Georgics,' where the pen was fitted to the matter as the plough is to the furrow."[12] That kind of exactitude in dealing with a hard and basic subject matter is her own kind of perfection. An austere exactitude can provide an intellectual exhilaration well enough, but does it amount to a passion, even a "stern" passion, and what has it to do with poetry? Her express view of poetry in the *Georgics* and in general is puzzling but worth working out if you can do it.

Jim Burden is interrupted in his study of the *Georgics* by a visit from Lena Lingard, and when she has gone, she and her laughter have reminded him of other girls back home in Black Hawk, who were beautiful and easygoing but not the "nice" girls of the town. He says, "It came over me, as it had never done before, the relation between girls like those and the poetry of Virgil. If there were no girls like them in the world, there would be no poetry. I understood that clearly, for the first time. This revelation seemed to me inestimably precious. I clung to it as if it might suddenly vanish." When he returns to his book the memory of an old dream he had about Lena coming toward him across a harvest field "floated," he says, "on the page like a picture, and underneath it stood the mournful line: *'Optima dies . . . prima fugit.'* "[13]

The idea, or the fugitive revelation, is put with great emphasis and its importance to Willa Cather is evident, but its meaning is not. There are no pretty girls to speak of in Virgil, he is anything but a love poet, so the relation must be to poetry in general. She may mean that the sources of poetry are ultimately sexual, which is all right and would have been worth saying at the time of writing, 1918, but I think she means more. In the context of Black Hawk the pretty laughing girls would be defined against Puritanism, or the bleak respectability of the Protestant churches. They would embody a kind of paganism and, in spite of their race, a Latinity—the life of the flesh, the senses, and finally the arts, as against virtues and sins and a supernatural attitude toward the perceptible world. Virgil's poetry would stand for the highest or most essential utterance of that pagan world, of which the girls are part, and the image of Lena in the harvest field floating on the page like a picture would make an apt enough illustration of the *Georgics*. But here we are in difficulties with Lena again. Her image is rather portentous and mysterious, the memory of a dream in the midst of a reverie, and part of a "revelation." Willa Cather may mean her to represent Venus or Aphrodite, in a number of her aspects, beauty and the fertility of nature as well as love proper, and in that case the relation of Lena and girls like her to the poetry of Virgil would be clear. Venus Genetrix, or the Lucretian Venus, the goddess who makes things grow, would infuse even the hardest facts of farming with a numinousness, and the poetry of the *Georgics* would come out of those facts, like wheat from the ground.

I do not like this much. There are schools of criticism which like symbols and working out mythical structures behind anything at all. Today they would spot Lena Lingard as the White Goddess at once, and go on from there, but I think Lena is a great myth in her own right, and does not need Venus or Calypso or Camille behind her. Still, it does look as if Willa Cather is suggesting Venus, and the critical question is how the suggestion works, whether it implies a whole structure of thought and detailed lore, or is simply an allusion in passing, a sort of elaborated adjective modifying the noun Lena. I think the latter, and that there is, in the narrative, as much economy of depth as there is economy of explicit statement. That, I think, would be classic, if classicism likes things simple and mainly flat. It may have what is called a depth of passion, but I would call that rather strength of passion and locate it not far from the explicit surface.

Some of Willa Cather's classical allusions are easier to deal with. In *The Professor's House*, the Professor, in despair over his impossible daughters, asks himself, very funnily, "Was there no way but Medea's?" (p. 126). One had best laugh and go right on reading, without making more of Medea than the archetype of infanticide, because if you think it over nothing more works out: Medea did not kill her children because they were impossible, she killed them for revenge on Jason, and they were sons, not daughters, in the first place. In an early story, a sort of parable, "The Way of the World" (1898), children build little towns in play, one of them is destroyed and its builder, says Willa Cather, "sat down with his empty pails in his deserted town, as Caius Marius once sat among the ruins of Carthage."[14] Except for the tone of antique grandeur, its vocal value, so to say, that will not do at all. Marius was not a Carthaginian and had nothing to do with either the building or the destruction of Carthage. He just happened to take refuge there when driven from Rome, and Marius sitting among the ruins of Carthage, a fugitive, is simply a proverbial case of desolation redoubled. The full story, in Plutarch, does nothing at all for "The Way of the World."

But the tone of antique grandeur, the solemnity of the very names, Medea, Caius Marius, and Carthage is, or was, quite genuine, in a culture which took the history of mankind as seriously as it did religion. Names from cultural history were almost exactly like names from the Bible, Jezebel, Abraham, or Absalom, which have a handsome sound and a lofty archetypical meaning, perhaps accompanied by an image, but without much connection with the detail of their stories in the Bible. Invoking them was enough. The best thing one can do with them in reading now is to listen, with all one's ears, catch the vibration in passing, but not to stop and look or do research.

The best example I know of what not to look into is in *O Pioneers!*, the title of Part IV, "The White Mulberry Tree." It seems to invite the reader to recall the story of Pyramus and Thisbe in Ovid, where the blood of a dying lover stains the white mulberry tree red. About eleven years ago the late L.V. Jacks tried to work out parallels between the Pyramus and Thisbe story and the story of Emil and Marie, as if there might be a thematic substructure or counterpoint.[15] He did find a few correspondences of detail, but the differences are very great. In manner, the story in Ovid has the charm and lightness of a fairy tale, while the story of Emil and Marie and her husband is a fairly realistic tragedy, with strongly motivated characters. Pyramus and Thisbe are suicides; Emil and Marie are murdered by her jealous husband. They are adulterers, while the love of Pyramus and Thisbe is unconsummated. One difference is comic: Ovid, to solve the difficulty of getting blood up into the tree to stain its berries, compares the spurt of blood from Pyramus's wound to the long whistling jet of water from a small leak in a lead pipe, which does well enough for a fairy tale. Willa Cather has some white berries lying already on the ground where they can be stained by the final writhings of Marie, which is more like realism. The story was originally, no doubt, a Babylonian myth connected with the death of a vegetation god, and getting the blood into the tree was probably done by a miracle, requiring no such ingenuity as Ovid's to make it appear plausible. What is one to make of all this in the chapter title and story by Willa Cather? The image of a white mulberry tree is certainly decorative, and even poignant, if you take into account the force of white and pallor at the time. If you take the detail of Ovid's story into account also you introduce a strident sort of comedy into Willa Cather's story and make an amusing technical problem of the tree which dominates it. If you take the

Babylonian vegetation myth into account, you turn the story of Emil and Marie into some sort of fertility rite. Since this was the time (1913) of *The Golden Bough*, and *The Waste Land* was to appear nine years later, Willa Cather, who was, in her way, a modern, until 1922 or "thereabouts," may well have wanted to suggest some kind of ritual out of anthropology. She certainly meant to poetize and enlarge her regional or even local story, and the white mulberry tree, taken as some vast vague symbol of immemorial tragedy, even a Wagnerian sort of love-death, would certainly increase the dimensions. But the text of Ovid certainly does not.

The great temptation of Willa Cather was her own virtuosity. She could and did write almost any kind of story, even what she calls a "manly battle yarn," in *One of Ours*. She could write fantasies and parables and, when symbols and mythologies were being used, indulge in them herself. But her real strength lay, I think, in another direction, in a special kind of concentrated realism, in reduction rather than complication or augmentation. In *A Lost Lady* she uses an expression which may help define this. She says that for Niel Herbert the books in his uncle's library were "living creatures, caught in the very behaviour of living,—surprised behind their misleading severity of form and phrase" (p. 81). She has just spoken of the *Heroides* of Ovid, which Niel has read over and over, so we are still with the classic Latin style as she felt it, severe but betraying "the very behaviour of living" behind it. Apart from the books themselves as living creatures, I would apply that expression to what it is that Willa Cather eminently catches in the characters of her major works. The behavior of living, not life; that is, the quick of the process, much rather than life as an aggregate of factual detail or life in a summary philosophical sense. The behavior of living especially in the course of a lifetime, long or short. Its "very" behavior—the actuality of living—not its conditions of causes or mythic significances, is her prime subject, and it has no need of symbols or ideas to sustain or augment it, though it may indeed use them for embellishment. All it needs is to be uttered, in voice or gesture or event. In Willa Cather's work it is habitually remembered, rather than presented raw, but it is remembered vividly, and memory, or the device of retrospect, is a fine way of isolating the vital aspect of persons and events, and getting rid of the real but irrelevant facts around it.

You will surely remember the death of Count Frontenac in *Shadows on the Rock*. After the extreme unction she says,

> Then, very courteously, he made a gesture with his left hand, indicating that he wished every one to draw back from the bed.
> "This I will do alone," his steady glance seemed to say.
> All drew back.
> "Merci," he said distinctly. That was the last word he spoke. [Pp. 262–63]

The severity of that passage is obvious, and the strong emotion just under the irreducible wording, but there is a distinction worth making, that although the chivalric character of Count Frontenac is perfectly rendered by the gesture of the left hand, the less commanding hand, by the steady glance, and his last word, the virtue and energy of the passage is not in that rendition so much as in putting us into direct contact with the very behavior of living a few moments before dying, as anyone potentially might live them. This grasp of what a teacher of mine called "livingness" is, I believe, the greatest strength of Willa Cather, to which her many other talents are subsidiary, though they were indeed sometimes insubordinate.

Distinct from her characters, there is the writer herself as a living creature, a mind and a temperament and especially a voice, uttering its sense of the narrative events as they come along, inflecting them, selecting them, accenting them or muting them, as if they were in a song. The last sentence of *Death Comes for the Archbishop* will, I hope, be a clear example. The Archbishop has died, just after dark—a typical lighting—the cathedral bell has sounded the knell, with various effects on the people waiting at the cathedral in Santa Fé. Then comes this extraordinary sentence, which looks so casual: "Eusabio and the Tesuque boys"—I have to explain that these are Indians —"went quietly away to tell their people; and the next morning the old Archbishop lay before the high altar in the church he had built" (p. 299). I wish I had time to analyze the effects of that sentence, but a few will serve. First, the conjunction *and*, which looks as if it joined two events in a perfunctory way, actually joins two solemn and uncanny silences, the tread of the departing Indians and the body of the Archbishop. It is the joining of emotional qualities, as in a song, not the mere facts. Then he is called the old, not the dead, Archbishop, and there we have the Virgilian and Catherian interest not only in the fact of death but in the long process of living and aging before it. Most remarkable is the phrase "in the church he had built." Why not say cathedral, since in fact it is a cathedral? Well, I should say Miss Cather's voice is negotiating an awesome hush, and the word cathedral has too many syllables and too florid a meaning, so she uses the smaller word, church. But if it is small and commonplace, it is also the more universal word. It was not a cathedral that Christ founded, but a church, and indeed it was a church, a religious congregation, that the Archbishop had founded in New Mexico, by fair means or foul, depending on your politics, but not just a cathedral. All this, if you please, in the utterance of a single short word.

Let me give one more example, somewhat less funerary. In *My Ántonia*, the Widow Steavens is telling how Ántonia came to say goodbye to her before departing on her perilous adventure to marry Donovan in Denver. The Widow Steavens, you may remember, is now the tenant on the Burden homestead, living in the house that had "always been a refuge" to Ántonia. The Widow Steavens says, " 'She laughed kind of flighty like, and whispered, "Good-bye, dear house!" and then ran out to the wagon' " (p. 310). One should attend to the voices in Willa Cather, and read "kind of flighty like" as a musical notation, like, say, *agitato ma non troppo*, and the whisper as *mezzo piano* or softer. Then the words, "Good-bye, dear house," in all their simplicity, have the force of any devastating aria on the subject of parting and farewell. And she says "good-bye," not "farewell." Virgil himself would have used words as ordinary as that—something like *vale, cara domus*—spoken them with a vibrant whisper like Ántonia's, and made all Rome tremble.

[*Reference notes appear on page 263.*]

COMMENT

The discussion developed other ideas on Willa Cather's accuracy in Latin, on oral and silent reading, and on the general classical vision of her imaginative world.

JOHN HINZ: You brought out the cultivated simplicity and the Virgilian regret and the tone and luminosity in Willa Cather's prose, which may be Virgilian. I have difficulty reconciling that with other things you suggested about her—carelessness, let's say, in rendering the Latin, as though she has a beautiful ear and a very precise ear for things, and yet in some way she was not a classicist. I find that strange, because I think she's a very particular writer. I have difficulty persuading myself of the connection between somebody who's into Virgil but persistently misquotes everything, with the other part of Willa Cather where she arranges and executes things so perfectly. . . .

DONALD SUTHERLAND: I think it's quite possible to get the hang of something, the spiritual hang of something, before you have the finished idea of what the words actually are.

GEORGE GREENE: The paper as a whole verifies what Miss Cather herself well said in one of her newspaper interviews, that a Negro lad humming or playing on a fiddle airs from *La Traviata* may know more about the essences. It's associated with the will of the individual.

VIRGINIA FAULKNER: A relatively simple explanation for some of the errors is that Willa Cather frequently quoted from memory. And it wasn't only in her recollection of Latin poetry that she got things a bit off, but in English as well, as we know from the collections of the early writings. Early as a journalist she was in a hurry; and I think in *The Professor's House* one quatrain of Longfellow's poem is quoted wrong. It's corrected in the Brown-Edel book—the four lines beginning "For thee a house was built." She misquotes Shelley, and so on, and she just didn't check it out. She was not writing a thesis.

GEORGE GREENE: Yes, Dr. Johnson was capable of misquoting, too.

PAUL OLSON: If you have an aural sense for the poetry your inclination would be to quote it as you remembered it, as it rings in your imagination.

MARGARET O'CONNOR: In relation to Cather's fine ear, I was thinking of my own interests in the early short stories and a sense that I find there of Cather trying to master dialogue in her work. There's a great deal of dialogue in the early stories, and in fact in the later stories there is very little dialogue. The phrases are short and the characters are really undifferentiated in their speech. They really don't demonstrate an idiolect, the individualized dialect. We see perhaps in the commentary around the phrases themselves the real character—"she said in a hushed tone"—this kind of concept that really makes the character individual. It's in the descriptive passages that she describes the spoken word.

DONALD SUTHERLAND: We have to read Willa Cather as if there were a temporal continuity rather than a structural one. That's what I mean primarily by the voice. . . .

180

Donald Sutherland

RICHARD GIANNONE: I think we read every author differently. Sometimes the first sentence of the text sets up stylistic cues, which are almost moral cues, as in Jane Austen in the beginning of *Emma* or *Pride and Prejudice*. Long before we reach the end we've already ratified reasons, parallelisms, paradoxes—those things that the narrative represents. It's not accidental in Cather that the "wisdom figures," the moral centers, are generally pre-literate—not necessarily illiterate —people. I think that's the model behind the voice. . . . All of the performance implies a particular relationship between auditor-reader and text. . . . It seems to me you imply a way in which we are to read Cather, which is authentic to that Cather voice. . . . It seems to me that the art invites participation. The page only implies sound, but sound is itself, so that when we hear we are "in" rather than "with." And that, I think, asks us to ignore inflections, ignore mistakes in dates. . . . The true voice provides inner access. It seems to me that knowing is only one form of being. Moby Dick knows more about being a whale than all of that business at the beginning of Melville's book knows about being a whale. Knowing is not necessarily living. Cather was interested in living. . . . In some passages even a shift in syntax, such as from verbal adjective to substantive, is revealing.

DONALD SUTHERLAND: She was very conscious of just those things, the emotional effect of the part of speech, the thrilling adjective or magnificent conjunction.

JOHN HINZ: You said that she didn't do the social novel, she didn't do the experimental novel, she didn't do the psychological novel. All that was left, in a sense, were the old things, the old ways to be new, as Frost said about Robinson. But *The Professor's House* seems to me pretty close to being a psychological novel.

DONALD SUTHERLAND: I think you can find at least one work of Willa Cather's in contradiction. I think she does work out some psychology in the Professor. He's having a very nervous time of it. But I don't think the interest in the thing is psychological. I don't think it is typical of Willa Cather's world.

WARREN FRENCH: I think *The Professor's House* is not only much more psychological than the rest of her novels, but it is also much more a society novel, a social novel, and an experimental novel than the other things she wrote. It's totally atypical of her work and it has over-bothered critics. They don't quite know what to do with it. As a matter of fact, it violates the dramaturgical limitation. It's not a stage-able novel, but it's a highly filmable novel. . . . I have found that *Shadows on the Rock* is a much better novel read aloud than read silently, read in the study. It is flat in the study, but it comes to life; and there's no complexity in *Shadows on the Rock* which you can't follow from listening to it. This is not true of *The Professor's House*. . . . Her

181

later novels are quite beautiful read aloud, and it's too bad that they are not done that way.

DONALD SUTHERLAND: I think they're beautiful read silently.

PAUL OLSON: Willa Cather's classicism can be contrasted with Joyce's. In Joyce you are called upon constantly to look at parallelisms. With Willa Cather, what one is asked to look at is a vision of how the world is put together, which to me is in some ways close to Virgil's vision. The theme of exile and of creating a new civility is central in Willa Cather's work. . . . There are also ordinary people who suddenly become almost more than themselves, who become somehow divine, which I think is part of the apotheosizing tradition of the novel. Ántonia becomes that sort of thing, or the Archbishop. A New Critic can't do very much with that. There are not levels upon levels of allusion, but I think there are parallels of vision which are terribly important. If criticism began with Willa Cather as an epic writer as opposed to a novelist, people would come closer to the heart of what she is doing.

Part II

Recollections

Homage to Willa Cather

Leon Edel

Tonight the world comes to the parish to pay homage to Willa Cather. She was a child of both. Within the landscapes of her youth, the matrix of her creativity, we will seek to understand how the artist was formed, and how she formed her art. To be sure, the landscapes of her youth are much changed; they were changing during her lifetime and she resented the alteration. But that story belongs elsewhere. What we must note tonight is the loyal pride of Red Cloud and Lincoln and the University she attended, which has given impulse to these observances so thoughtfully and gracefully planned: observances local, national, international. How much Willa Cather's place in the world has been enlarged may be seen by looking at the audience gathered here. We have come from all corners of America, even from outpost states, like Hawaii, which I happen to represent. We have present scholars from the European countries Miss Cather knew and loved; and from the Orient which she never knew, but which knows her.

This testifies to a grateful parish and an inquiring one. I would like personally to thank the planners for the honor they have done me in asking me to pay the initial homage. The occasion calls, I would suggest, neither for eulogy, nor indeed for elegy. It asks us, with the distancings of time, to try to see the reality of this bright-eyed daughter of the prairies, who traveled westward from Virginia when young, and who went

185

her way eastward, first in anger at the narrowness of local horizons, and who then returned in profound love. She was lively,
alert, abrasive as only the young can be, drawn always, always
drawn, to the Bright Medusa. She lived out the words of Sarah
Orne Jewett to which I made allusion, "One must know the
world *so well* before one can know the parish." Miss Cather had
to get to know the world as precocious children do, in revolt
against family and establishment. She was in her salad days
spirited, ebullient, untried; and in the end she filled her art
with an ache for her prairie years, which she called "the best
years," the years of her youth, and tried to face the truth that
they are the first to flee. We are involved thus in a drama—the
drama of a woman from the provinces who had to learn the
illusions of the great wide world as well as its glories. It is a
Balzacian drama of which Miss Cather made herself the
heroine.

Our presence here is a direct response to the high individuality of Miss Cather's work and her life as a responsible artist. I
need not return to familiar ground. This audience knows the
world of Willa Cather. You have read her novels and tales; you
have reflected on her essays and early writings, exhumed in
such abundance and with so much piety in recent years. I
would like to speak instead of certain ironies and paradoxes in
her life, and some of its mysteries. I speak out of my
biographer's workshop, where I recently reread the papers,
notes, and letters that go back to the time, more than two dec-
ades ago, when it fell to my lot to finish the biography of Willa
Cather begun by my friend Edward Brown and left incomplete
at the time of his death.

I have used the word mystery. We stumble upon one at the
very start. We know that Miss Cather died in 1947, on April 24,
and that four days later she was buried in the sloping ground of
the Old Cemetery of Jaffrey Center in New Hampshire. In due
course a white headstone was placed on the grave by Miss
Cather's friend of many years, Edith Lewis, carrying these
words from *My Ántonia*: "That is happiness, to be dissolved
into something complete and great." Carved into the marble as
is customary, are the years of Miss Cather's life, 1876–1947. You
will ask at once, and quite rightly: why are we here in Lincoln
in 1973, if the birth year on the grave says 1876. Are we three

years early? It seems a curious discrepancy at any rate and yet the planners of our observances obviously knew what they were about.

It is not my intention to attach too much importance to this mystery. Yet behind it there is a story, one of those little stories that gives light and life to the biographical process. Three years, one way or another, in the length of any century, mean very little. There are, moreover, many illustrious figures whose birth dates and death dates are wholly unknown. We celebrate their span of mortality by a process of educated guesswork. A biographer, however, in the very nature of his job looks at facts. He is confined to a garden where he must see real toads, not imaginary ones. The only imagination allowed him, as I have often said, is his organizing imagination. Moreover, a biographer must learn to rise above his facts. Uninterpreted fact is like a town meeting without a chairman, a packet of seeds without a label. Dry uninterpreted facts make up a *curriculum vita*, an entry in *Who's Who*, scribbles in a datebook. Behind the facts, in any biography, lies the mystery of life itself. And we try, in our clumsy ways, to fathom a little bit of the mystery. The headstone in the burial ground near Mount Monadnock affirms in gleaming marble the years of Willa Cather's life. We may, I repeat, legitimately ask: what are we doing here in 1973? The date of her death is beyond question: it is attested in the most official way in our over-documented modernity. About the birth year given there has to be a great deal of questioning, for we had, to begin with, no documents at all. Professor Brown, in his unfinished manuscript, wrote 1873. (Let me say, in parenthesis, that his death robbed us not only of the completion of the book by the mind and hands of its original author, but of one of our most sensitive critics of fiction; a finely-tempered scholarly spirit and mind.) His life of Miss Cather, I am sure, is known to most of this audience. I think it has stood the test of its twenty years. It contains inevitably, certain verifiable slips and errors as all biographies do. We know so much more about Miss Cather now than he could have known, thanks to the work of many scholars here tonight. The details they have given us, the retouching of the portrait, does not alter, I believe, its essential lines. New letters and a great many little facts about the folk that surround an artist, do not change the nature of the artist, or

187

the vision we have of him. The central myths of Miss Cather's life, as probed originally by Professor Brown, were clearly defined. And even though his was an authorized work, which presupposes certain restrictions, and hindrances and obscurings of the story, I can testify that he wrote in relative independence. His book would have been even more independent had he lived to finish it.

Brown's manuscript, his marked copies of Miss Cather's novels, his papers and correspondence, the few letters he had received from Miss Cather, his notes made in Red Cloud, in Virginia, in Pittsburgh and New York confronted me with an extremely delicate problem. I refer not only to the devilish difficulty of finishing someone else's book, which in itself would be task enough. A book is as organic as the human body. I had learned this only too well in writing the first volume of my life of Henry James which I had almost completed when my living room became filled with the Cather papers assembled by Brown, including a large map of Nebraska and another of Lincoln. I knew only too well how many subtle threads bind every chapter to the chapter that precedes it, and to the rest of the book. The threads might as well be the veins and arteries of the human body. I accordingly went over every inch of Brown's manuscript and retraced his pages to their sources. I studied the way in which he had handled his facts. I talked with a number of persons he had consulted, among them Miss Sergeant and Dorothy Canfield Fisher. I came on new material. And I learned how he observed the principal tabu: he was not allowed to quote from Miss Cather's letters. This was her testamentary decree. And I came on the noticeable birth date which Brown gave as 1873—though I had not yet had a chance to hunt for his documentation of that date.*

But all this was as nothing beside the delicate diplomacy in which I found myself involved, for I also met Edith Lewis. Brown had had the help of Miss Lewis, Miss Cather's intimate friend, from the start. It was she who had proposed that he write the biography; and he had told me of some of his conversations with her, and some of his difficulties in straightening out fact from legend. (It was she, by the way, who got me fixed

*Mildred R. Bennett's *The World of Willa Cather* (1951) also gave the birth year as 1873.

188

in the habit of speaking of Miss Cather—or Willa Cather—but *never* Willa. She did not even want the little Willa of the child-hood years to be on a first-name basis to her biographer.) I am not suggesting that Edith Lewis was a sort of dragon guarding a sacred shrine. She was the exact opposite: a lady of charm and delicacy, quiet, dignified, sentient. The lapse of the years gives me the liberty now to speak of our relation and our work to-gether. I liked her very much, and we became very good friends. She possessed the same lively rigidities as Miss Cather—that is, the Willa of the late years. She was beautifully loyal to her memory and her loyalty applied both to fact and legend, as Brown had told me. She knew all the stories of their days, their travels, their adventures. And she rightly believed it was her duty to guard the approaches to Miss Cather's privacy. She had the same sense of fun, the same love of food, and some of the same heartiness, though perhaps on a less demanding scale. She was alert, cultivated, intelligent; if it did not sound condescending I would use the word civilized. She had had her own career in magazine work and publicity. She knew the ways of the world. My relations with her as Brown's surrogate were pleasant but complex from the start. The first difficulty arose from the spontaneity with which she had offered—as we can understand—to complete Brown's book after he died. This was some weeks before I came into the picture. It was an impulse of loyalty and of generosity, a desire to make certain that the book, three-quarters done, should be properly finished. Professor Brown's widow was reluctant to consent. I think most biog-raphers would understand that Miss Lewis's role in Cather his-tory was that of memorialist rather than biographer; she could illuminate the personal life, but she had been too close to her subject. She might have written a Boswellian biography, but that is quite different from the critical biography Brown had brought into being. There was danger of an overlay of folklore; there were all the dangers resulting from a close interpersonal relation. Miss Lewis could only write a worshipful life, and it would no longer be the life of Brown's researches. Her decision made, Mrs. Brown asked me, as Brown's old companion in scholarship and his one friend who consistently practiced biog-raphy, to finish the job. I did not answer promptly. I studied Brown's materials; and I went to see Alfred Knopf, who had given Brown a contract for the book. It was the occasion of our first meeting and the beginning of a friendship I have deeply valued. Mr. Knopf was devoted to Miss Cather and to Miss Lewis; he had never forgotten how Miss Cather chose him to be her publisher, when he was beginning the great career we all know. He hoped very much I would be able to undertake the completion of the unfinished book; he made it clear he thought so highly of the manuscript that he would have published it in its incomplete state. He also made it clear that Miss Lewis had to be consulted about its completion. I would have to be *persona grata* in my relation to her; she was the guardian of Miss Cather's papers, a guardianship Mr. Knopf shared. In this way, I had my first meeting with Edith Lewis.

We met in Miss Cather's apartment on Park Avenue, which Miss Lewis had shared. Everything had been kept as it was at the hour Miss Cather died. It was touching, and I think noble, to see Miss Lewis's piety; yet it was a realistic piety: one might say that she had moved into a state of curious exaltation since Miss Cather's death three years before. The realities of the posthumous job, the posthumous reputation, were before her. I remember looking at the bookshelves, with every book—so she told me—in its accustomed place; I remember the large etching by Couture of that first of the feminists, George Sand, on the wall where Miss Cather had placed it. I sensed Miss Lewis's hurt feelings that the widow of Professor Brown had not allowed her to finish the book; and I felt myself in the invidious role of a rival, in the place Miss Lewis felt to be rightfully hers. If she had such feelings, she concealed them by her cordiality; and she was perfectly frank. After a few minutes she admitted that she had felt hurt; that the confidence she had shown in Mr. Brown had, so to speak, not been returned once Brown was gone. She questioned me about my reading of Miss Cather; wasn't I involved in the world of Henry James?—why did I feel I could come into the Cather world? I passed that examination rapidly. I had lived on the Canadian prairies; I was married to a girl from Lincoln who had attended the University of Nebraska; I had written about Miss Cather—and then I was not a biographer who confined himself to any one subject, although James was, and would remain, my major undertaking. Miss Cather had always interested me. I think I finally settled matters between the two of us when I said to her that we each were mourning a friend: that we each were trying to be loyal to that friend, she to the subject and I to the biographer. In some such way we arrived at a truce of courtesy and respect that later led to a friendship. But on one point, given the hurt feelings, Miss Lewis drew a sharp line. She had written considerable memoranda to guide Professor Brown. This had been a personal link between them. She felt that she could not let me see that series of documents. To that extent I was on my own. But we arrived at our *modus vivendi*; I recognized that it provided salve for Miss Lewis's wounded feelings. I never would know during my work how much Brown had used or planned to use, from her then unpublished pages, and how much further research on them was needed. Moreover, she took an ultimate revenge, though perhaps that may be regarded as too strong a word. She published her memoranda in a book which she called *Willa Cather Living*—a kind of Gallic title, *Willa Cather Vivante*—and it came out at the same time as Brown's biography. This will explain the overlap in the two books. Brown had used her materials freely, not expecting that they too would be published; and doubtless they would not have been had he lived. But I did not feel any essential conflict—save as to some discrepancies of fact—between the two volumes, and I took Miss Lewis to a Village restaurant to revive her memories of Bank Street and we celebrated her emergence as an author. In her way she did write, on a small scale, the Boswellian memoir.

But enough of these ancient diplomacies. We know that in middle life Miss Cather disliked the way in which the world was moving; in spirit and word she very early anticipated the "ecological" feeling of our time: she did not like to see trees torn down to be chopped into matches or newsprint; she would have liked to keep the primeval forest; and she felt that machinery made for softness in men and women, weakened their physical and moral fiber. She preferred trains to airplanes in the way in which old prairie dwellers do, remembering how important the single train from the east used to be when it passed through the small town in the morning, and then passed again on its backward trip in the evening.* She shrank at the

*I speak here out of personal prairie memories. I am told there were as many as a dozen trains passing daily through Willa Cather's Red Cloud during her childhood.

191

ravage of the land; she shrank also from the flight of youth, the ravage she saw in her looking glass. Miss Cather for some years practiced what we can only describe as a harmless deception: it is said usually to be practiced by women, but I know men who deceive in the same way. This deception became an issue between Miss Lewis and myself. There I was, a biographer, seeking in a methodical way to determine all the elements of Professor Brown's story; and there was Edith Lewis, determined to protect the text carved into the marble in the Jaffrey burial ground. We had no argument about Miss Cather's birthday. Everyone agreed it fell on December 7. Today we would of course add that she was a Sagittarius. But Brown's manuscript said in bold numbers 1873; and Miss Lewis pointed to *Who's Who*, a volume with which we usually don't argue, and it said 1876. This was the official date; and there had, up to this time, been no way of absolute verification. Births in the 1870s in Frederick County in Virginia had been recorded in a haphazard manner, when they had been recorded at all. Vital statistics were reported at that time, it would seem, by the tax collector, I suppose the individual most concerned with capturing the living and writing off the dead. The first of Miss Cather's younger brothers was registered with the date of June 24, 1877; that was of some help; it established at any rate that Miss Cather could not have been born in December 1876—the Cather mother was hardly capable of the feat of bearing a daughter just before Christmas and a son six months later, in June. On the face of it therefore 1875 made sense. Nevertheless Brown's manuscript had to be respected until it could be proved wrong; due allowance made of course for a possible slip of the pen on his part. I promised Miss Lewis I would do my best to settle the matter. "Must you?" queried Miss Lewis, looking at me very straight. I felt that so far as she was concerned, the matter *was* settled.

It was some time before I found Brown's evidence. It lay in a box of papers dealing with Miss Cather's Virginia years. There I came on a photostat of a letter dated January 22, 1874. It was a legible, straight up and down hand, and I saw from the address and signature that it was written by Willa Cather's father from Virginia to his brother in Nebraska. This is what I read in the middle of the letter: "Jennie and I were at town today, the first time she has been out. We left the baby at home with its

Grandma; she is just as good as she is pretty. She is not old enough yet to have that picture taken. We call her Willie after our little sister." Mr. Cather's sister had been named Wilella and she had died some years before of diphtheria.

My first impulse was to question the date on technical grounds. January dates are always suspect. We tend to slip back into the previous year until we become accustomed to the new one. If there had been a slip it would mean Miss Cather had been born in 1872. But fortunately I did not have to speculate long, for I found a further letter, in the same box, from Miss Cather's cousin, Mrs. Blanche Cather Ray, to Professor Brown who had asked her to check her correspondence. She had discovered a letter from an old schoolmate to the Nebraska uncle which reported "Charley and Jennie are getting along splendidly. Charley don't get to Church till it is half out on account of having to rock the babe to sleep—that's the way of the world." This letter was dated February 1, 1874. The birth year seemed settled beyond dispute; and the documents gave us the original and well-concealed name of Wilella. I summarized this data in a letter to Miss Lewis. She accepted it without question and replied, "Mr. Cather's letter does seem to me conclusive evidence." But when I next saw her and raised the question of how to deal with the discrepant dates, her first words were, "She hated the name Wilella. She changed it after much reflection. She would be most unhappy to have that name revived. Professor Edel, is it really necessary to mention that name?" And she added in a voice that was almost a wail, "Miss Cather always said she was named after her uncle who was killed in the Civil War, William Lee Boak." I confessed that the name Wilella was of secondary importance to me. I was concerned with the exact birth year. Birth dates are usually where biographies begin; and if I accepted a date that did not fit the documentary evidence, the biography would be vulnerable.

I had some further thoughts, however. Miss Lewis needed time to absorb the shock of Wilella, this scraping off of a layer of legend. No immediate decision was necessary; I would think about the problem and find a proper way of handling it. With a sense of gained time, Miss Lewis then volunteered information she had not given me before. Miss Cather, she explained, had first changed her age in response to a joke made by Sam Mc-

Clure, her boss on *McClure's Magazine*. When she had become sufficiently famous to be included in *Who's Who* and was filling out the forms, he said to her: "Willa, let me give you some advice. Knock a year or two off your age—you'll be glad later on."

Imagine me, then, a few days after this in the New York Public Library with a pile of *Who's Who* issued during Miss Cather's lifetime in front of me. I had no difficulty finding her first entry in 1909. She had certainly taken McClure seriously; the birth year she gave was 1875, instead of 1873. The question now was how did it ultimately get to be 1876? My feeling was that I should continue to look at *Who's Who*, volume by volume, and follow Miss Cather down the years. A few volumes later, in 1919, when Miss Cather was in middle life and the world, as she said, "broke in two" for her, the birth date of 1875 was changed to 1876. And so it remained.*

Let me say that all this is not of the essence. I don't think I would have argued too hard with Miss Lewis about it but for the fact that I was rereading *Death Comes for the Archbishop*. I was reading my way through her novels chronologically in order to have them fresh in my mind. I had forgotten since my first reading many years before that one of the most delightful chapters in that novel is the tale of Doña Isabella. Most of you will remember how in the story the devout Antonio Olivares has built a fine house, over which his wife Isabella, and his daughter Inez, preside; and how Father Vaillant and Bishop Latour like to spend evenings there—evenings of music and talk, the life of the Old World grafted into the abundance and wealth of the New. When Antonio dies suddenly, he leaves his large fortune to Isabella and Inez, and after them—for he was deeply devout—to the Church. Antonio's brothers were more secular. They promptly got a lawyer to challenge the will. They based their case on the fact that Doña Isabella claimed she was in her forties, and that this meant her daughter would have had to be born when she was six or eight years old. At stake thus was not only the inheritance, but ultimately the benefaction intended for the Church. As I reread this chapter, I realized that

---

*The family Bible preserved in Red Cloud shows that the name Wilella was tampered with, and there had been some doctoring of the 1873 to convert it into 1876.

Miss Lewis and I had been acting out a scene from *Death Comes for the Archbishop*. In his talk with Doña Isabella the vicar is however more direct than I had been. " 'To prevent this outrage to your husband's memory,' " says Father Joseph, " 'you must satisfy the court that you are old enough to be the mother of Mademoiselle Inez.' " And then he adds, as if to help her out —but it sounds as if he is rubbing it in—" 'You must resolutely declare your true age; fifty-three is it not?' " (p. 190).

We remember how Doña Isabella becomes pale, how she shrinks into one end of the sofa, and her shriek " 'Fifty-three!' " She is indignant, enraged. " 'Why, I never heard of anything so outrageous. I was forty-two my last birth-day.' " (Let me insert in parenthesis that the real-life num-bers seem to have been running around in Miss Cather's mind—fifty-three for 1873 and the number forty-two—the two being the number of years Miss Cather had first knocked off her own age. Moreover, we discover that Doña Isabella's birthday also falls in December, Miss Cather's birth month. Doña Isabella you see is also a Sagittarius.) Bishop Latour, with his greater finesse, checks his impetuous vicar. His tone is a tone of compromise; he is experienced in the ways of feminine feeling. " 'Forty-two to your friends, dear Madame Olivares, and to the world. In heart and face you are younger than that. But to the Law and the Church there must be a literal reckoning. A formal statement in court will not make you any older to your friends; it will not add one line to your face.' " And the Bishop, in his quiet voice adds, " 'A woman, you know, is as old as she looks.' "

Doña Isabella listens and smiles through her tears. The words are encouraging. But she is firm. She would rather not have the money than testify that she is older than she is. The Bishop then tests her on a note of responsibility. She certainly is entitled to give up the money if she wishes, he says, but has she a right to make a beggar of her daughter? Doña Isabella reminds the Bishop that her daughter talks of going into a convent. And lapsing into French, the Bishop's mother tongue, she adds, " '*Ah, mon père, je voudrais mieux être jeune et mendiante, que n' être que vieille et riches, certes, oui!*' " Doña Isabella would sooner be young and a beggar than old and rich, decidedly. So at least she says.

195

As I had done with Miss Lewis, the Bishop lets the facts sink in. And after a while Doña Isabella has a second thought. " 'What is the youngest I could possibly be, to be Inez's mother?' " Her lawyer is ready with the answer: fifty-two would satisfy the needs of justice. The Bishop, leaving the distraught lady, remarks to his vicar, " 'I would rather do almost anything than go through such a scene again.' " Thus the little drama of Sam McClure, in the office of his magazine, and the *Who's Who* forms, is translated from a joke into witty comedy. And thus fiction and life strangely intermingle. The denouement is simple enough and it has a graceful curtain line: Doña Isabella goes to court; in a hushed whisper that only the judge can hear she gives her age as fifty-two. She wins the case and that night there is a great fiesta in the big house, music and song and dance. At the end of the evening, saying good-bye to her guests, Doña Isabella turns to the vicar and the Bishop and says: " 'I shall never forgive you, Father Joseph, nor you either, Bishop Latour, for that awful lie you made me tell in court about my age!' "

Here transformed in the most charming way with a great deal of humor and *savoir-faire* is Miss Cather's change of age. Apparently she felt some need to do something with it, perhaps get it out of her system. Her fundamental honesty, her Puritan conscience, had felt a touch of guilt; or perhaps, using an old theme, Miss Cather could arouse quiet laughter, in a sense laugh at her own little bit of vanity. I thought I had my data, but I found still more. Reading on, in chronological order, I came to the posthumous volume published by Mr. Knopf the year after Miss Cather's death, *The Old Beauty*. In it there is a tale called "The Best Years." It is about a young girl who graduates too young to get a job as teacher; so she *adds* two years to her age. When finally she confesses this deception to the lady who is superintendent of schools, and explains that she had also changed the high school records because " 'I didn't want to be the class baby,' " the lady takes the matter with a casualness that surprises the young girl. " 'If your age is wrong on both records,' " she says, " 'why do you tell me about it now?' " The girl replies that she has always felt guilty at breaking the law. The older woman rejoins, " 'There's nothing very dreadful

about it. You didn't give your age under oath, you know.' "
And she adds she can never be sure about the ages applicants
give; she has always used her judgment. " 'Some girls are older
at thirteen than others are at eighteen,' " she says (pp. 88–90).

It came to me, after reading these two episodes, with their
touch of equivocation, both churchly and legalistic, that the
wisest thing I could do would be to insert a footnote at the point
at which E. K. Brown gave Miss Cather's birth year as 1873, and
explain the discrepancy between that date and the official, the
graveyard date in New Hampshire. In this note I would link the
whole matter to Miss Cather's fiction. I worded it with caution
and you may read it in the book.[1] I also initialed it to make it
clear that it was my handiwork, not Brown's. Filled with the
bargaining spirit of Bishop Latour I brought it to Miss Lewis.
The question of Miss Cather's juggling of her age in *Who's Who*
I said was not important. What she did with it in her work
seemed to me at the heart of my biographical inquiry. Cultivat-
ing something of the manner of Bishop Latour, I also pointed
out that a judiciously worded footnote would unobtrusively
end idle speculation and cut short further discussion of the
subject. When Miss Lewis seemed to hesitate, I made my con-
ciliatory gesture, for I saw how much feeling was invested in
this matter. In plain words, I proposed some old-fashioned
horse-trading. I would forget about Wilella if she would accept
the footnote. After all, I said, Miss Cather remained Willa to all
the world—and, I added, surely everyone was entitled to be
called by the name of their choice. I at once regretted saying
this, because I thought Miss Lewis would reply that everyone is
entitled to be called by the age of their choice as well. She was
silent for several minutes: but the swap seemed to satisfy her.
Anything to avoid the revelation of the horrid name of Wilella.*
The small print of the footnote made the whole matter seem
parenthetical. It ministered to Miss Lewis's comfort. I was
happy that we had in this way resolved this irksome and em-
barrassing matter.

The documents notwithstanding, I note that Miss Lewis in

*Miss Lewis was perhaps unaware that the name Wilella had already ap-
peared in Mrs. Bennett's book. She seemed determined at any rate not to have it
appear (or reappear) in the biography. It is to be found, of course, in the latest
biography of the novelist, James Woodress, *Willa Cather: Her Life and Art* (1970).

her memoir stays with legend. Even though Miss Cather's father clearly wrote that Willa was named after "our little sister," Miss Lewis's text reads: "They named her Willa after . . . William Lee Boak, who was killed in the Civil War."[2] I checked the other day for the first time to see how Miss Lewis handled the age question. She avoided it. No birth year is mentioned, but several vaguenesses are permitted in her text. At one point Miss Lewis tells us Willa was "about thirty" in 1906 which would have meant a birth year of 1876. She is closer to the facts when she says that in 1883 Miss Cather was nine, in other words born in 1874. But a truce on these matters. At heart I agree with Miss Lewis: it is not the age that matters, it's the life—and the myth of the given life.

Let me add a personal note. I was touched in picking up the volume, to read again the inscription she wrote in the book after our celebration in the Village. "For Leon Edel, who would be a good comrade on any difficult undertaking." I could say now, as I look back to those months of work, to the way she read the proofs and checked everything and asked me to verify matters about which she had been vague, that *she* had been a delightful if sometimes difficult comrade in this difficult task, though my younger self were he here this evening might not agree with me.

I have dwelt on this real-life cautionary tale because it is at once a part of the delight of biography and a part of its serious responsibilities. Biography is a thoughtful process. It asks us to be judicial, so long as we do not sit in judgment on the subject. We do have to consider human reticence and man's innate need for privacy, so frequently violated today. I had to recognize also that biographical fact may point in one direction, while feelings point in another; a biographer dare not override feelings in too cavalier a fashion. Bishop Latour had shown great flexibility in Miss Cather's novel; so had the charming school superintendent. I do not believe Wilella's formal absence made the least difference to Brown's splendid portrait.

Look at Steichen's photograph of Miss Cather. She is in the prime of life. It captures her clear untroubled eyes facing directly into the camera, that is, looking directly at us; the repose of her shoulders and crossed arms; the simplicity of her garb

—the eternal middy blouse of those years, the loosely knotted tie that reminded Katherine Anne Porter of a girl-scout costume; and she noted that the hair was parted in ragged fashion: something loose, informal, easy about her aspect—something sisterly, or perhaps a maiden aunt; a hearty woman with hearty appetites.[3] No, Miss Cather must not be seen as anything like the frail lady novelists—say Emily Brontë—or the intellectual ones, George Eliot, or the passionate ones, George Sand. One feels that she would relish a good workout in the kitchen, a bit of gardening or even a game of golf quite as much as a stint at her writing desk. But never be misled by the appearance of writers. Max Beerbohm once asked a friend to join him and several writer friends at a certain bar, and he added words to the effect that the friend had simply to walk in and look for the most depressed faces in the room. Those would be the writers, Max said.

Miss Cather did not have the complexity of art in her; she was an exquisite painter of surfaces, and I think Rebecca West found an apt image when she spoke of the paintings by Velasquez which show tapestry-makers in the shadow "and some of their fellows working behind them in shadows honeycombed with golden motes, and others still further back working in the white wine of full sunlight." That could be a Cather scene. Miss West, in her brilliant essay on *Death Comes for the Archbishop*, said that Miss Cather was not unaware of the fissures in the solid ground of life, "but to be aware of them is not her task." And she went on to say that hers was "to move on the sunlit face of the earth, with the gracious amplitude of Ceres, bidding the soil yield richly, that the other kind of artist, who is like Persephone and must spend half his days in the world under the world, may be refreshed on emergence."[4] I find this a just as well as a subtle appreciation. The depths of the abyss are not in Miss Cather's work; and, unlike women writers both in America and England, love is not her primary subject. Her subject is the land, conquest, achievement, success, the primary finding and making of daily life, and then the elegy for things past. "To note an artist's limitations is but to define his talent," said Miss Cather in a memorable essay on Sarah Orne Jewett;[5] and when we call over to ourselves the list of her limitations we seem at the same time to be reciting, quite as she said, what was heroic and noble in her work. She believed in simplicity; she believed in directness. In her vigor, her zeal, her love of the work of human hands—and her hatred of the machines that deprive human hands of their function—I find myself wanting to place her with those hearty figures in Dutch and Flemish paintings, buoyant, drinking, eating, laughing, amid heaps of oysters, game, and flagons of wine. There is bright red in the cheeks and a kind of carefree clutching of the moment, an energetic hedonism. The passions of love are subsumed in the energies of the everyday task. One cannot associate Miss Cather with the impressionists, or the subjectivists. She doesn't know the meaning of chiaroscuro. When the new poetry was being created in our time by Pound and Eliot, she was admiring Housman and responding to Kipling. I doubt whether she would have warmed to Virginia Woolf: there is too much implied in Mrs. Woolf of the trouble that lies beneath surfaces, of the dark wood, the lost road. Mrs. Woolf however read Miss Cather; I find her in one of Mrs. Woolf's essays,[6] an admirable survey of the American fiction of her time. She remarks that there are now American writers—unlike Hawthorne or James—"who do not care a straw for English opinion or for English culture, and write very vigorously none the less—witness Mr. Lardner; there are Americans," she adds, "who have all the accomplishments of culture without a trace of its excess—witness Miss Willa Cather; there are Americans whose aim is to write a book off their own bat and no one else's—witness Miss Fannie Hurst." She goes on then to say that the shortest tour and most superficial inspection of American fiction offers the important fact "that where the land itself is so different, and the society so different, the literature must needs differ, and differ more and more widely as time goes by."

This suggestive observation needs to be applied to Miss Cather. It is one thing to speak of her devotion to Flaubert, or of her invoking other English and European writers, whom she certainly read, perhaps with more enthusiasm than critical objectivity; but her writing I find indeed free of that "excess of culture" of which Mrs. Woolf spoke: there is the landscape, and the sense of men and women moving within it: there is the plow against the sunset, the mesa, the prairie, the rock—and the characters who are held in the grip of soil and climate which they can either attempt to tame, as the Professor does by creating his little formal garden in alien surroundings, or else bow to its will and accept a kind of eternity of unremitting toil and adversity and the simple joys of fertility. This directness and plainness has great virtues, especially when we remember how suitable it was to the material of her stories. Lacking the complexity of modern art, she lacked also a sense of experiment. Even *The Professor's House*, which might be written down as experimental, turns back to glimpses of Dutch interiors and beyond, to the story within the story of Cervantes and the insets of Smollett. And yet I have always felt that this novel may have provided a hint to Virginia Woolf when she was writing *To the Lighthouse* for it possesses an analogous structure. But when we have pondered this, we have exhausted Miss Cather's inventiveness. Edmund Wilson went so far as to speak of her "anemia of the imagination"[7] and I think that the explicator of *Axel's Castle* found indeed that Miss Cather's art required little explaining. Still his praise for her, very early, will strike us as eminently fair and accurate. He wrote after reading *A Lost Lady* that Miss Cather was "one of the only writers who has been able to bring any real distinction to the life of the Middle West. Other writers have more enthusiasm or animation or color or humor, but Miss Cather is perhaps unique in her art of imposing a patina on that meager and sprawling scene." He found "exquisite pages of landscape" in her; he characterized her work as containing two currents of profound feeling, "one for the beauty of those lives lived out between the sky and the prairie; the other . . . for the pathos of the human spirit making the effort to send down its roots and to flower in that barren soil."[8] Of course the soil was not barren: Edmund knew New England better than the prairies.

I began by wanting to find Miss Cather's limitations and have strayed into her essential character. Certainly Miss Cather did not have the larger imagination; she had to attach herself to stories she had heard, people she had known, figures in history: that quality of using given material which belongs to her journalism and was carried over by her into her art. She had also in her writings—and I find this a serious limitation—a disagreeable vein of sadism, a kind of brutality and violence (as in the Aztec story interpolated irrelevantly in "Coming, Aphrodite!") which makes her readers shudder. This said, we must recognize that in her preserved sense of adolescent being, its mercurial moods, its heights of joy and depths of despair, she achieved a lyrical note and a simplicity of art that touches us deeply, even in its sentimentalities. She was a born story-teller. That is a great thing to be able to say of any writer. Her prose at its best contains a pulsing rhythm and distills a unique purity. I would celebrate her in particular for the unchangeable ideal of art reflected in her early writings. These show among her youthful dogmas the belief that culture is not an ornament in a wild land, but a crying need. She reminded us in another quotation from Virgil, that she was the first to woo the muse in this land, *Primus ego in patriam mecum . . . deducam Musas*. She wooed the muse, and the muse answered not in sylvan garb or in classical draperies, but decked in the prairie's wild roses, doubtless mixed with a few dandelions, and carrying a cornucopia of grains and a great deal of native corn. But that muse had mixed up in her bag also European memories, memories that went back hundreds of years, pleasant memories. In this kind of fusion, and with early memories of the South, Miss Cather embodied a great deal of pioneer feeling, the democratic desire of Americans transplanted, whether from the East or South, or from Europe, to create new worlds and to succeed in life; and strangely enough success was enshrined by Miss Cather more in the performing arts than in the difficult art she practiced. The artist as performer interested her most; such persons act out their talent and discipline, in a very concrete way. Their careers require neither reflection nor meditation. Miss Cather always was a writer of "success" stories; we remember *The Song of the Lark*, for example. But success is a limited subject. In her prairie tales, which are also success stories, she expresses more than the drive to power; she feels deeply what it means to be uprooted and to go in quest of new roots in a new land carrying a few household gods and certain memories of a life that can never be relived. Her own migration at a tender age from Virginia to the Divide made her aware of things lost, of the poetry of absence, that provided the elegiac note and the lyricism in her melancholy. "Life began for me when I ceased to admire and began to remember," she once said.[9] Beyond these experiences of her childhood and youth, she possessed what I can only describe as a large human reach: her curiosity about people, her love of anecdote, her craving for detail, her way of cross-examining friends and neighbors about their lives and adventures—how things are done and what was the recipe. Within all this, within the frame of success, the quest for new roots for the uprooted, the sense of finding and making, was her strong masculine drive to conquest. She was a woman who early had to make her peace with a man's world, especially among her brothers, and within the extreme masculinity of the frontier. In recording the dramas of the frontier, she spoke with a voice so authentic that it holds us still, even in its most contrived moments. And then we remember her later phase, her despair at the way in which the pioneer's handiwork was exploited by the middleman, the still-present rape of the land; this will remain beyond the era of a school of fiction addicted to cinema-violence and television immediacy. If ever the printed word is able to assert itself against the crushing visuality of the camera, we will be able to feel once more Miss Cather's human drama of the quest for civilization as against the voice of an achieved society, and the story of its ultimate corruption in America. I suspect Willa Cather will retain this modest place, and I do not diminish her role by calling it modest, in the American literature of our century. For within her tales she is also highly documentary, in the way in which novelists become historians, as Balzac told us long ago. Her repudiation of that master in her essay on the *roman démeublé** was simply a way of asserting her own need to deal with the smaller provinces of life.

Miss Cather clung to the rock as "the utmost expression of human need" and I long ago suggested this was indeed to reduce human needs to stratification. Her quest, in the flux of life, was for the durable, the unyielding, the steadfast; she was a creature of old and fixed habits and she could not swim with the stream. This made for deep loyalties and abiding affections. It also tended to dry up the fount of her inspiration; there was no sustenance in the present. But there was in her stubbornness and pride and in her immovable and monumental being, a classical American individualism. If this sometimes diminished

*I prefer to translate this as "the disfurnished novel" rather than the "unfurnished."

her work, it gave strength to her voice which calls to us even now across the wide land over which the jumbo jets fly. It is the voice of stillness, the voice of the old unravaged prairie and the human spirit. She possessed, as E. K. Brown said, "the power of the picture, the power of symbol, the power of structure, the power of style." This power speaks to us in Tom Outland's passion for the life of the ancient cliff dwellers in the South-west, or in the courage of the French missionaries of *Death Comes for the Archbishop*. Reading words of Thymokles in Meleager's *Garland* the other day I came upon certain apposite lines; it seemed to me that thousands of years ago he sketched an archetypal artist and the classic art to be found in the elegies of Willa Cather:

> *Springtime is loveliest, time most elusive,*
> *Quicker than the quickest bird in the sky,*
> Look, your blossoms
> all scattered on the earth.[10]

And since we look to the East as well as the West tonight, I might borrow another epigraph for our occasion from Sei Shonogon's *Pillow Book:*

> Things which pass
> a sailboat
> the years of a life
> spring, summer, autumn, winter.[11]

These elegies by other hands I read in homage to Willa Cather, writer of elegies, for whom there was always anguish in the things which pass, and in their passing. These words out of remote time help us express what she was: and what she will remain:

> Look, your blossoms
> all scattered on the earth.

[*Reference notes appear on page 264.*]

Miss Cather

Alfred A. Knopf

Until the autumn of 1918 I had never heard of Willa Cather (or
Willa Sibert Cather, or Willa S. Cather, as she variously signed
herself), much less read anything by her. Like tens of thousands
of other Americans I was home recuperating from the influenza
that was epidemic (we had just moved from Hartsdale in
Westchester to West Ninety-fifth Street), when one day I was
attracted by an oddly dignified advertisement of Houghton
Mifflin's for a new novel, *My Ántonia*, which I read with great
enjoyment and admiration although I had never been west of
the Missouri.

About a year later, there happened to me the sort of thing a
publisher dreams about but doesn't often experience. Willa
Cather just walked in, unannounced, to our small offices in the
Candler Building on West Forty-second Street. Even more
amazing, perhaps, she expressed surprise when she learned
that I knew her work. She liked the kind of advertising we were
doing—it must have been on a very small scale, because we
were very small publishers in those days—and I'd been given a
good character, although he had never met me, by the husband
of her closest friend.* Out of this first meeting there developed

*This was Jan Hambourg, the violinist brother of Mark, a pianist well known
in England and abroad (but not in the United States), and Boris, a cellist. Jan
had married Isabelle McClung, daughter of the Pittsburgh judge before whom
Alexander Berkman was brought after his attempted assassination of Henry C.
Frick. Miss Cather met the McClung family when she was on the staff of the
Pittsburgh *Leader*, and indeed lived for some time with them.

205

a relationship that was unique in my experience. From small beginnings it grew into something so close that to the day of her death some twenty-seven years later, we never wavered in our respect and affection for each other.

On February 1, 1920, we made a contract with Willa Cather for *Youth and the Bright Medusa*. Later I told her that I had done something unusual when I accepted a collection of short stories without asking for any commitment to us of her future work. She replied that while she felt obliged to give her next book, a novel, to Houghton Mifflin, I would certainly become her publisher after that. But she never went back to the Boston house. One evening at a party at our home she took me into our bedroom and handed me a letter to read. It was from Ferris Greenslet, the partner and senior editor at Houghton Mifflin with whom she dealt, and it acknowledged a letter from her in which she told him she had decided to come over to us.

The new novel was *One of Ours*, first called *Claude*—a most unattractive title. As late as August 1921 she wrote me at length defending *Claude* and insisting on its use. But shortly thereafter she wrote from Nebraska that a long talk with her friend, and mine, Fanny Butcher of the *Chicago Tribune*, had shaken her and that she was satisfied to call the book *One of Ours*. At the same time she decided to drop the Sibert and the middle initial, S, from her name except in signing checks.

She was greatly concerned that no word should get abroad in advance of its publication that this novel touched on the war at all; she wanted it to be regarded as the story of a boy's life and said that anything else was secondary. Through all her correspondence at this time ran requests for my opinion of the manuscript as I read it, and when I wired her enthusiastically about it, adding "I shall be proud to have my name associated with it," she, with characteristic modesty, thanked me and even added that I had taken a load off her mind.

In October Paul R. Reynolds, the dean of American literary agents, wrote me that a publisher had told him that there was no reason why Cather's work shouldn't be as well known as that of Edith Wharton and that he would like a chance to make it that well known. Reynolds asked if Miss Cather would not like to meet this publisher. Nothing came of this, for when I sent Miss Cather the letter she returned it to me after writing across it, "I wonder who?"

Alfred A. Knopf

We tried to sell the serial rights in *One or Ours* to all the big magazines including the *Saturday Evening Post*, then edited by the great—and I mean great—George Horace Lorimer, who would have none of it. Blanche and I came to know Lorimer in a friendly way through Joseph Hergesheimer, and always called on him at his office when we were in Philadelphia. As Hergesheimer lived in West Chester, Pennsylvania, and you had to go to Philadelphia on your way to visit him, these calls were rather frequent. Lorimer had bought Joe's first story and virtually supported him in the years of his lush and extravagant living, but he told me once that Joe was "the icing on the cake," and I suspect he felt his cake could stand but one "icing." True, he also supported Thomas Beer regally for years, but Tom's stories, good as they were, had a very wide following among readers of the *Post*.

To get back to *One of Ours*. We published it in March 1922. Miss Cather was interested in our advance orders and hoped they would come to something between eight and ten thousand copies. We printed fifteen thousand, our advance came to about twelve thousand, and we went to press immediately with another ten. This pleased her greatly and she wrote that she hoped we wouldn't get stuck with overstock and that such an expression of faith in her book ought to impress booksellers.

In September I wrote her that it seemed to me too soon to run any advertising that would make it clear that *One of Ours* was a war novel. "Now at any rate we must advertise it as a fine novel and leave it to its opponents to emphasize the war aspect of the book." Late in the year she wrote me that it helped to publish with people who can like a thing for what it is and not worry because it hasn't the Rex Beach quality.

Meanwhile she had finished *A Lost Lady*. Apparently she felt it was too short to make a book and should be published together with some other stories, for I wrote her after reading it: "Mrs. Knopf and I both agree that you ought to be restrained by law, if necessary, from publishing this book, with anything else. It belongs alone, exactly as 'Ethan Frome' belongs, alone, and you are very unjust to it and to yourself, I think, for feeling otherwise." She asked us to try to sell it to a magazine that would pay well, because she needed a really competent secretary which she could not afford. Blanche did finally sell *A Lost Lady* to the *Century*, then edited by Glenn Frank, who later

207

became president of the University of Wisconsin. We published the book in February 1923 and did very well indeed with it.

Blanche and I sailed for England early in 1923 and so for the first time my father dealt with Miss Cather and his first letter to her accompanied the contract for *A Lost Lady*. She was planning a trip abroad and by mid-March S. K., as he was usually called, was offering her his help and that of our customs broker, advised her how best to get her baggage to the pier, and took care of getting a typewriter sent to her in Paris.

In May *One of Ours* was awarded the Pulitzer Prize. Miss Cather was at Ville d'Avray, near Paris, at the time, staying with her old friends the Hambourgs. She was delighted with the news and wondered who the judges were. She said that if William Lyon Phelps had been one (he wasn't) the prize would never have been awarded to her. She also wrote me that Houghton Mifflin had sold three thousand copies of *My Ántonia* in the previous six months. Her chariot was indeed beginning to roll. In 1923 her books on our list alone earned her nearly $20,000.

Miss Cather had gone back to Nebraska the Christmas before—presumably to Red Cloud—for her parents' golden wedding anniversary. All her sisters and brothers were there. She said she got more thrills out of this cornfield country than she could get from any other country in the world. Her parents were absurdly young, drove a hundred miles any day, and would not be tired the next.

An amusing note: Early in 1923 the North American Newspaper Alliance (better known as NANA) planned to run a feature, "Which Ten Books Have You Enjoyed the Most?" We were asked to pass this invitation along to Miss Cather and to ask her to address her reply directly to M. Lincoln Schuster, 250 West Fifty-second Street. He was a partner in the publishing firm of Simon & Schuster. I doubt very much that she replied.

In 1923 we also published a revised and enlarged edition of her only volume of verse, *April Twilights*. This had first appeared in 1903 over the imprint of Richard Badger in Boston, a firm that would nowadays be regarded as a vanity publisher. Our first edition comprised only 450 copies, designed and printed by that master craftsman Elmer Adler of Pynson Printers fame, all signed by the author. In the gorgeous days of the twenties there was a lively demand among collectors for limited first editions of the better authors. So of *One of Ours* we printed 35 copies on Imperial Japan Vellum and 310 on handmade Italian paper; of *A Lost Lady*, 220 copies on a specially made all-rag paper that bore the Borzoi watermark.

In 1924 Miss Cather wrote an introduction for our reissue of Defoe's *The Fortunate Mistress* in the Borzoi Classics, a series long forgotten but which was quite popular in the twenties. Others who wrote introductions for those rather handsome volumes were: Carl Van Doren, Havelock Ellis, Arthur Machen, Wilbur L. Cross, Burton Rascoe, Ernest Boyd, and H. L. Mencken.

In 1925 Miss Cather for the first and only time permitted a motion picture to be made from one of her books—Warner Brothers' silent film of *A Lost Lady*. That year we published *The Professor's House*, the first of her novels that gave full expression to her love of the Southwest. It sold well and this delighted her. She spent part of the summer in Santa Fé, no doubt brooding over Archbishop Lamy and his story. In the fall she was back at another favorite spot, the Shattuck Inn in Jaffrey, New Hampshire, where much of her best work was done.

Next year we published another short novel, *My Mortal Enemy*. The first edition consisted of only 220 copies, of which 20 were not for sale. The entire format was designed by W. A. Dwiggins, and the books (printed on handmade paper) were made by the Pynson Printers of New York. Each copy was signed by the author. Of the regular edition we made a first printing of ten thousand copies. Miss Cather regarded this story as exceptional. It meant a great deal to her, and the reviews—and this was to happen over and over again—disappointed her. She told us that many of the reviewers simply didn't know what the book was about. Indeed, she even wrote out an advertisement for us in which she quoted Fanny Butcher, and asked us to run it several times, especially in the *New York Times Book Review*.

Early in 1926 she brought me the manuscript of *Death Comes for the Archbishop*. Paul Reynolds sold it as a serial to the *Forum*, then edited by Henry Goddard Leach. This was the only time, to my knowledge, that she used an agent. I think she cared more for Archbishop Lamy's story than for any other book of

hers we published. She never asked for an advance and, I feel
certain, would have regarded publishers who offered them (all
publishers did and do) and authors who accepted them as
equally immoral. But she knew the worth of this new novel
and, remarking that our son would some day be paying royalties on it to her niece, she asked for special terms: an increase of
one percent over the customary maximum 15 percent which we
had always paid her. She never again asked for the higher rate
or accepted it when we offered to pay it.

By mid-September 1927 *The Archbishop*, as we came to call it,
had been out for a month and had sold nearly thirty thousand
copies. Miss Cather followed the reviews and our advertising
carefully and was pleased with neither. She thought the quotes
we were using dull and uninteresting. So again she made up an
advertisement for us to use. But in November she was still
unhappy about the reviews and by mid-December, when the
sales had passed fifty thousand copies, she complained for the
first and only time about the amount of advertising we were
doing (and I must say with justice) and about the failure of
friends to find the book in stock when they tried to buy it.
Many of the complaints came from people in smaller towns and
cities, where bookshops usually bought from wholesalers
rather than direct from publishers. So it is amusing to recall that
the second largest of these jobbers, the Baker and Taylor Company, cut their original order for five thousand copies in half
after reading the book!

Miss Cather had given up her old home on Bank Street in
September 1927. When in New York she stayed at the Gros-
venor on lower Fifth Avenue. Later she moved to an apartment
on Park Avenue. It was unlike any Park Avenue apartment I
have ever seen. In the rear of the building—away from the
bustle of the avenue and even from the cross-town street—it
was a quiet and comfortable retreat which suited her perfectly.
She never moved again, though she bought a summer home on
the island of Grand Manan, in the Bay of Fundy. She visited
Jaffrey regularly, and once while she was there wrote me that
she was walking six or eight miles a day and doing nothing
else. It was in 1927, too, I think, that she took a long horseback
trip through the Big Horn Mountains in Wyoming. She worked
slowly, and we had no new manuscript from her in 1928, '29,
and '30.

Alfred A. Knopf

At its commencement in 1929 Yale gave her an honorary degree, and by October she had begun calling me "Alfred." But *we* never called her anything but Miss Cather, and I cannot say why. Somehow it just didn't seem fitting (note that all Thomas Mann's friends called him "Tommy"), and after her death even her close friend and trustee Edith Lewis always spoke and wrote to me about *Miss* Cather.

She was very enthusiastic about the wrapper which Harold Von Schmidt had made for *The Archbishop*, and in 1929 we brought out a newly designed and reset edition with illustrations by this artist, who has since become famous in the Southwest. Blanche and I were abroad when copy was prepared for the wrapper of this edition. It outraged her and she was more upset by it than I ever knew her to be in her dealings with us. But she was right again, for writing the copy had somehow been assigned to a young and inexperienced editorial assistant. So once more she sent us copy and instructed us to print exactly what she gave us. Though she never said so right out, I have always suspected the hand of her friend Edith Lewis in much of the copy about her books that she supplied from time to time, for Miss Lewis was an important copy writer in that great American advertising agency, J. Walter Thompson. Miss Cather said, wisely, that a wrapper should tell the public what they want to know—something about how and why a book was written since that, she said, is what novelists get letters about.

Also in 1929 she allowed my very capable secretary Manley Aaron to lease *Death Comes for the Archbishop* to the Modern Library, but when this contract expired she refused to permit us to renew it. She never wanted any kind of cheaper editions of her books. She felt that they would be used in schools and colleges and that boys and girls would grow up hating her because they had been compelled to read her. At this time, too, Warner Brothers was trying to secure the sound rights in *A Lost Lady*. She was willing, provided that the only use they made of her name would be to state that the picture had been "adapted from the novel of that name by Willa Cather." They would have to agree to this in writing and agree, too, to use that same phrase in all their advertising. She did not wish her name attached to dialogue written by a person or persons unknown to her. But by now she used to say that if she had wanted a motion picture she would have written a motion picture scenario. She

211

didn't, and she hadn't, and that was that. I remember our dear friend and long-time lawyer Benjamin H. Stern (he also drew Miss Cather's will) telling me in his office one day that he had an offer from Hollywood for her that ran into six figures. Ben's office was on the thirty-fifth floor of the French Building, and I told him that I would as soon jump out the window as even mention this offer to Miss Cather. I added that I thought if he wished to retain her good will he should not mention it to her either. He didn't. And of course she felt the same way about any dramatization of her works. I suppose that some day in the far-off future when her copyrights have expired *A Lost Lady* will be made into whatever will then be the equivalent of a Broadway musical.

Meanwhile she was working on her next great novel, *Shadows on the Rock*, which, like *Death Comes for the Archbishop*, drew on the history of the Roman Catholic Church in the New World. But when through a Catholic attorney in California (where she was staying to be near her ailing mother) she discovered some troublesome errors in the page proof she said that with this book she would bid adieu to Rome—that otherwise our good production man, George Stimson, and I would have to become converts to keep her out of trouble.

Miss Cather was also opposed to book clubs, for she felt most strongly that she wanted only people who really *wanted* to read her books to have them. She was an old, old friend of Dorothy Canfield Fisher—they had first met when Miss Cather was an undergraduate at the University of Nebraska—and Mrs. Fisher was one of the judges of the Book-of-the-Month Club. Harry Scherman, head of the club, with that shrewdness which was by no means uncharacteristic of him, had Dorothy write Miss Cather a long and eloquent letter explaining and defending the club's policies and practices. She brought this letter to me and asked my advice, for she was reluctant to offend Henry Seidel Canby, chairman of the judges and himself a distinguished critic.

The booksellers were waging a constant verbal war against the book clubs. I sympathized with and respected Miss Cather's point of view, and indeed I felt that the fact that her books were not available to any of the clubs helped their sales in the stores. But I decided to let a few booksellers answer the question she was asking me. We wired each of our salesmen, instructing each to ask the most important account he called on that day whether we should sell Miss Cather's new novel *Shadows on the Rock* to the Book-of-the-Month Club. All but one urged us to do so, saying a BOMC selection would mean increased sales in their stores; and since the one who objected spoke for a comparatively unimportant department store it was apparent that Mr. Scherman's maneuver had succeeded. And indeed it turned out that *Shadows on the Rock* had the largest sale of any novel by Miss Cather published by us: over 183,000 copies through 1963. But then I should not really have been surprised, for I had grown used on my visits to stores in the Middle West to hearing the proprietor inveigh against the book clubs while he displayed generously and conspicuously the current selections of the Book-of-the-Month Club and the Literary· Guild, the two leading clubs of the time.

Shadows on the Rock started off with an advance sale, exclusive of book club editions, of fifty-five thousand copies. By late August ten thousand more had been sold, and I wrote Miss Cather: "I am glad you feel as I do about the New York reviews. I am pretty sure that it has taken the better part of four years for most of these people to become convinced of the greatness of 'The Archbishop'. I suppose when your next novel comes out they will be writing what a grand novel 'Shadows on the Rock' was."

She had written me that the New York reviews had not disturbed her and recalled that when *The Archbishop* came out the reviews, with few exceptions, were very nasty. I wrote her that unless she strongly disapproved it was my intention to ignore the critics entirely in our advertising: "You and the book are both so much bigger than any of the critics that I think we will do the best job by being high-hat and continuing to put little more in our advertising than the announcement your new novel is now ready." She told me that the worst reviews she ever had were of *My Ántonia*—that in the whole country there were only three enthusiastic ones. She said the reviewers really liked only *Youth and the Bright Medusa* and *A Lost Lady*. But of course *Shadows on the Rock* did get some very favorable notices, especially those by Governor Wilbur L. Cross of Connecticut (earlier a *very* distinguished professor at Yale), the ever discerning Fanny Butcher, the *Atlantic*, and the *San Francisco Chronicle*. By early September the sale of *Shadows* had passed seventy-four thousand.

At about this time Miss Cather sent me two new stories which she asked me to read *as a favor*. These were "Two Friends," which she regarded as the best short story she had ever written, and "Old Mrs. Harris." Later Miss Aaron sold "Old Mrs. Harris" to the *Ladies' Home Journal* as a three-part serial for $15,000, and "Two Friends" to the *Woman's Home Companion*, which was edited by Miss Cather's old friend Gertrude Lane, for $3,500. And this was in the midst of the depression!

Her mother had died in Pasadena on August 30, 1931, and by mid-December Miss Cather was back in Red Cloud in her parents' home and with her mother's maid. I wrote her that this promised to be the dreariest Christmas ever and that she was lucky to be away from New York. "There just isn't, generally speaking, any Christmas business this year, but despite it all, 'Shadows' continues on its way. It hasn't quite reached one hundred and fifteen thousand, but doubtless will cross that figure before Christmas eve."

Early in 1932 the Frigidaire Corporation sponsored a broadcasting program that would be devoted to the discussion of women's names. Miss Cather was asked permission for the use of the following: "Willa Cather, the famous Nebraska novelist, is the only person I have ever met bearing the name Willa. I presume it is a contraction of Wilhelmina or just a feminization of William. But it's an attractive name." She told us to inform the gentleman that she did not and never would give him permission to use her name.

That midsummer we published *Obscure Destinies* in a first printing of twenty-five thousand copies. A few days before publication I told Miss Cather that I thought we would have an advance sale of over fifteen thousand. It turned out to be just over nineteen thousand. When the reviews began to come in, I wrote her that "on the whole reviews become less and less important except as selling instruments. And the only review that seems able to sell a lot of books is a front-page enthusiastic one in the *New York Times Book Review*." Before the end of September we had sold over thirty thousand. Incidentally, at about this time George Stimson, our production manager, wrote her:

214

Alfred A. Knopf

"One of the durable satisfactions in my particular life is that of serving you. The rest is silence." That gives an indication of how people in our organization felt about her.

In November Scribner's proposed to do a subscription edition of her works—not more than a thousand sets of ten or twelve volumes, the first volume of each set to be signed by her. Nothing came of this as Houghton Mifflin, who had a subscription department of their own, refused to allow Scribner's the use of their titles. Later on, the Boston firm did bring out a very beautiful set designed by that great typographer Bruce Rogers. Miss Cather was not keen about it, and seemed to take a genuine satisfaction in the failure of the set to do very well, though I think it has since become a collector's item.

In December 1932 Miss Cather moved to what became her permanent home, the apartment at 570 Park Avenue which she shared with Edith Lewis.

Late in October 1933 she wrote Blanche that she had just finished the first draft of *Lucy Gayheart.* She said it would take a hard winter's work to finish the book and counted on us to continue, as she put it, to keep the dogs off her—meaning, of course, demanding people whom she didn't want to see. Sometimes I think that perhaps the greatest service I rendered her —apart from publishing her books and promoting them in a way that pleased her—was my zealous regard for her desire for privacy. This of course is always difficult in the case of a popular writer, and I believe that anyone who abhors contact with members of the public is best advised not to produce work which has public interest. She never quite realized how widely known, admired, and respected she was, and how many people were eager at least to shake her hand. Thus she resented the fact that she could not sit on a bench in Central Park for long before being recognized and spoken to by strangers; and when she returned on a visit to Winchester, Virginia, in the spring of 1938, she registered at the hotel under an assumed name and tried to disguise herself by wearing dark glasses. This was difficult in a place where a good many Cathers were still listed in the local telephone directory.

By this time our treasurer, Joseph Lesser, was handling all of her federal and state income tax returns and payments. She made out checks in accordance with his instructions and then sent them to him for mailing. The Ryerson Press, then our

Canadian agents, proposed manufacturing an edition of *Shadows on the Rock* to retail at one dollar. Miss Cather refused to allow it.

She continued her interest in the design of her books —typography and wrappers, that is, for the binding had become uniform: a green cloth with labels designed by Dwiggins. When I wrote her that we had worked long and hard over *Lucy Gayheart* and sent her a sample page, she did not approve it. She felt that the type was too large and monotonous, and explained her feelings at length. She had wanted *Death Comes for the Archbishop* to look a little as if it had been printed on a country press, an impression that she did not want *Lucy Gayheart* to give. She said that if I would meet her wishes—how she could even have imagined that I mightn't I don't know—she'd write me another romantic story that would be even better than *Lucy Gayheart*. She even wrote Blanche saying how good we were to consider her preferences.

Later CBS, apparently in conjunction with BBC, telegraphed her about a broadcast. She asked me whether this was a compliment or an attempt to get something for nothing. I wrote her that I thought it might be a bit of both, but even if she were to receive a fee I advised her to refuse, which she did.

In July 1935 an agent approached her on behalf of a client who wished to dramatize *Death Comes for the Archbishop*. We replied that "on no account does Miss Cather permit dramatization of any of her books, and Mr. Knopf also would refuse to grant his permission . . . . neither Miss Cather nor Mr. Knopf is willing to have her books presented in this way." Late in July I wrote her that my brother Edwin at MGM said that they were interested in *Lucy Gayheart* and wanted to see proofs or an advance copy. "I told him that you would not be interested in any sale of motion picture rights." But on July 31 I wrote her that "a Mr. Samuel Marx, head of their scenario department, telephoned me from California and I did my best for you. I told him that you were not interested in any sale, that you were just about to leave the country, and I could vouch no sale would be made to any other company while you were away. He asked if you had an agent and I said you did your business direct with me. He said further that he thinks the book has great motion picture possibilities, that no one could do it as well as Metro Goldwyn Mayer and that no one could play Lucy so well as

Norma Shearer. That it was unfair for you to judge the company's standards of today by what Warners' did several years ago with 'A Lost Lady' . . . . I shall continue to assume that you do not want to do any business with any motion picture producer."

Miss Cather was traveling in Italy at this time. I wrote her in late August that "Lucy pursues the even tenor of her way —without benefit, as usual, of the reviews." Next month when the sale had passed just over forty-seven thousand I wrote, "I hope you don't read many of the American reviews—vicious is the only word to be applied to most of them. I almost wish we had sent out no copies of the book for review at all." Later that year Sigrid Undset told me that her publishers, Nygaard, were going to do *Lucy* in Norway and that her sister was to do the translation.

Nineteen thirty-eight was an uneventful year. I had become friendly with a Westchester neighbor, Professor W. L. Westermann of Columbia University. He had known Miss Cather in the old Nebraska days, but had lost all touch with her. It gave me great pleasure to bring these old friends together in Miss Cather's apartment. Their talk became so private and personal that I soon left them.

She was having trouble with the French translation of *Death Comes for the Archbishop*, though the publisher, Stock, interestingly enough employed Mme Marguerite Yourcenar, whose *Hadrian's Memoirs*, published years later, was such a distinguished success, to do it. Miss Cather found the translation unsatisfactory, and there was apparently very little meeting of minds when the two ladies saw each other. Early in 1939 W. A. Bradley* died and his widow, Jenny, decided to carry on their literary agency, which she has done brilliantly ever since. Mrs. Bradley and Miss Cather agreed that still another French translation of *The Archbishop* was very bad indeed.

It was in this year that Vernon Loggins stated in his *I Hear*

*Bie, as he was always known to his friends, came to me right after the first World War with a letter of introduction from Electus Litchfield, a distinguished architect whom my father had employed to design some houses which he and several friends built in Jamaica, Long Island, as a speculation. They were before their time: the Long Island Railroad delayed the construction of its new station in Jamaica, and the houses were much too superior for the class of people who might have been expected to buy them. The result was disastrous for all who had invested in the development.

America that Miss Cather had recently entered the Catholic Church. This was untrue (although many readers of *The Archbishop* and *Shadows on the Rock* were quite prepared to believe it), and caused her and us considerable embarrassment, since no denial of a statement of this kind ever catches up with the statement itself. Robert Crowell, Loggins's publisher, behaved extremely well and did what he could to help, but Mr. Loggins, despite our protests, kept silent for a long time. Finally, in late March of 1940, he wrote to me that the source of his information was a literary agent whose name he was unwilling to disclose as "she could not possibly have started the rumor" and could not recall from whom or under what circumstances she had heard it. We had finally to send out a publicity release stating that Miss Cather was a communicant and active member of the Episcopal Church.

Meanwhile the question of the use of her work in anthologies came up with increasing frequency. She made it clear that she was never willing to have any but a very tiny selection from her published writings reprinted in any anthology, and when in 1940 the L. W. Singer Company wanted to include *Death Comes for the Archbishop* in an anthology intended for high school students, we told Mr. Singer that she would never consent to the use of any important work of hers in any anthology intended for the use of schools and colleges. She even refused a request of Archibald MacLeish, then Librarian of Congress, to record for the use of the blind some of her books (many had of course already been produced in Braille). She felt after listening to several recordings of fiction that these often misrepresented the writer, that plain statements were often much ornamented by the reader in ways which it was clear the writer of the book did not intend.

Another Hollywood agent wanted to have prepared at his own expense a screen treatment of *Death Comes for the Archbishop* for submission to Miss Cather. At her request I wrote him asking him not to do any such thing.

On September 3, 1940, Sigrid Undset and her son, who had escaped from occupied Norway, reached New York by way of Siberia, Japan, and San Francisco. Mrs. Undset was very eager to meet Miss Cather, whose work she greatly admired, and I soon brought this about. The two ladies had much in common and became very good friends.

Alfred A. Knopf

Motion picture people continued to pursue her and we had to inform a representative of MCA that she would under no circumstances meet him to discuss the utilization of her work for motion pictures.

Later that year I had a letter from Charles G. Burlingham, the grand old man of the New York bar: "I have just finished 'Sapphira and the Slave Girl', non sine lacrimis. You may well be proud to be the publisher of such a book . . . what a marvelous book it is."

Nineteen forty-one was uneventful, but early in '42 another gentleman from the motion picture world argued with Miss Cather that in book form *The Archbishop* "could reach so few people who would enjoy it." So we checked our sale and found that it had just passed 178,000. It had reached quite a good many people. In mid-1943 the agent Jacques Chambrun approached Miss Cather indirectly with a proposal that "would involve the sum of roughly $100,000." She was not interested and did not even ask what the proposal was for. Later, Whit Burnett, who was working on still another anthology—"of religious experience written by outstanding world authors"—asked her for the use of at least part of *The Archbishop*. She wrote me that she wouldn't want him to use any of her novel at any price. Later Dent in Canada wanted to include *Shadows on the Rock* in a new series of English literature texts for pupils in secondary schools. I wrote them that Miss Cather never allowed any of her books to appear in text editions for school use.

That summer she settled for a time at the Asticou Inn at Northeast Harbor, Maine, another place to which she became very devoted.

Next year she received a medal from the National Institute of Arts and Letters, though she had already—I think thirteen years earlier—received a gold medal from the Academy. This was the Howells Medal, which was awarded every five years. Governor Cross had taken her to the Hall on that occasion and she had enjoyed herself. It was also in 1944 that a Canadian lady representing "The Committee on Missionary Education of the United Church of Canada," without a by your leave made a condensation of two chapters of *Shadows on the Rock*. We informed her that neither we nor Miss Cather ever permitted any condensation of, or extract from, her books to be published.

She was following the war with great concern, for she was an inveterate Francophile. She was particularly impressed by Joseph Kessel's *Army of Shadows*, which Blanche had bought in 1943, and I think for the first and only time gave us a blurb to use in advertising. Eisenhower had publicly acknowledged the assistance rendered the invasion of France by the Maquis. Miss Cather said that in many western cities where *Army of Shadows* ought to be read, the word *Maquis* would mean nothing, that all middle westerners hate foreign words, especially French, because they are uncertain how to pronounce them. Of *Army of Shadows* she wrote: "Congratulations on your good fortune in securing Kessel's 'Army of Shadows'. Here at last is a book that tells us *how the French underground worked*; incident by incident, sacrifice by sacrifice. The courage and constancy (and the resourcefulness) of all the unconquered and un-bought people of France—this Russian has found a way to bring it all before one's eyes. If this book is made into a film it will surely stir the country."

Nineteen forty-five was uneventful, but in '46 Miss Cather was worrying about the use of her work on the radio. I had to write her that "anyone can read you verbatim over the radio with or without your consent. But they cannot adapt or dramatize what you have written."* She refused to have a *Portable Willa Cather* published by Viking. At the time I wrote her, "I feel as you do about anthologies, too, but we have had to go into the field ourselves to some extent. You would be amazed at how many authors who ought to know better feel actually flattered when they are included in an anthology, and often write the publisher warning him not to charge too large a fee for fear the editor will use something else instead."

Next January Greenslet was again writing to "my dear Willa," this time about a motion picture offer for *The Song of the Lark* which would bring as her share somewhere between forty and fifty thousand dollars. While he said he knew she hated all ideas for motion picture productions of her novels he asked her to think this over. In reply she asked him to do everything he possibly could to discourage the project, adding that the money offered meant absolutely nothing to her. It is true that by this time she was prosperous, and since she never lived extrava-

*In 1952 the Copyright Law was amended to make a public reading for profit on a non-dramatic work an infringement of copyright.

gantly had all the money she needed. But she arrived at this happy condition relatively late in life, and all those young people who always tell you that Willa Cather could afford to take the "noble" attitude she did toward all subsidiary income from her books because she was wealthy, simply do not know the facts. But she was unreasonable to expect her earlier publishers to see things as she did. After all, they controlled the motion picture rights in *The Song of the Lark* and had a financial stake in any sale of such rights. However, Greenslet wrote her that "all of us here fully understand and appreciate your feeling. . . . we are prepared, *for the present at least*, not to urge you further in the matter of a motion picture sale of *The Song of the Lark*." She had shown me her agreement with Houghton Mifflin for that novel, and I told her that in fairness to them she had to realize that this was the normal kind of agreement made between author and publisher back in 1915. In those days a common clause which listed the grants made by the author to the publisher included the all-inclusive words "and all other rights of said work or parts thereof." The great development of motion pictures, especially with sound, of radio and television had not yet been dreamed of.

It is characteristic of Miss Cather that when Katherine Anne Porter asked to use some of her work in an anthology she remarked that she thought Miss Porter would be much more usefully engaged completing her own long-promised novel. This was 1946, sixteen years before *Ship of Fools* finally burst on an expectant world.

One afternoon in April 1947 Rudolph Ruzicka, an old friend of mine and of Miss Cather, telephoned us that she had just died, suddenly and quietly. We were about to leave for Winchester, Virginia, our first stop on a trip south, but stayed on to attend the simple services that were held in her apartment. She was buried in her beloved Jaffrey, leaving her literary affairs in the devoted hands of her old, old friend Edith Lewis, who also was to receive the royalties from her books. No one could have been more unselfishly devoted to her memory, and every question I had to raise with Miss Lewis in connection with the Cather Estate was answered exactly as Miss Lewis thought her friend would have done had she still been there to speak for herself.

RECOLLECTIONS

A POSTSCRIPT

When Miss Cather made her agreement with Houghton Mifflin for *The Song of the Lark* she not only assigned to them book
rights but virtually all other rights in the novel, including motion picture and dramatization (radio and television were still
not in the picture at all). To assign such rights to the publisher
was common practice in those days, and I have seen
contracts—in all probability some of our own early ones which
were based on what I had learned at Doubleday, Page and
Company—in which the clause ended with "and all other rights
of and in the said work." Some months before her death Miss
Cather had been concerned about the possibility that Houghton
Mifflin Company might dispose of the motion picture rights in
The Song of the Lark. It was not very long after Miss Cather's
death that the devoted and selfless Edith Lewis asked me if I
thought that if she offered the firm "a considerable sum"—she
mentioned twenty-five thousand dollars—it would be willing
to assign back to the estate all other rights than book rights so
that she could prevent any motion picture based on the book
from being made. I told her I thought it would be unwise to
volunteer such an offer. But early in 1948 I arranged for her to
meet with Henry A. Laughlin and William E. Spaulding,
Chairman and President of the Boston publishing house, in an
attempt to "arrive at some arrangement for handling Miss
Cather's work that would satisfy my feeling of responsibility
toward her and would enable me to carry out the wishes she
had expressed in her will."

Messrs. Laughlin and Spaulding met with Miss Lewis and
agreed to a ten-year moratorium on any sale of motion picture
rights, in return for her permission to reissue *My Ántonia* and *O
Pioneers!* in educational editions for high schools and to include
My Ántonia in college anthologies. They carried out this agreement loyally and indeed the matter was not referred to again
until July 1960, when they felt inclined to extend the motion
picture moratorium if in return Miss Lewis would make conces-
sions which would permit them to develop further the market
for Miss Cather's work in book form. They proposed the extension of the motion picture moratorium for another five years if
they would be allowed to publish paperbound editions of their
four Cather novels over their own imprint.

Miss Lewis countered with a proposal that if Houghton Mifflin would agree *never* to offer for sale motion picture rights in the Cather books on their list, she would accept all their other proposals. The publishers in return said they felt they should be granted more latitude on "reprints, special editions, selections, abridgements, condensations, and so forth."

I replied on my own, tentatively and without consulting Miss Lewis, that I felt that no book by Willa Cather should be subjected to an abridgement or a condensation "and I am inclined to believe that your own artistic conscience would support me in this opinion."

Mr. Spaulding very handsomely expressed immediate agreement with my position. An associate was still concerned about the possibility of unauthorized motion pictures being made from the novels once they came into public domain, so it was agreed that Houghton Mifflin would make no attempt to *sell* any motion picture rights "nor to accept an offer for them without the consent of Miss Cather's executor."

Finally on August 15 these long-drawn-out negotiations came to an end to the satisfaction of all parties. They were extremely gratifying to me, not only because they brought great relief to Miss Lewis, but because they brought me into close contact with Henry Laughlin, who became an intimate friend for whom I soon developed a warm feeling of respect and affection.

Then one day a Louise Stegner of Omaha wrote me that several years earlier she had purchased a collection of Cather letters, photographs, manuscripts, and ephemera which she would like to sell us. Miss Lewis expressed an interest in buying this material, more especially as Miss Stegner wrote that she had been advised by her lawyer that she could publish it. Benjamin Stern, our attorney, wrote her most emphatically that she could not publish anything by Miss Cather and would be dealt with harshly if she made any such attempt. Then, writing that she had had inquiries regarding the purchase of the material from several quarters, Miss Stegner suggested that we work out a contract with her whereby we would have the exclusive publication rights while she retained the originals with complete freedom to sell them elsewhere. This was a useless suggestion as we knew we could never publish any of this material. Finally, since we insisted that we would have to see what she was trying to sell before we could decide whether or not to buy it,

Miss Stegner sent it to a friend in White Plains, where Miss Lewis and I were able to inspect it. Apart from the letters which could neither be printed nor published under the terms of Miss Cather's will, there was nothing of much interest or value in the material. But Miss Lewis bought it lest it fall into other hands, and I *suspect* burned it.

By the end of the sixties it was clear that Miss Cather's sales were declining and that the young were no longer reading her as we felt they should. The prices of hardbound novels had gone up by leaps and bounds, and those that were not available in paperback were not used in classes. I explained the situation to Miss Lewis (this was the last time I saw her; she was bedridden and very frail). She quickly saw the point of our belief that it was greatly to the benefit of her friend's memory that the best of our Cather books should be brought out in paperback form, and soon we published six of them in the very distinguished series we had founded many years earlier, Vintage Books.

Miss Lewis died on August 11, 1972.

December 7, 1973

Part III

Afterviews

Definitions and Evaluations

From the concluding Seminar Panel discussion

BERNICE SLOTE: In her short essay "On the Art of Fiction" Willa Cather writes: "Art, it seems to me, should simplify. That, indeed, is very nearly the whole of the higher artistic process. Finding what conventions of form and what detail one can do without and yet preserve the spirit of the whole, so that all that one has suppressed and cut away is there to the reader's consciousness as much as if it were in type on the page." How do you interpret this comment on simplification and suggestiveness in art? In fact, what does she mean by "simplify"?

BRUCE BAKER: There is the famous scene in *A Lost Lady* where Niel Herbert learns the truth about Mrs. Forrester which all others, the readers and her husband, have known right along. One of my students wrote, "Other writers would have taken us into the bedroom." Willa Cather simply has Niel drop the roses he has chosen for her as a tribute. It's obviously a symbolic scene and builds, it seems to me, throughout the entire novel from the very first chapters where we see Marian Forrester first with roses. That flower motif is associated with her throughout the novel, so that at that particular symbolic moment much of which we are completely unaware is there beneath the consciousness of the reader. In that way simplicity is used in order to suggest. . . .

LEON EDEL: I think that Willa Cather's statement is very good, but then we have to go beyond it and ask ourselves whether it is, or can be regarded as, the last word. I think not. Picasso simplified, too. He simplified in a very complex way by shuffling his eyes, putting the parts of the anatomy wherever he wanted to put them. He made a new structure, a totally new structure. That statement on simplification, of course, we've had from other Americans. Thoreau used to say, "Simplify, simplify, simplify." But we've had Ezra Pound in our century who didn't simplify, and we've had T. S. Eliot who didn't simplify. So that we have to ask ourselves, what did she mean exactly by the word "simplify"? Is it a case of omission? Is it a case of stripping down? Or is it a case of finding what Eudora Welty said last night—"getting at essence." And each writer gets at that essence in his or her own way.

EUDORA WELTY: I agree with Mr. Edel. I think in a sense it would be more obvious in the short stories, perhaps, where the form demands the simplification that a novel doesn't. I think about that story of the Wagner matinee in which the whole past life comes into complete picture at the visit of the old lady when she comes to Boston after many years on the prairie, when you see these details of her life, so that nothing needs to be told ahead of time. And, instead of a whole lot of children, for instance—who can beat one? That's the kind of simplification where one thing speaks for a whole lot of things, not necessarily a detail but a condensation of a situation into one bigger one. Don't you think that's what she meant?

BERNICE SLOTE: A condensation . . . a selection of exactly the right thing. That is a very good correction to our first impulse to say, yes, it means stripping away. Perhaps if we say "essences" and "the necessary things to convey the whole" we will have something closer to what is meant.

EUDORA WELTY: She meant stripping away, though, too, didn't she—like throwing the furniture out the window . . . because it wasn't useful.

MARCUS CUNLIFFE: I was thinking of a quotation which has been attributed to Oscar Wilde, and no doubt plenty of people said it before him, which is to the effect that art is the removal of the superfluous. This is clearly a notion which becomes powerful at the end of the nineteenth century, and would be carried through by a remark by Hemingway—to the effect that interior decoration is to be dispensed with. There is, of course, the other side of the statement—as always, everything is double —and I can recall a famous quatrain by the South African poet Roy Campbell, writing about some other South African writers whom he despised. He said, "You praise the firm restraint with which they write, / I'm with you there, of course. / They use the curb and snaffle well, / But where's the bloody horse?" Now you have the problem of how you remove the superfluous. I think one of the most striking things visually about Willa Cather is to see one of those pages of her typescript. I think there's one as the frontispiece of the edition I read of *Shadows on the Rock*. And this is extraordinary. I can't imagine a better way to teach, for example, than to set before a group of students a page as she had originally done it, and then say, "Make something better of this." The changes she makes are on various levels—avoiding a little clumsy repetition, perhaps a particular noun that she doesn't think should occur twice in two successive sentences, making a verb do more work by taking a less banal one, and then, sometimes, putting a more apparently commonplace word in because she thinks that the one she's already got for the phrase is a little bit too ornate. . . .

JOHN ROBINSON: In the seminar that Professor Celli led, a good deal of the talk was spent on simplicity—the complex simplicity of Willa Cather's language. Professor Celli had some fine quotations to show passages which really were extraordinarily simple, monosyllabic throughout, almost, a minimum of punctuation and then plain words, and yet passages which would sustain a long, hard look because patterns would emerge in the language. And the same thing is true about the subject matter of some of the novels. So we were talking about simplicity, but it was almost archetypal simplicity which had a lot more complicated results when you came to actually judging the novels as a whole.

ALDO CELLI: My impression is that a writer, whether a poet or a novelist, as well as any other artist, the painter or the musician, struggles with the instrument of his art. A novelist struggles with words. I wonder whether by "simplicity" you would mean not just revisions of words—which she has done, obviously, rewriting passages—but the struggle of finding the word which to her carried the meaning of what she intended to do and which would go together with the other words which she has used. In a sense, silence would come together with the

229

words. She said almost exactly so—find words that by themselves, without the accompaniment of other useless words, would carry on whatever she intended to say. I have ten words to say something, and I will try to find the one or the two words, leaving the others in silence, in order to say the things that could be said in the ten words. This is my impression of what she perhaps meant.

BERNICE SLOTE: You're suggesting that the silence has weight. The things that are unsaid take on a heavier quality, even, than if they were said.

ALDO CELLI: I'm convinced that this is true of art.

[Response to comments from the audience on writing short poems]

ALDO CELLI: . . . I don't think that a poet walks in some place and then gets the idea of doing something, but it was already with him. And I don't think it's his own decision whether it be one line or ten lines or twenty lines.

EUDORA WELTY: What you were talking about was, need length of lines have anything to do with the simplicity? I think things come ready-made with their own length belonging to them, just as a seed would make a sprout of a certain number of inches high. The thing is for the writer to know when it gets there. But I think everything has its right length and its right everything; and it can be very different from person to person or from time to time.

LEON EDEL: I have a question I'd like to ask of Professor Gervaud. Would it be possible that we have been mistranslating *roman démeublé*. Should it be the "*un*furnished novel" or the "*dis*furnished novel"?

MICHEL GERVAUD: I cannot feel the difference. I should ask you that question.

LEON EDEL: In my mind, "disfurnished" might be slightly more accurate, because "unfurnished" means "empty the house of all the furniture." I don't think Willa Cather meant to have an empty house.

MICHEL GERVAUD: To remove the useless species of furniture. This is the way I understand it. The ugly pieces of fashion, and so on—whatever has no place.

LEON EDEL: I leave this to the semanticists, but I would opt for disfurnished.

EUDORA WELTY: In the context in which that was said she quoted Dumas, that all you need is four walls and a passion.

BERNICE SLOTE: Yes, the passion is the important thing, and some kind of form to contain it. . . . I'd like to ask Miss Sato if the idea of simplicity of form is one thing in Willa Cather that appeals to the Japanese.

HIROKO SATO: Yes, I think so. You have mentioned four walls and one passion . . . our poetry, of course, is very similar. Like Miss Cather's style, one word suggests so many things. This similarity appeals to us very much. Also, the four walls to me suggest a kind of restriction. Of course it's very simple, but it is still being surrounded by four walls. The world is kind of small in this case, and this idea also appeals to me.

ROBERT HOUGH: In Miss Sato's paper she called attention to the image that so many of us have seen, that of the plow against the sun, as being particularly evocative and suggestive of the idea of man and nature going together to create civilization. . . . The image is somewhat like a Japanese picture, very sparse and very bare, and just kind of sitting there. . . . It did seem to me that the kind of simplicity that Cather gains through her images carries a great deal of weight in most of the novels.

[*Response to question from the audience: Why did Willa Cather use so many male narrators?*]

BERNICE SLOTE: Of course she also used women narrators. I think she was catholic—meaning universal—in being able to do a great many things. She was also a very great play-actor. She loved to take parts. On male narrators—she also explained that sometimes men can get around in ways that women can't; she felt that that kind of expansion was more possible in the male narrator.

JAMES E. MILLER, JR.: . . . I would adopt the term "androgynous." I think Willa Cather was an androgynous writer in the Virginia Woolf sense, so that she could project herself imaginatively into either the male or the female point of view—as she used Nellie Birdseye, for example, in *My Mortal Enemy*; as she produced *My Ántonia* so that she could also use Jim Burden and see things from his point of view; as she could see into the mind of the Professor in *The Professor's House*. I think she was capable, as all great writers are, of projecting themselves into male or female points of view, just as Henry James was able to see things from the female or male point of view. In *Portrait of a Lady* we get a tremendous vision from the female point of view.

JAMES WOODRESS: I think the real question to ask is whether or not it comes off, and I think it does. But it's also interesting that this was the thing that Sarah Orne Jewett warned her against doing. . . . Once when Willa Cather was asked why she used Jim Burden's point of view in *My Ántonia* she said, Well, I've been practicing by writing McClure's autobiography, and people wrote me and said this was McClure himself speaking, and so I thought I could pull it off. I think that is a valid explanation, but not the real one.

DONALD SUTHERLAND: She has an article, done when she was very young, in which she lambasts the typical lady novelist largely for the narrowness of the point of view, that it always has to be a sensitive sort of love story. And I think that whatever other reasons she had for taking the masculine point of view, one of them must surely have been that it broadened her range, both of manner and of content. And—emotionally, I mean—she did have a tomboy phase herself. If she's going to have a hard, simple style, it is a little more suitable, I think, to make a sort of masculine masquerade. I don't press that, because there's not very much evidence, but she does have some awfully sharp things to say about the feminine normal.

EUDORA WELTY: Behind that would be simply Willa Cather as a fiction writer. The point of view of the story is always told. It's told from a person. It's already leaped the greatest hurdle of all, which is not from one sex to another but from one person to another person. And if it's told by another person, that person has a character, so that's a creation to start with. It's not the voice of Willa Cather but the voice of Jim Burden, a character, telling it. That is the character, just as if it were a stage and he were a character on the stage—he's that much of a creation. He could have any sex you wanted to give him. And I think she chooses the sex which is the proper point of view for the story she is telling. It's a functional decision she's made. The leap in the imagination comes simply from being able to imagine what's inside any other person. That's the hardest.

DEFINITIONS AND EVALUATIONS

From the teletaped discussions

ROBERT KNOLL: . . . Willa Cather was not simple at all.

ALFRED A. KNOPF: She was not simple. . . . The virtues she believed in were simple.

ROBERT KNOLL: Yes. And the prose is simple. Oh, but those are not simple stories.

ALFRED A. KNOPF: No. She worked over that prose, you know. She was more like Turgenev than she was like Tolstoi.

ROBERT KNOLL: Or like Flaubert. Chopping and chopping and chopping—chiseling it down, and when you finally get through, it's exceedingly evocative. And that isn't simple.

ALFRED A. KNOPF: . . . She was a great story-teller. When you read the first two or three sentences of one of her books, you're right in. . . . She learned the hard way. . . .

ROBERT KNOLL: Did she talk to you about the books as they were in progress?

ALFRED A. KNOPF: I don't recall her ever asking advice or an opinion about anything. Well, Thomas Mann didn't either. Good writers, really good writers, shouldn't. They should know what they want to do. It's all right in the case of nonfiction for somebody to say, "Do you think a life of Jones would be a good idea, or would Smith be better?" But I don't think Miss Cather would be even interested in my opinion or Blanche's opinion of her work she was starting or working on. It was sufficient for us to know that she was working on something.

ROBERT KNOLL: But she valued your opinion once it was done.

ALFRED A. KNOPF: Oh, once it was done our opinion meant a great deal to her. . . . My relations with her were perfect because our attitudes meshed about most things. She believed in those old stern virtues, decencies, and what I suppose today we call civility . . . and we did, too.

❧

JAMES E. MILLER, JR.: Which of Willa Cather's novels would you recommend to a friend as having the greatest impact?

DONALD SUTHERLAND: One of my favorites is precisely the one that people more or less apologize for, *Sapphira and the*

Slave Girl. I think it's a very beautiful piece of work. . . . It has an intensity just by reduction that reaches you, or it doesn't. . . . I find it very beautiful, like a drawing, and never a wasted word, and always a great modesty about making rhetorical effect. But if you read it carefully the thing is very highly finished and, I think, a triumph of craftsmanship. It may not be a great book, but as craftsmanship I have nothing but admiration for it. . . .

JAMES WOODRESS: For teaching next spring I've narrowed my choice down to *My Ántonia, A Lost Lady*, and *The Professor's House*. In California, I would like to use *The Professor's House*, because of the Southwestern material in the Tom Outland story. . . . My favorite is *My Ántonia*. . . . *A Lost Lady* is perhaps almost a perfect short novel, the best example of her own technique described in her essay "The Novel Démeublé."

LEON EDEL: I think I would settle for *Death Comes for the Archbishop*. I like *A Lost Lady* very much. I not only like it but I like to talk about it because it links up in my mind with all the novels of lost ladies in the nineteenth century that preceded it. I think of Tess and I even think of Anna Karenina. I think of, in a sense, Isabelle Archer. But the lost lady in the provinces, that's the one that I think of—Madame Bovary, though she is quite different . . . the woman whose society is gone. The life she has been accustomed to is gone. She's sort of living on, on her memories, on her past, and reaching still for life. That makes it to me a very poignant story. I remember its effect on me when I read it when I was young. But *Death Comes for the Archbishop* I like because it's a beautifully composed series of scenes and I like its historical depth. It has more depth, it seems to me, than some of her other novels.

JAMES E. MILLER, JR.: "Serenity" is the word that comes to my mind when I think of *Death Comes for the Archbishop*.

LEON EDEL: Yes. Of course if anyone asked me where to start I should say "Tom Outland's Story" from *The Professor's House*. . . . To me, it stands as a great short story.

JAMES E. MILLER, JR.: I like all of the novels you've mentioned, but one of the pleasures of rereading Cather's work was to come upon *One or Ours* in a new way. . . .

DONALD SUTHERLAND: I think that *One of Ours* is a much better novel than people give it credit for. . . . I think the battle

234

scene is extremely good. People reproach it for being heroic because the fashion is to have no heroes in a war novel. Well, in war there are heroes, and to give that particular quality its due in a book is good. I think it's handsome. . . . She doesn't idealize warfare for the fun of it. She knows all about it, but she does allow an ingredient of reckless heroism in the big battle scene, and I think she's quite right . . . not for sales, but she's right about life.

JAMES E. MILLER, JR.: I had expected the war scenes to be more romantic than they turned out to be. There is that quality of cruelty or horror that is offhand and casual and that gives the war scenes a kind of stark reality that seems to me as good as some of the Hemingway war scenes I've read. As for the romance, I think that she does make a distinction between the way Claude Wheeler in the novel sees the war and the way she as the tale-teller sees it. *He* romanticizes it.

JAMES E. MILLER, JR.: Where would you place Willa Cather in American literature?

JAMES WOODRESS: I'm perfectly content to have her as one of the authors represented in the volume *Fifteen Modern American Authors*, which includes Steinbeck, who is certainly lesser than Cather, and includes Thomas Wolfe and Hemingway . . . William Faulkner, of course. . . . It doesn't include Dos Passos or Farrell or Sinclair Lewis or Erskine Caldwell. . . . Dreiser is there. . . . Clearly I couldn't rate Willa Cather as high as Faulkner, and probably not Hemingway. But certainly she is right there below the two or three most important twentieth-century writers, in my opinion.

DONALD SUTHERLAND: I don't have a sensible opinion. It's just that when I'm reading her I think that she's it, and these others are on the wrong track. Of course, when I close the book and go on to something else they get their stature back, but she is so absorbing to me that I just don't care about her rank. She's the first.

LEON EDEL: I'm going to put myself out on a limb, but I think the time will come when she'll be ranked above Hemingway. . . . But I've got her below Faulkner.

Directions:
Additional Commentary

"The Art of Willa Cather: An International Seminar" contained two strains, one forward and the other backward looking. The old ideas about Cather were reiterated: the similarity of her novels to the Turner thesis, her decline after the "Red Cloud" novels, the limitations of imagination that kept her close to life sources, etc. The other strain was largely evident through cracks, as it were, exhibiting itself in polite questioning during sessions and more outspoken comments between sessions.

James Woodress, while equating Willa Cather's successful period with her Nebraska material, contradicted himself by proclaiming *Death Comes for the Archbishop* her most artful novel and thus weakened his "Nebraska" theory. Giving this matter more thought, one finds other exceptions: *The Professor's House* and *My Mortal Enemy* can hardly be categorized "Nebraska" novels; the former might just as well be set in Buffalo and the Professor's window overlook Lake Erie. We can only go so far in Woodress's direction without approaching Michel Gervaud's thesis that there is a French myth, and it frequently complements but sometimes opposes the Nebraska myth.

France served as a filter for Willa Cather's Nebraska memories. In her travel notes of 1902 she noted mud and stone huts at Barbizon, prairies of wheat and Millet-type women of battered beauty who had raised many children and worked in the fields, long before the Nebraska counterparts of these appeared in her novels. Her initial delight in the American Southwest was linked to France. Elizabeth Sergeant tells us that the country around Albuquerque was to Willa Cather "something like the country between Marseilles and Nice but more luminous. Even finer than the Rhone Valley . . . ." When she set a complete novel in this area, she chose two thoroughly

French main characters. Her interest in Quebec was its French link, its rough Norman outline, as well as its frontier setting. France as well as Nebraska defined Cather as a novelist. France and what it meant to her showed her Nebraska and eventually drew her away and made her more than a regionalist. While Willa Cather's connection to France has been frequently noted, its mythic implications are important to remember in treating novels emphasizing France, especially *One of Ours*, where Cather's myths both complement and oppose each other.

A refreshing aspect of James Miller's paper is his acknowledging that *One of Ours* is far better than its reputation. In fact, Miller's opinions on individual novels, some of these mistaken truisms in Cather criticism, might stimulate more response than his comparing Cather's theory of fiction to James's. For example, while commenting on Tom Outland's "idealism, frankness, and primitive wisdom," Miller seems to forget that Tom was a miserable failure in human relationships, refusing to communicate with Roddy Blake and then rejecting him because he failed to understand what Tom was doing. Like Woodress, Miller sees a falling off after *Archbishop*, which is ironic in a paper on James's theory of fiction. When Cather took advantage of the freedom James insisted on for novelists and developed her plotless "Catholic" novels, she was condemned because of what she wrote about rather than how she wrote it. Perhaps Miller has forgotten one of James's main points: "We must grant the artist his subject, his idea, his donnée: our criticism is applied only to what he makes of it. Naturally I do not mean that we are bound to like it or find it interesting: in case we do not our course is perfectly simple—to let it alone."

The future direction of Cather criticism is suggested in Aldo Celli's paper and frequently stressed by Bernice Slote. We must get to the specifics of the text and refrain from generalizations. Celli urges that Cather's modes of narration, the archetypal substructures and the language of the novels be carefully explored. While Willa Cather needs no justification among those whom Katherine Anne Porter called "her faithful friends and true believers," she is in need of the kind of justification that will prevent her exclusion from courses in American literature and from studies like Chase's *The American Novel and Its Tradition*, Bewley's *The Eccentric Design*, and Fiedler's *Love and*

Death in the American Novel, only three of several books that omit her but contain ample discussions of several of her contemporaries. The uncovering of the complexities of her fiction and her relationship to Howells and the realistic movement, to the themes of Hawthorne, James, Faulkner, and perhaps even Cooper, need exploration rather than recital. All this will not make us love her less but introduce more readers to the joys of her fiction.

JOHN J. MURPHY

Professor Edel speculates that Willa Cather never developed the kind of conscious theory of fiction that Henry James did, but was rather an intuitive story-teller. I concur in the first observation, but I take vigorous exception to the second. I think that Willa Cather was a highly self-conscious artist who—after getting off on a wrong track in *Alexander's Bridge*—conceived her major works through *Shadows on the Rock* as, among other things, a series of progressive experiments that can best be understood not through the example of a writer like James, but rather through the successive experiments of some of the most significant painters of the late nineteenth and early twentieth century. "There are hopeful signs," she wrote in "The Novel Démeublé" (1922), "that some of the younger writers are trying to break away from mere verisimilitude, and, following the development of modern painting, to interpret imaginatively the material and social investiture of their characters; to present their scene by suggestion rather than by enumeration." Certainly one of the major efforts of artists from Manet to Matisse was to "disfurnish" (as Professor Edel brilliantly suggests we might best translate "démeublé") their canvases—to eliminate the clutter of the mid-nineteenth-century genre painters as Willa Cather suggests young novelists are trying to escape the clutter of Balzac's fictions.

From Willa Cather's letter comparing the design of *The Professor's House* to certain Dutch domestic paintings and her statement in an open letter to the *Commonweal* that she wished to try in prose in *Death Comes for the Archbishop* something "a little like" the Puvis de Chavannes' frescoes of the life of Saint

Geneviève, we know that she was much interested in painting and consciously tried to employ painterly techniques in some of her most successful fiction. (In "My First Novels," she also even compares *Alexander's Bridge* to the rejected style of "studio picture.") I suspect that this effort extends much further than these references suggest and that Willa Cather saw herself as one of those "younger writers trying to break away from mere verisimilitude" and follow developments in modern painting. Clearly a thorough study of this intriguing and, I think, important matter would require a study on the scale of Richard Giannone's *Music in Willa Cather's Fiction*, which I could not pretend to provide on short notice even were space available. Yet I think that the relationship between Willa Cather's novels and modern painting is too significant to an appreciation of her art to go unmentioned in this centennial tribute. I would like, therefore, simply to sketch the line that such an investigation might follow in the hope that these speculations may stimulate detailed study.

The history of significant experimental painting since just about the time of Willa Cather's birth tells of efforts, as I have already commented, to "disfurnish" the canvas. Up through much of the nineteenth century, painters first made elaborate underpaintings in monotones of projected works in complete detail; then the final painting was produced by coloring in this "corrected" draft. Even when artists like Constable began to work out-of-doors, they often did so only to make preliminary sketches that became bases for the kind of "studio paintings" to which Willa Cather compared her apprentice novel. (Today these sketches are often preferred to the finished products.) With the impressionists, especially Monet, however, painters began to produce the final work directly on the bare canvas, attempting to recapture—sometimes even in a whole sequence of studies of the same subject in changing light—the direct "impressions" of nature that distinguish their work.

That Willa Cather had an appreciation for what these experimenters were doing is shown by a passage in *Lucy Gayheart*. Lucy has taken her home-town beau to an early Chicago loan exhibition of the French impressionists, and he points out that some figures are not correctly drawn. Lucy agrees, but goes on,

"I don't think it matters. I don't know anything about pictures, but I think some are meant to represent objects, and others are meant to express a kind of feeling merely, and then accuracy doesn't matter."

"But anatomy is a fact," he insisted, "and facts are at the bottom of everything."

She did not answer him impatiently, as she would have done once, but bent her head a little and spoke in a quiet voice which disconcerted him. "Are they, Harry? I'm not so sure." [P. 101]

Like the early impressionists, however, Willa Cather had to break away from traditional artistic practices before launching her own experiments. She faced first a fundamental problem that had challenged the "factual" painter since the introduction of perspective during the Renaissance to achieve in paintings a three-dimensional illusion, especially in the kind of landscape paintings closest in feeling to Willa Cather's early prairie novels.·

This principal problem is fusing successfully foreground, middle distance, and background to create an integrated whole, so that the painting does not seem to separate into a succession of receding planes like an unsuccessful stage set.

James E. Miller, Jr., in his remarks on "Willa Cather and the Art of Fiction," comments on the novelist's difficulty with this problem of integrating the planes of action in O Pioneers!, observing that although the melodramatic plot of a hotheaded husband's killing his wife in her lover's arms stands out in bold relief in the foreground, it is not "emotionally integrated" into the panoramic background of the novel. As Miller puts his finger on a major problem about this never-quite-satisfying novel, we perceive that its shortcomings are more easily understood from the viewpoint of painterly technique than in terms of the customary verbal logic of literary criticism. Miller's objectives in his discussion do not lead him, however, to pursue his survey of Willa Cather's achievement principally in terms of pictorial "distancing"; but I think that the varying success of her later major writings may be most quickly—though, of course, by no means thoroughly—comprehended by comparing them in terms of pictorial compositional techniques.

The remarkable thing about Willa Cather's career looked at from this perspective is that her greatest success comes so relatively early in her career. In *My Ántonia* she succeeds in solving the problem of integrating foreground, middle distance, and background as she presents a picture of the world in Jim Burden's head—Ántonia towering in the foreground like a husky peasant in a Breughel painting, Jim himself mingled with yet set apart from the surging humanity of Black Hawk and Lincoln (like the revelling villagers in many Breughel paintings), and both set against the background of the prairie vividly epitomized by the already much-quoted picture of the plow against the sunset—a golden brown distance in contrast to Breughel's serene blues. Perhaps a reason why *The Song of the Lark* and *One of Ours* are less interesting than *My Ántonia* is that they are less successful experiments in organizing fundamentally the same kind of traditional compositions. The problems of integrating foreground and background plague the earlier novel as there is no special connection between Thea Kronborg's inner life and the backgrounds against which she moves. In "My First Novels" Willa Cather herself later acknowledged that the "overcrowded" picture can destroy "a very satisfying element analogous to what painters call composition." The later novel, *One of Ours*, really marks no advance over the compositional techniques of *My Ántonia*.

In *A Lost Lady*, however—as David Stouck has pointed out—Willa Cather begins consciously to "disfurnish" the novel, producing a distinctly Cézannesque effect. Cézanne's great contribution to the movement beyond impressionism was his simplification of scene—his elimination of extraneous objects—coupled with a commanding emphasis upon the forms of the objects presented. Attention to form—as Lucy Gayheart's beau objected—had practically disappeared in impressionist paintings. The paintings became all background—or perhaps all foreground, depending on how one looks at them —especially those studies of water lilies to which Monet devoted his last years. In Cézanne's paintings of subjects like Mont Sainte-Victoire, on the other hand, one is strongly conscious of receding planes, though the middle distance especially is cleared of all clutter, so that the mountain in the background dominates and unifies the scene. Willa Cather indicated her acquaintance with the post-impressionist painters' techniques by comparing Stephen Crane to them in her preface for his

Wounds in the Rain and Other Impressions of War. She, too, worked not like Monet, but like Cézanne in creating in *A Lost Lady* a group of powerful, arresting foreground figures against the brooding background of the exploited prairie. But the rich sense of communal life that provided the middle distance in *My Ántonia* is gone, just as Willa Cather considered it to have vanished, though spectral figures still went their empty ways.

Another characteristic of Cézanne's paintings is that his strong forms seem perilously poised on the verge of collapse—a strong shove would send them tumbling into the scrambles of Picasso's and Braque's cubist works. Cézanne's powerful, isolated forms seem a last refuge against encroaching chaos —surely exactly the effect that Willa Cather sought in *A Lost Lady*, her drama of a deteriorated heritage.

Curiously, the two works that David Stouck studies as the best examples of "the novel démeublé" are separated by *The Professor's House*, which may appear a reversion to more conventional pictorial techniques. Even this book, however, moves in one of the two directions that painting took as it passed beyond impressionism. Besides Cézanne's experiments, there were those of van Gogh, Gauguin, Toulouse-Lautrec, who shared a common interest in vivid, distorted, upsetting forms. With *A Lost Lady* Willa Cather had just about exhausted the pictorial (as well as for a time the emotional) potential of impressions from her prairie childhood. To move in the direction of "disfurnishing" beyond Cézanne's austere formalities would have involved creating word structures analogous to the formal experiments of Picasso and Braque, with the background disappearing altogether into a single, flatly-conceived plane. Willa Cather would later move tentatively in this direction, but she was not ready yet for such bold abandonment of conventional techniques.

Gauguin and others exemplified the drive toward expressionism—an attempt to present through pictorial distortions internal states of mind (a movement that provided great impetus in designing plays as well as paintings). Willa Cather's remarks about the influence of an exhibition of Dutch paintings on the overall design of *The Professor's House* are likely to make us think immediately of the serene Dutch paintings of the Age of Vermeer; but she mentions both "old and modern" works, and the novel is anything but serene. Even though she does not specify what modern Dutch paintings were included, if van Gogh was represented his canvases could surely have left a vivid impression, especially upon one in the disturbed state of mind that Willa Cather was at that time. The first and third sections of the novel share the nightmare qualities of some of van Gogh's famous interiors, especially the famous presentation of an evilly-lit cafe. Most of the characters, too—except the Professor himself and Augusta (an early van Gogh peasant)—might have been drawn from van Gogh's works or the even more grotesque distortions of the German expressionists. Indeed, one of Professor St. Peter's particular discomforts is that he is a substantial figure from the clearer, earlier work of traditional Dutch painting trapped in the nightmare city of the expressionists. Although "Tom Outland's Story," the second part of the novel, is marked by a serenity rarely found in van Gogh's restless work, even it is expressionistic in its description of the nightmarish Washington bureaucracy (much like the society in Elmer Rice's play *The Adding Machine*), while the Blue Mesa sections evoke the same kind of joy that van Gogh occasionally projected through his glowing canvases of bright fields and especially the dazzling blue of his "The Starry Night."

My Mortal Enemy is an astonishing jump. The artist picks up where she had left off in *A Lost Lady* to produce her supreme example of the "disfurnished" novel that she had argued for. Like the major works of Matisse in the first quarter of the century, *My Mortal Enemy* is almost entirely foreground. Perhaps it can be best compared to Mondrian's work at that stage when he had abandoned traditional realism but had not quite achieved the form of abstractionism most frequently associated with him. For a time, he created stripped-down but still recognizable forms teetering on the verge of dissolving into their constituent elements. Willa Cather was never to go so far as Mondrian did, but the juxtaposition of his early work against his near-abstractions conveys visually the same feeling one gets from the juxtaposition of *O Pioneers!* and *My Mortal Enemy*.

With this last novel, however, Willa Cather faced an even more challenging crisis than the one she had gone through in settling upon a design for a new novel after *One of Ours*. Except

for a few pages in the first section of the novel, the middle
distance is sketchy and the background has disappeared in the
mists of the characters' self-absorption. The final scene with
only a single tree providing any perspective against which to
measure the human actors calls for a stage as disfurnished as
that in Beckett's *Waiting for Godot*—a work with which *My Mortal Enemy* has also many thematic similarities that lie beyond
the scope of these remarks. Beckett's subsequent work, however, provides insight into the problems that Willa Cather faced
at this point. Beyond *My Mortal Enemy*, there was nowhere to
progress in the disfurnishing of the novel unless Willa Cather
created works that might be foreshadowings of Beckett's own
further experiments in *Endgame* and *Happy Days* and in his
novels. Action would have to be totally abstracted from outside
reality. Willa Cather goes this far at last in the final section of
Lucy Gayheart after the principal characters have disappeared
from the scene; but she was not at home in this kind of static
work. She remained too restless and probably too conservative
to be attracted to the ultimate inertness of a work like *Happy
Days*, from which action and at last even language are absent.
Without plunging like her contemporary Gertrude Stein into
experiments in creating with language analogues to the work of
the cubist painters, there was no place to go beyond *My Mortal
Enemy* in the direction that she had been moving.

She chose instead to move in another direction—to return to
more nearly conventional forms of composition in *Death Comes
for the Archbishop* and *Shadows on the Rock*; but even in this
effort she paralleled the work of certain modern painters with
whom she may well have been familiar.

Middle distance had not, after all, entirely disappeared even
from *My Mortal Enemy*. Early in the novel we get a picture of a
serenity that the forground characters sadly lack:

> When I was older I used to walk around the Driscoll place alone
> very often, especially on spring days, after school, and watch the
> nuns pacing so mildly and measuredly among the blossoming
> trees where Myra used to give garden-parties and have the band
> to play for her. I thought of the place as being under a spell, like
> the Sleeping Beauty's palace. [P. 17]

It was to recapturing the spell of this serenity that Willa Cather turned in her next two novels, placing the foreground characters once again against a middle distance and serene background, the contemplation of which freed them from the neurotically confining worlds of the characters in *A Lost Lady*, *The Professor's House*, and *My Mortal Enemy*.

The opening paragraph of *Death Comes for the Archbishop* illustrates—one might say announces—the technique and establishes the compositional style of these contemplative works:

> One summer evening in the year 1848, three Cardinals and a missionary Bishop from America were dining together in the gardens of a villa in the Sabine hills, overlooking Rome. The villa was famous for the fine view from its terrace. The hidden garden in which the four men sat at table lay some twenty feet below the south end of this terrace, and was a mere shelf of rock, overhanging a steep declivity planted with vineyards. A flight of stone steps connected it with the promenade above. . . . Beyond the balustrade was the drop into the air, and far below the landscape stretched soft and undulating; there was nothing to arrest the eye until it reached Rome itself. [P. 3]

I have tried to draw extracts from the passage to illustrate the three planes established by the four men at table, the flight of stone steps, and the undulating landscape, but only a single sentence can be removed without utterly destroying the composition. One can no more take apart the passage than he could cut a section of the canvas from a landscape by John Sloan without destroying the whole.

I have mentioned John Sloan because, even though Willa Cather's remarks about the influence of the Puvis de Chavannes' frescoes on her conception of the novel suggest the kind of retreat to the past that the story told in the novel represents, her effort has an exact parallel in the painting of the 1920s and 1930s. Van Deren Coke's *Taos and Santa Fé: The Artist's Environment, 1880–1942* (1963) documents the way in which the artists of a region Willa Cather loved were employing traditional techniques to conjure up a sense of their environment in a way analogous to that she employed in her novel. Sloan's "Picnic on the Ridge" (1920), for example, is organized in precisely the same manner as the opening paragraph of *Death Comes for the Archbishop*. Even more in the spirit, as well as the style, of the novel is "Sangre de Cristo Mountains" (1926) by Ernest L. Blumenschein, an artist who had illustrated some of Willa Cather's works. *Shadows on the Rock* had also its neglected painterly analogue in Preston Dickinson's Quebecois landscapes of the same period as Willa Cather's novel, bringing out the dramatic effects of the oblique northern lighting on the quaint old structures lining the steep streets.

One would expect *Lucy Gayheart* to be the masterly culmination of Willa Cather's painterly progress. After essaying her new techniques in treating Southwestern and Canadian subjects, she returned again to the region of her youth to apply her matured compositional theories to it. A problem was that she had already created her prairie masterpiece. If *My Ántonia*'s and *Lucy Gayheart*'s places among Willa Cather's productions were reversed, her career would make entire logical sense; but art rarely has much truck with such dehumanized logic. *Lucy Gayheart* would also make entire sense if *Death Comes for the Archbishop* and *Shadows on the Rock* didn't exist, for it is in some measure a move beyond *My Mortal Enemy* into further abstraction. I have already commented that Book III, which really takes place entirely in Harry Gordon's head, is uncharacteristically static. Book I takes place mostly in Chicago, but the city scarcely exists in the book. The author even remarks that because of the "strange kind of life" Lucy was leading, for periods, "the city was blotted out."

But the effect of the novel is uneven, for the abstractness is exchanged for the melodramatic realism of D. W. Griffith's *Way Down East* when the action shifts to the Platte River and its sidewaters. Willa Cather had contrived a work most nearly analogous to some of those collages of later years that incorporate realistic photographs into largely abstract paintings. But this time the foreshadowing of Tom Wesselman seems inadvertent and unwanted. Willa Cather's painterly progress culminated in her serene pictures of a Santa Fé and Quebec that had held to a past that had vanished elsewhere, and they have the timeless charm of paintings like those of John Sloan that we may also be just beginning to appreciate.

Like *Alexander's Bridge, Sapphira and the Slave Girl* is, I think, another matter, a return to the studio, though I expect closer study to illustrate further painterly qualities in all of Willa

Cather's work. I have not been able here to speak at all of the short stories that may contribute much to the filling out of this outline, although I cannot resist one final passing reference to the resemblances of "The Old Beauty" in subject, style, and setting to many of Matisse's paintings of striking women almost caricatured against flat, two-dimensional backgrounds.

What I do argue is that from the imperfect success of *O Pioneers!* and the triumph of *My Ántonia* to the triumph of *Death Comes for the Archbishop* and the confused design of *Lucy Gayheart* Willa Cather pursued in the formal design of her fictions—though many forces influenced other facets of them—a program of restless, innovative experimentation most nearly analogous to the experiments of a varied group of twentieth-century painters from the French avant-garde to the New Mexican regionalists for whom she felt a sympathetic kinship. She did indeed "interpret imaginatively the material and social investiture" of her characters in the ways that she found these painters did.

WARREN FRENCH

A Gathering of Nations

Bernice Slote

Whatever adds to our knowledge of the artist's creativity enriches our concept of man himself; what the artist shows us of the human experience deepens our understanding of our own lives and the lives of others. So by studying the art of Willa Cather—both its means and its end—we may find some illumination of a peculiarly American, and yet very personal, experience. Like her own country, she was herself and she was everyone. Her art combines an absorbing individuality with the scope of both traditions and new perceptions, of single fields and many nations. That people from all the world gathered, in the luck of history, to create America was one of her great themes. It is right that in 1973, the centennial year of Willa Cather's birth, there has been a meeting of scholars from seven countries, including all regions of the United States, to consider, even partially, the work of this American writer.

For several years after she was nine years old Willa Cather lived on the prairie of Webster County, Nebraska, where, according to census records of 1885, the population was a mosaic of Scandinavian, Bohemian, German-Russian, and French-Canadian immigrants, along with English settlers from Virginia or Pennsylvania or Illinois. This was her first international storehouse of the material she used in fiction from 1892 on. In 1921 she recalled "the old women, who used to tell me of their home country . . . . Their stories used to go round and round in my head at night. This was, with me, the initial impulse" (Latrobe Carroll, "Willa Sibert Cather," *Bookman*, May 1921, p. 212). Both the old women and Willa Cather understood homesickness—for the "old country" or for Virginia, where the Cathers had lived until they came to Nebraska in 1883. She observed, too, in addition to the perils of settling, the conflicts of backgrounds, of language, of abilities on that frontier. Much of her early fiction was, in fact, international.

In a half dozen of her published stories between 1892 and 1900 Willa Cather portrayed the Nebraska immigrants, or their children: the tragedy of the Bohemian violinist in "Peter," the madness of a Dane in "Lou, the Prophet," the violent loneliness of Norwegian Canute Canuteson on Rattlesnake Creek in "On the Divide." Serge Povolitchky in "The Clemency of the Court" was born of a Russian girl, "one of a Russian colony that a railroad had brought west to build grades." Mexicans, Bohemians, and French entangle in "The Dance at Chevalier's." In "Eric Hermannson's Soul" there is Eric, a big, silent Norseman like a young Siegfried, and with him and other Norwegians we hear something of the "rude, half mournful music, made up of the folksongs of the North."

It is not true that Willa Cather began using her prairie material only with *O Pioneers!* in 1913. In the twenty years before that, half of her stories were about the West. In some of them after 1900 the country was portrayed darkly, as in "A Wagner Matinee" and "The Sculptor's Funeral"; in others it was made beautiful, as in "The Treasure of Far Island" or "The Enchanted Bluff." But it is true that after "Eric Hermannson's Soul" in 1900 she did not write again of the immigrants—the various nationalities on the plains—until "The Bohemian Girl" in 1912. (A companion story of 1912, "Behind the Singer Tower," portrays the fate of Sicilian immigrants in the industrial East.) From that time on, almost everything Willa Cather wrote had some element of the meeting of the different nationalities, or cultures, of the world. A few examples will illustrate: In "The Bohemian Girl" there were the Norwegian Ericsons and the Bohemian Clara Vavrika, with other Swedes and Danes of the Nebraska farming country. *O Pioneers!* has the Swedish Bergsons, the Norwegian Ivar, the Bohemian Shabatas. In the country of *My Ántonia* the smell of dried mushrooms from Europe blends with the odor of sunflowers: Joining lives with the Bur-

dens, from Virginia, are the Bohemian Shimerdas, Russian
Pavel and Peter, Scandinavians like Lena Lingard, and eventually Ántonia Cuzak and her family. *The Song of the Lark* has the
Swedish Thea Kronborg, whose teachers include the German
Wunsch, the Hungarian Harsanyi, and—a teacher in his own
way—"Spanish Johnny" Tellamantez. There are the cultured
German Erlichs in *One of Ours*; other German-Americans, who
were persecuted by the Americans at home in World War I, are
also depicted. (And in that book Claude Wheeler is himself a
kind of immigrant in wartime France.) There are Godfrey St.
Peter in *The Professor's House* with a Canuck grandfather; Irish
John Driscoll in *My Mortal Enemy*; the Spanish, Mexican, Indian, French, and English mingling of *Death Comes for the
Archbishop*; the French-German-Jewish Rosens in "Old Mrs.
Harris"; the Bohemians of "Neighbour Rosicky"; and, finally,
Southern whites and blacks in *Sapphira and the Slave Girl*. Other
characters and themes are also used, but the strands which
represent the intertwining of nationalities and races are strong
in the Cather fabric.

From her childhood Willa Cather grew accustomed to an international literature. In her kind of education, of course, one
had to know the *Aeneid*, the *Iliad*, the *Odyssey*, and the Bible.
She also had very early a deep affinity for Continental literature, especially French and Russian, which she found in translation. Her French interests have been well discussed in the
International Seminar; however, Russia also appealed to her,
and she read widely in Dostoevski, Tolstoi, Turgenev, Chekhov.
She frequently noted similarities to Russia in both the American blending of peoples and in the American landscape, though
she never visited a Russian steppe except through fiction. The
special interest in the lands and cultures of central and eastern
Europe continued through most of her life, from articles in her
McClure's Magazine years to the epigraphs for her first
novels.The epigraph for *O Pioneers!* ("Those fields, colored by
various grain!") is taken from the folk-epic of Lithuanian Po-
land by Adam Mickiewicz, *Pan Tadeusz*; that of *The Song of the
Lark* ("It was a wond'rous lovely storm that drove me!") is from
the Hungarian-Austrian Nikolaus Lenau's *Don Juan*. And in the
thirties, said Yehudi Menuhin (in interviews in Lincoln, December 1973), one of the books Willa Cather gave him and his

sisters, Hephzibah and Yaltah, was another Russian folk-epic, Nekrasov's *Who Can Be Happy and Free in Russia?*.

Willa Cather's novels and stories were extensively translated from the first, and she had special recognition among the Scandinavians. The regard commanded by her name is suggested in a letter from one of her old friends, Mrs. George Seibel, who wrote that when she and her husband were in Sweden and were identified as friends of Willa Cather, they were "treated like royalty."

Since those who came to the International Seminar on "The Art of Willa Cather" were from a number of different nationalities and cultures, their views of her work necessarily emphasized different elements; but among the variations were many points for meeting. Some of these comments came in a panel discussion taped for television. Hiroko Sato of Japan, for example, spoke of the nostalgia among some in her own country for traditional values that seemed lost after World War II, and the Japanese reader finds it in Cather; they like especially the reminders of the old values of man's affinity with nature. Philip Siggins, from Australia, felt that he could relate immediately to Cather's landscape, though both he and Canadian David Stouck, commenting on Cather's pioneer books, agreed that their countries differ from America. In Australia and Canada, they thought, people came more for refuge than for conquest. David Stouck noted the special response in Canada for *Shadows on the Rock*, "a much more intimate kind of novel to the Canadian because there the primitive world is a refuge . . . it's clinging to a rock." Michel Gervaud, speaking as a French scholar, agreed that *Shadows on the Rock* shows the attitude of the French immigrants in early Quebec as "defensive. They are trying to maintain old ways; they see the rest of the country, the forest in particular, as a threat." It is almost, he said, "a negative vision of the pioneering experience."

Many readers in other countries are, of course, dependent on translations. What of translation into Japanese? According to Hiroko Sato, "When you really want to transfer what she's writing into the exact equivalent, it's almost impossible. . . . Her real quality is very difficult to translate." French translations are less difficult, said Michel Gervaud, but he made somewhat the same distinction: "There is no major problem, really, in finding the equivalent of the words she uses. The difficulty is in preserving the rhythm of her prose."

What books are most popular in other countries? In Canada, said David Stouck, *Death Comes for the Archbishop* is generally first on university lists, but *Shadows on the Rock* has, of course, a special place in Canadian interest. (I can add that *Shadows on the Rock* is taught in schools in the province of Quebec.) Most participants agreed, however, that *My Ántonia* has a primary interest, in Japan as well as in France or Australia or, as Sister Isabel Charles added, in America. "So," said Robert Knoll, the moderator of the panel, "Willa Cather really does seem to reach out across the water and touch hands."

There are many different, and genuine, ways of reading Willa Cather, as the participants in the seminar have shown. Differences of opinion came especially on two points: whether Cather was an intuitive or a conscious artist, and whether the later books, after those of the twenties, are of lesser quality or of a different quality, not yet fully defined. Most agreed that the Cather style is one of external simplicity, internal complexity; and, as John Murphy and Warren French indicate in their comments in the preceding chapter, many areas are still unexplored.

But it may be best to let Willa Cather herself have the last word. Although she said a few things about her art in published essays of the 1920s and 1930s, such as the familiar "The Novel Démeublé," one cannot stop there if he is to define Cather's own view of the art of fiction. For eight years, until 1900, she wrote voluminously of the arts and observed many times what makes a good book, or a bad play, or mediocre poetry. Much of this comment was supported in later years; some of it developed in new directions. And she said a great deal more in interviews than has been noted.

Willa Cather's first important personal statement in 1896 emphasized the difficulty of her own kind of "translation":

> Art is not thought or emotion, but expression, expression, always expression. To keep an idea living, intact, tinged with all its original feeling, its original mood, preserving in it all the ecstasy which attended its birth, to keep it so all the way from the brain to the hand and transfer it on paper a living thing with color,

odor, sound, life all in it, that is what art means, that is the greatest of all the gifts of the gods. And that is the voyage perilous. [*Nebraska State Journal*, March 1, 1896; reprinted in *The Kingdom of Art*, p. 417]

Some twenty years later she was stressing the idea of control, simplicity: Not until young writers "learn to write will they learn to let writing alone. . . . Not until writers learn to do very elaborately will they learn to do with simplicity" (Denver *Times*, August 16, 1915). And in another 1915 interview: "Young writers must care vitally, fiercely, absurdly about the trickery and the arrangement of words, the beauty and power of phrases. But they must go on and on until they get more out of life itself than out of anything written" (Lincoln *Star*, October 24, 1915). In 1921 it is the writer's self that vanishes; all that remains is the created thing: Objects and people could tell their own story "by juxtaposition, without any explanation on my part. Just as if I put here on the table a green vase and beside it a yellow orange. Now, these two things affect each other. Side by side, they produce a reaction which neither of them will produce alone . . . . [from] the relation they have to each other and the effect they have upon each other. I want the reader to see the orange and the vase—beyond that, *I* am out of it." And, she concluded, "I'd like the writing to be so lost in the object, that it doesn't exist for the reader—except for the reader who knows how difficult it is to lose writing in the object. One must choose one's audience, and the audience I try to write for is the one interested in the effect the green vase brings out in the orange and the orange in the green vase" (Carroll, "Willa Sibert Cather," p. 216). Although both Willa Cather and her readers have noted the central place of memory in her kind of work, one important part of the artist's creativity cannot be overlooked: "Your memories are like the colors in paints," she said in 1925, when she was mature in her art, "but you must arrange them" (New York *World*, April 19, 1925).

There is in Willa Cather a certain magic, found through a life, a consciousness, an art, both primitive and civilized, a response to wildness ordered by the shaping hand of her creativity. Because she was many-colored, her readers too respond to an art that gives them freedom and depth, for richness.

Bibliography of Works Cited

I. WORKS BY WILLA CATHER

The listing is chronological by date of first publication. If the edition cited in this volume is other than the first, it is indicated in the entry. Out-of-print works are indicated by an asterisk(*). If all editions are out of print, the most recently published is the edition cited. Only the title, or a short form of the title, appears in the footnotes and reference notes.

The Kingdom of Art: Willa Cather's First Principles and Critical Statements, 1893–1896. Selected and edited with two essays and a commentary by Bernice Slote. Lincoln: University of Nebraska Press, 1966.

The World and the Parish: Willa Cather's Articles and Reviews, 1893–1902. Selected and edited by William M. Curtin. 2 vols. Lincoln: University of Nebraska Press, 1970.

Willa Cather's Collected Short Fiction, 1892–1912. Edited by Virginia Faulkner. Introduction by Mildred R. Bennett. Lincoln: University of Nebraska Press, 1965; revised edition 1970.

Willa Cather in Europe: Her Own Story of the First Journey. With an introduction and incidental notes by George N. Kates. New York: Alfred A. Knopf, 1956. A more accurate text of these letters appears in *The World and the Parish* (see above), pp. 889–952.

*April Twilights. Boston: Richard G. Badger, 1903. References are to *April Twilights (1903).* Edited with an introduction by Bernice Slote. Lincoln: University of Nebraska Press, 1962; revised edition 1968.

*The Troll Garden. New York: McClure, Phillips and Company, 1905. The stories are included in *Willa Cather's Collected Short Fiction, 1892–1912* (see above), pp. 147–261.

*Alexander's Bridge. Boston: Houghton Mifflin, 1912. *Reprinted with

the 1922 preface by Bantam Books (New York, 1962). References are to the Bantam edition.

O Pioneers!. Boston: Houghton Mifflin, 1913. References are to the Sentry edition (1962).

*The Song of the Lark. Boston: Houghton Mifflin, 1915. References are to the new edition which includes the 1932 preface and the revisions made by the author in 1937. (The pagination in this edition is the same as in the Sentry edition, which, at this writing, is out of print.)

*My Ántonia. Boston: Houghton Mifflin, 1918. References are to the Sentry edition (1961).

Uncle Valentine and Other Stories: Willa Cather's Uncollected Short Fiction, 1915–1929. Edited with an introduction by Bernice Slote. Lincoln: University of Nebraska Press, 1973.

Youth and the Bright Medusa. New York: Alfred A. Knopf, 1920.

One of Ours. New York: Alfred A. Knopf, 1922. References are to the Vintage Book edition (1971).

April Twilights and Other Poems. Alfred A. Knopf, 1923.

A Lost Lady. New York: Alfred A. Knopf, 1923. References are to the Vintage Book edition (1972).

The Professor's House. New York: Alfred A. Knopf, 1925. References are to the Vintage Book edition (1973).

My Mortal Enemy. New York: Alfred A. Knopf, 1926. References are to the Vintage Book edition (1961).

Death Comes for the Archbishop. New York: Alfred A. Knopf, 1927. References are to the Vintage Book edition (1971).

Shadows on the Rock. New York: Alfred A. Knopf, 1931. References are to the Vintage Book edition (1971).

Obscure Destinies. New York: Alfred A. Knopf, 1932.

Lucy Gayheart. New York: Alfred A. Knopf, 1935.

Not Under Forty. New York: Alfred A. Knopf, 1936.

Sapphira and the Slave Girl. New York: Alfred A. Knopf, 1940.

The Old Beauty and Others. New York: Alfred A. Knopf, 1948.

Willa Cather on Writing: Critical Studies on Writing as an Art. Foreword by Stephen Tennant. New York: Alfred A. Knopf, 1949.

N.B. An article on Willa Cather's unfinished novel, *Hard Punishments*, "Willa Cather's Unfinished Avignon Story," by George N. Kates, appears in *Five Stories* (New York: Vintage Books, 1956), pp. 175–214.

II. SECONDARY SOURCES

The following list includes biographical, bibliographical, and critical sources cited more than once in this book. Only the author's or editor's name and a short form of the title of the works listed below appear in the footnotes and reference notes. Complete bibliographical information for other sources cited is carried in the footnotes and reference notes.

Biographies

Mildred R. Bennett. *The World of Willa Cather*. New York: Dodd, Mead, 1951; Bison Book edition revised with notes and an index, Lincoln: University of Nebraska Press, 1961. References are to the Bison Book edition.

E. K. Brown, completed by Leon Edel. *Willa Cather: A Critical Biography*. New York: Alfred A. Knopf, 1953.

Edith Lewis. *Willa Cather Living: A Personal Record*. New York; Alfred A. Knopf, 1953.

Elizabeth Shepley Sergeant. *Willa Cather: A Memoir*. Philadelphia: J. B. Lippincott, 1953; Bison Book edition, with a new foreword, Lincoln: University of Nebraska Press, 1963. References are to the Bison Book edition.

James Woodress. *Willa Cather: Her Life and Art*. New York: Pegasus, 1970.

Criticism

N.B. In the case of studies reprinted in James Schroeter, ed., *Willa Cather and Her Critics* (Ithaca: Cornell University Press, 1967), page numbers in the footnotes and reference notes are to that collection.

Latrobe Carroll, "Willa Sibert Cather." *Bookman* 53 (May 1921): 212–16.

David Daiches. *Willa Cather: A Critical Introduction*. Ithaca: Cornell University Press, 1951. Reprinted by Collier Books (New York, 1962). References are to the Collier edition.

Leon Edel. *Literary Biography*. Toronto: University of Toronto Press, 1957.

———. *Willa Cather: The Paradox of Success*. Washington, D.C.: The Library of Congress, 1960. Reprinted in Schroeter, ed., *Willa Cather and Her Critics* (see note above).

Richard Giannone. *Music in Willa Cather's Fiction*. Lincoln: University of Nebraska Press, 1968.

Bernice Slote. "Willa Cather." In Jackson R. Bryer, ed., *Sixteen Modern American Authors: A Survey of Research and Criticism*. Durham: Duke University Press, 1973. Paper edition published by W. W. Norton (New York, 1973). References are to the paper edition. (This volume is a revised and expanded edition of *Fifteen Modern American Authors* [1969]).

Lionel Trilling. "Willa Cather." *New Republic*, February 10, 1937. Collected in Malcolm Cowley, ed., *After the Genteel Tradition: American Writers, 1910–1930*. New York: Viking Press, 1937. Reprinted in Schroeter, ed., *Willa Cather and Her Critics* (see note above).

BIBLIOGRAPHY AND REFERENCE NOTES

Dorothy Van Ghent. *Willa Cather*. University of Minnesota Pamphlets No. 36. Minneapolis: University of Minnesota Press, 1964.

Rebecca West. "The Classic Artist." New York *Herald Tribune*, September 11, 1927. In *The Strange Necessity* (New York: Viking Press, 1928). Reprinted in Schroeter, ed., *Willa Cather and Her Critics* (see note above).

Edmund Wilson. "Two Novels of Willa Cather." In *The Shores of Light: A Literary Chronicle of the Twenties and Thirties*. New York: Farrar, Straus and Young, 1952. Reprinted in Schroeter, ed., *Willa Cather and Her Critics* (see note above). The review of *One of Ours* originally appeared in *Vanity Fair*, October 1922; the review of *A Lost Lady* in the *Dial*, January 1924.

258

Reference Notes

PART I

The House of Willa Cather

Sources of quotations from the writings of Willa Cather are listed in the order in which they occur on the text page.

Page 3: *My Antonia*, p. 16.
Page 4: *The Song of the Lark*, pp. 6, 51; "The Novel Démeublé," in *Willa Cather on Writing*, p. 41; *My Ántonia*, pp. 119–20; *The Song of the Lark*, p. 276.
Page 5: *The Song of the Lark*, pp. 59–60, 376; *A Lost Lady*, p. 168.
Page 6: *O Pioneers!*, p. 65.
Pages 6–7: *My Ántonia*, pp. 352–53.
Page 8: *The Song of the Lark*, p. 378; *The Professor's House*, p. 194.
Page 10: "On *The Professor's House*," in *Willa Cather on Writing*, p. 31; *The Song of the Lark*, p. 374.
Pages 10–11: *The Song of the Lark*, p. 374.
Page 11: *The Song of the Lark*, p. 251.
Pages 11–12: *My Ántonia*, p. 245.
Page 13: *O Pioneers!*, p. 307.
Page 14: *The Song of the Lark*, pp. 177, 198–99, 199; *O Pioneers!*, p. 17.
Page 15: *The Song of the Lark*, pp. 272, 254–55, 570–71.
Page 17: *O Pioneers!*, p. 19; *The Song of the Lark*, p. 42; *The Professor's House*, pp. 201 (3), 203–204, 213, 220, 221.
Page 18: *The Professor's House*, p. 272.
Page 19: *The Song of the Lark*, pp. 571, 221, 273; "The Best Stories of Sarah Orne Jewett," in *Willa Cather on Writing*, p. 51.

The Two or More Worlds of Willa Cather

1. Ray Allen Billington, *Frederick Jackson Turner: Historian, Scholar, Teacher* (New York: Oxford University Press, 1973), pp. 491–92.

2. Lewis, *Willa Cather Living*, pp. 138–39, 143.

3. Examples cited in Richard Hofstadter, *The Progressive Historians: Turner, Beard, Parrington* (New York: Vintage Books, 1970), pp. 54–55, 67.

259

BIBLIOGRAPHY AND REFERENCE NOTES

4. George R. Stewart, *Bret Harte: Argonaut and Exile* (1935; repr. Port Washington, N.Y.: Kennikat Press, 1964), pp. 150–51, 175.

5. Hofstadter, *The Progressive Historians*, p. 54.

6. G. Edward White, *The Eastern Establishment and the Western Experience: The West of Frederic Remington, Theodore Roosevelt, and Owen Wister* (New Haven: Yale University Press, 1968), pp 191–92.

7. Stewart, *Bret Harte*, p. 159.

8. Wilbur R. Jacobs, ed., *The Historical World of Frederick Jackson Turner* (New Haven: Yale University Press, 1968), pp. 55–62.

9. Billington, ed., *"Dear Lady,"* pp. 147–49. The full citation is on p. 29 n, above.

10. Ibid., p. 448.

11. Ibid., p. 365.

12. Jacobs, ed., *Historical World of Turner*, p. 164.

13. Billington, *Frederick Jackson Turner*, pp. 426–27. The Emerson allusion is from Emerson's 1844 lecture, "The Young American"; see Hofstadter, *The Progressive Historians*, pp. 56–57.

14. Vachel Lindsay, *Collected Poems* (New York: Macmillan, 1925), p. 99. He notes having written this poem at the Guanella Ranch, Empire, Colorado, in August 1919.

15. Van Ghent, *Willa Cather*, pp. 5, 22–23.

WILLA CATHER: AMERICAN EXPERIENCE AND EUROPEAN TRADITION

1. Mildred Howells, ed., *Life in Letters of William Dean Howells*, 2 vols. (Garden City, N.Y.: Doubleday, Doran, and Co., 1928), 2: 350.

2. Lionel Trilling, "The Meaning of a Literary Idea" in *The Liberal Imagination* (New York: Viking Press, 1950), pp. 295–96.

3. Philadelphia *Record*, August 9, 1913; reprinted in *The Kingdom of Art*, p. 449.

4. Quoted in an interview in the Lincoln *Daily Star*, October 24, 1915; reprinted in *The Kingdom of Art*, p. 452.

5. This quotation is from James's often-reprinted essay "The Art of Fiction." It appears in James E. Miller, Jr., ed., *Theory of Fiction: Henry James* (Lincoln: University of Nebraska Press, 1972), p. 35.

6. Originally published in the *Home Monthly*, August 1896; reprinted in *Collected Short Fiction, 1892–1912*, pp. 475–76.

7. Giannone, *Music in Willa Cather's Fiction*.

8. A photograph of this inscription appears between pp. 222–23 in Bennett, *The World of Willa Cather*.

9. See Woodress, *Willa Cather: Her Life and Art*, p. 196.

10. See Edel, *Literary Biography*, pp. 56–80.

11. See "On *The Professor's House*" in *Willa Cather on Writing*, pp. 30–32.

12. See "On *Death Comes for the Archbishop*" in *Willa Cather on Writing*, pp. 5–13.

13. Quoted by Willa Cather in her 1922 preface to *Alexander's Bridge*, p. vi.

WILLA CATHER AND FRANCE: ELECTIVE AFFINITIES

1. Willa Cather to Carrie Miner Sherwood, June 28, 1939. Archives of the Willa Cather Pioneer Memorial, Red Cloud, Nebraska.

BIBLIOGRAPHY AND REFERENCE NOTES

2. Latrobe Carroll, "Willa Sibert Cather," *Bookman* 53 (May 1921): 215.

3. *The World and the Parish*, p. 939.

4. Information kindly given by Mildred R. Bennett.

5. Mildred R. Bennett, "Willa Cather: Is She Relevant Today?," Omaha *Sunday World-Herald Magazine of the Midlands*, April 4, 1971, p. 18.

6. *Not Under Forty*, p. 5.

7. *The World and the Parish*, p. 921.

8. Willa Cather to Dorothy Canfield Fisher, April 7, 1922, Guy W. Bailey Library, University of Vermont.

9. Brown, *Willa Cather*, p. 64.

10. *Not Under Forty*, p. 23.

11. Ibid.

12. *The Song of the Lark*, p. 571.

13. *The World and the Parish*, p. 594.

14. Ibid., p. 142.

15. Ibid., p. 340.

16. George Seibel, "Miss Willa Cather from Nebraska," *New Colophon* II, Pt. 7 (September 1949): 197.

17. *The Kingdom of Art*, p. 394 n 71 and p. 397.

18. Woodress, *Willa Cather: Her Life and Art*, p. 103.

19. Brown, *Willa Cather*, p. 99.

20. Lewis, *Willa Cather Living*, p. 55.

21. *The Professor's House*, p. 104.

22. *The World and the Parish*, pp. 928–29.

23. Ibid., p. 373.

24. Brown, *Willa Cather*, p. 217.

25. *Willa Cather in Europe*, p. 92.

26. Lewis, *Willa Cather Living*, p. 190.

27. *The World and the Parish*, p. 373.

28. *Willa Cather in Europe*, p. 130.

29. Edward Wagenknecht, *Cavalcade of the American Novel* (New York: Holt, Rinehart, and Winston, 1952), p. 337.

30. Sergeant, *Willa Cather: A Memoir*, p. 145.

31. Brown, *Willa Cather*, p. 270.

32. *One of Ours*, p. 390.

WILLA CATHER IN JAPAN

1. *Willa Cather on Writing*, p. 28.

2. This point is discussed in Tony Tanner, "Notes for a Comparison between American and European Romanticism," *Journal of American Studies* 2, no. 1: 83–103.

3. Edel, *Literary Biography*, pp. 73 ff.

4. "On *Shadows on the Rock*" in *Willa Cather on Writing*, p. 16.

5. Tony Tanner, *Problems and Roles of the American Artist as Portrayed by the American Novelist* (London: Oxford University Press, 1971), p. 22.

6. *The Song of the Lark*, p. 380.

7. Woodress, *Willa Cather: Her Life and Art*, p. 234.

8. "On *Shadows on the Rock*," p. 15.

9. *Death Comes for the Archbishop*, p. 39.

261

Bibliography and Reference Notes

10. Ibid., p. 272.

11. *The Song of the Lark*, p. 251.

12. Daiches, *Willa Cather: A Critical Introduction*, p. 45.

13. *The Song of the Lark*, p. 380.

14. *Death Comes for the Archbishop*, p. 275.

15. Trilling, "Willa Cather," reprinted in Schroeter, ed., *Willa Cather and Her Critics*, p. 149.

Italian Perspectives

1. *Collected Short Fiction, 1892–1912*, pp. 210–11.

2. Reprinted in *Collected Short Fiction, 1892–1912*, pp. 43–54.

3. *Uncle Valentine and Other Stories*, pp. 58–59.

4. *Collected Short Fiction, 1892–1912*, p. 214. The reference is to the last words of Francesca in the famous episode of Paolo and Francesca, *Inferno* V, 137–38.

5. Cesare Pavese, *Saggi Letterari* (Turin: Einaudi, 1968), pp. 173 ff. Reprint of an article, "Ieri e Oggi," *L'Unità*, August 3, 1947.

6. *Americana: Raccolta di narratori dalle origini ai nostri giorni, a cura di Elio Vittorini, con un introduzione di Emilio Cecchi* (Milan: Bompiani, 1942). A previous edition, published in April 1941, was banned by Fascist censorship. See Elio Vittorini, *Diario in Pubblico, 1929–1956* (Milan: Bompiani, 1970), p. 119.

7. Vittorini, *Diario in Pubblico*, p. 151.

8. Cesare Pavese, "Maturità Americana," in *La Rassegna Italiana*, December 1946. Reprinted in Pavese, *Saggi Letterari*, p. 159.

9. Review of *Obscure Destinies* by Michele Prisco, *Idea* 8 (July 1956): 4.

10. Salvatore Rosati, *L'ombra dei Padri* (Rome: Edizioni di Storia e Letteratura, 1958), p. 97.

Willa Cather and the Art of Fiction

1. Bernice Slote, "Willa Cather," in Bryer, ed., *Sixteen Modern American Authors*, p. 57.

2. See Leon Edel's treatment of her stories of artists in *Willa Cather: The Paradox of Success*, reprinted in Schroeter, ed., *Willa Cather and Her Critics*, pp. 257–59.

3. *The Kingdom of Art*, p. 40.

4. "Miss Jewett," in *Not Under Forty*, p. 91.

5. *Nebraska State Journal*, September 23, 1894; reprinted in *The Kingdom of Art*, p. 406.

6. James E. Miller, Jr., ed., *Theory of Fiction: Henry James* (Lincoln: University of Nebraska Press, 1972), p. 43. All Henry James quotations are from this source.

7. *Willa Cather on Writing*, p. 103.

8. Ibid., p. 40.

9. Ibid., pp. 42–43.

10. Lionel Trilling, "Willa Cather," reprinted in Schroeter, ed., *Willa Cather and Her Critics*, p. 148.

11. *Willa Cather on Writing*, p. 37.

12. See especially "The New Novel," excerpted in Miller, ed., *Theory of Fiction: Henry James*, pp. 158–60.

13. *Willa Cather on Writing*, p. 40.

Bibliography and Reference Notes

14. Ibid., p. 97.

15. "The Novel Démeublé," in *Willa Cather on Writing*, pp. 41–42.

16. *Willa Cather on Writing*, p. 102.

17. Ibid., p. 91.

18. *Nebraska State Journal*, March 29, 1896; reprinted in *The Kingdom of Art*, p. 362.

19. Sergeant, *Willa Cather: A Memoir*, p. 139.

20. *A Lost Lady*, pp. 171, 169.

21. *My Mortal Enemy*, p. 95.

22. Ibid., p. 105.

23. See especially Stanley Cooperman, *World War I and the American Novel* (Baltimore: Johns Hopkins Press, 1967), pp. 129–37.

24. *The Professor's House*, p. 169.

25. "On *The Professor's House*" in *Willa Cather on Writing*, pp. 31–32.

26. "On *Death Comes for the Archbishop*" in *Willa Cather on Writing*, pp. 12, 5.

27. Ibid., p. 9.

28. All quotations in this paragraph from "On *Shadows on the Rock*" in *Willa Cather on Writing*, p. 15.

29. *Willa Cather on Writing*, pp. 92–93.

30. Sergeant, *Willa Cather: A Memoir*, p. 225.

31. "On *Death Comes for the Archbishop*," pp. 9–10.

32. Martha Duffy, "The Old Sod," *Time* (August 13, 1973): 80.

33. See F. O. Matthiessen, ed., *The James Family* (New York: Alfred A. Knopf, 1947), pp. 602–14.

34. See Sergeant, *Willa Cather: A Memoir*, pp. 68–69.

Willa Cather: The Classic Voice

1. Willa Cather to George and Helen Seibel, July 17, 1901. See the introduction to *Collected Short Fiction, 1892–1912*, p. xxii.

2. Originally published in the *Hesperian*, January 15, 1893; reprinted in *Collected Short Fiction, 1892–1912*. See p. 528.

3. Originally published in the *Woman's Home Companion*, February and March, 1925; reprinted in *Uncle Valentine and Other Stories*.

4. *Nebraska State Journal*, September 30, 1894; reprinted in *The Kingdom of Art*, p. 217.

5. *Obscure Destinies*, p. 206.

6. *Tales of Edgar Allan Poe* (New York: Random House, 1944), pp. 341, 342–43.

7. *My Ántonia*, p. 261.

8. Ibid., p. 165.

9. *Shadows on the Rock*, p. 241.

10. Originally published in *The Troll Garden*; reprinted in *Collected Short Fiction, 1892–1912*.

11. Originally published in *Collier's*, May 18, 1912; reprinted in *Collected Short Fiction, 1892–1912*.

12. *My Ántonia*, p. 264.

13. Ibid., pp. 270–71.

14. Originally published in the *Home Monthly*, April 1898; reprinted in *Collected Short Fiction, 1892–1912*. See p. 404.

15. See L. V. Jacks, "The Classics and Willa Cather," *Prairie Schooner* 35 (Winter 1961/62): 292.

BIBLIOGRAPHY AND REFERENCE NOTES

PART II

HOMAGE TO WILLA CATHER

1. *Willa Cather: A Critical Biography*, p. 17.

2. Lewis, *Willa Cather Living*, p. 4.

3. Katherine Anne Porter, "Reflections on Willa Cather" in *Collected Essays and Occasional Writings* (New York: Delacorte, 1970), pp. 29, 30. First collected in *The Day Before* (New York: Harcourt Brace, 1952).

4. Rebecca West, "The Classic Artist," reprinted in Schroeter, ed., *Willa Cather and Her Critics*, pp. 63, 71.

5. "Miss Jewett" in *Not Under Forty*, p. 81.

6. Virginia Woolf, "American Fiction" in *The Moment and Other Essays* (New York: Harcourt Brace, 1947), p. 125. This essay was first published in 1925.

7. "The All-Star Literary Vaudeville" in *The Shores of Light* (New York: Farrar, Straus and Young, 1952), p. 232. This essay was originally published in *American Criticism* (New York: Harcourt Brace, 1926).

8. Edmund Wilson, "Two Novels of Willa Cather," reprinted in Schroeter, ed., *Willa Cather and Her Critics*, pp. 28–29.

9. Sergeant, *Willa Cather: A Memoir*, p. 107.

10. Translated by Peter Jay.

11. Translated by Ivar Morris.

Participants and Guests

Willa Cather International Seminar
October 25–28, 1973
University of Nebraska–Lincoln

Co-Principal Investigators

ROBERT E. KNOLL, Professor of English, University of Nebraska–Lincoln

BERNICE SLOTE, Professor of English, University of Nebraska–Lincoln

Principal Speakers

MARCUS CUNLIFFE, historian, Professor of American Studies, University of Sussex, Brighton, England

LEON EDEL, Pulitzer Prize-winning biographer, Citizens Professor of English, University of Hawaii, Honolulu

EUDORA WELTY, Pulitzer Prize-winning novelist, Jackson, Mississippi

Associate Investigators (Directors of Seminars)

ALDO CELLI, Professor of American Studies, Università degli Studi di Firenze, Florence, Italy

MICHEL GERVAUD, Professor of North American Literature and Civilization, Université de Provence, Aix en Provence, France

265

JAMES E. MILLER, JR., Professor of English, University of Chicago

HIROKO SATO, Assistant Professor of English and American Literature, Tokyo Woman's Christian College, Tokyo, Japan

DONALD SUTHERLAND, formerly Professor of Classics, University of Colorado, Boulder

JAMES WOODRESS, Professor of English, University of California, Davis

Discussants

BRUCE P. BAKER II, Professor of English, University of Nebraska at Omaha

MILDRED R. BENNETT, President, Willa Cather Pioneer Memorial and Educational Foundation, Red Cloud, Nebraska

EDWARD A. BLOOM, Professor of English, Brown University, Providence, Rhode Island

LILLIAN D. BLOOM, Professor of English, Rhode Island College, Providence

SISTER ISABEL CHARLES, O.P., Assistant Dean, College of Arts and Letters, University of Notre Dame

VIRGINIA FAULKNER, Professor of English, University of Nebraska–Lincoln

WARREN G. FRENCH, Professor of English, Indiana University–Purdue University, Indianapolis

BLANCHE H. GELFANT, Professor of English, Dartmouth College, Hanover, New Hampshire

RICHARD GIANNONE, Associate Professor of English, Fordham University, Bronx, New York

GEORGE GREENE, Professor of English, Boston State College, Boston, Massachusetts

VICTOR P. HASS, Book Editor, Omaha *World-Herald*, Omaha, Nebraska

JOHN HINZ, Professor of American Studies, Richmond College, Staten Island, New York

ROBERT L. HOUGH, Professor of English, University of Nebraska–Lincoln

Participants and Guests

Ellen Moers, Adjunct Associate Professor of English, Barnard College, New York City

John J. Murphy, Associate Professor of English, Merrimack College, North Andover, Massachusetts

Margaret A. O'Connor, Assistant Professor of English, University of North Carolina, Chapel Hill, North Carolina

Paul A. Olson, Professor of English, University of Nebraska–Lincoln

John H. Randall III, Associate Professor of English, Boston College, Boston, Massachusetts

John W. Robinson, Professor of English, University of Nebraska–Lincoln

Sister Lucy Schneider, Associate Professor of English, Marymount College of Kansas, Salina, Kansas

David Stouck, Associate Professor of English, Simon Fraser University, Burnaby, British Columbia

Auditor-Participants

Dalma Hunyadi Brunauer, Associate Professor of the Humanities, Clarkson College of Technology, Potsdam, New York

Philip L. Gerber, Professor of English, State University of New York, Potsdam

Philip Siggins, Department of English, Monash University, Clayton, Victoria, Australia

Distinguished Guests

Mrs. E. K. Brown, Rochester, New York

Alfred A. Knopf, Chairman Emeritus, Alfred A. Knopf, Inc., and Mrs. Alfred A. Knopf, New York City

William A. Koshland, Chairman of the Board, Alfred A. Knopf, Inc., New York City

Roger Lyons, Voice of America, Washington, D.C.

Professor and Mrs. Philip L. Southwick (Helen Cather), Pittsburgh, Pennsylvania

Mr. and Mrs. Frank H. Woods, Lake Forest, Illinois